Social work with unaccompanied asylum seeking children

Contents

The story of the little wave

A little wave in the ocean is rolling along and terrified that he is going to crash. 'I am so scared,' he says to the passing bigger waves, who reply, 'You are not a little wave. You are the ocean.'

Acknowledgements

This book is dedicated to a number of people. Firstly to the respondents in the study, who told their stories of practice. Secondly to June Thoburn at the University of East Anglia and Fiona Mitchell at the University of York for their intelligence and expertise. Thirdly to Gurmukh Singh Kohli, who generated the pulse of movement towards the United Kingdom for my family of origin, and to Surjeet Kaur Kohli and Preeti, with whom I migrated. And, finally, to Jane, Maya, and Rosh – who know that to be unaccompanied on any journey can be arduous, and that connection and companionship make the journey and its end worthwhile.

R.K.S.K.

Social work with unaccompanied asylum seeking children

Ravi K. S. Kohli

palgrave
macmillan

First published 2007 by
PALGRAVE MACMILLAN
Houndmills, Basingstoke, Hampshire RG21 6XS and
175 Fifth Avenue, New York, N.Y. 10010
Companies and representatives throughout the world

PALGRAVE MACMILLAN is the global academic imprint of the Palgrave Macmillan division of St. Martin's Press, LLC and of Palgrave Macmillan Ltd. Macmillan® is a registered trademark in the United States, United Kingdom and other countries. Palgrave is a registered trademark in the European Union and other countries.

ISBN-13: 978–1–4039–8965–9   hardback
ISBN-10: 1–4039–8965–6   hardback
ISBN-13: 978–1–4039–8966–6   paperback
ISBN-10: 1–4039–8966–4   paperback

This book is printed on paper suitable for recycling and made from fully managed and sustained forest sources.

A catalogue record for this book is available from the British Library.

A catalog record for this book is available from the Library of Congress.

10   9   8   7   6   5   4   3   2   1
16   15   14   13   12   11   10   09   08   07

Printed and bound in China

Introduction

The United Kingdom has provided sanctuary for many unaccompanied children seeking asylum at certain times in the twentieth century. These children came in relatively well-organised quotas, largely from specific parts of Europe (Bell, 1996; Harris and Oppenheimer, 2001). In contrast, unaccompanied children who began arriving from the late 1980s onwards often came alone, or sometimes in sibling groups, from many parts of the world. At the beginning of the twenty-first century, patterns of arrival indicate that they rarely come as part of a large community of children, but arrive suddenly, alone or in small clusters, from distant places, depending on the ebb and flow of war. Amongst them are children who are trafficked, and others who are attempting to escape from poverty and the collapse of civic order in their countries of origin. Whichever way they are deposited on UK soil, they require care and protection by social workers in order to resettle successfully within their new territories, as new manifestations of 'children in need'. Yet very little is reliably known about the details of how this requirement is met (Williamson, 1999; Mitchell, 2003). Even though the care and protection of 'children in need', as well as issues of resettlement for children seeking asylum, are established areas of academic enquiry they have tended to be developed separately, without much cross-referencing. In terms of contemporary social work however, these areas have intersected. The intent of this book is to shine a light at this intersection and to see what is revealed.

Specifically, the book seeks to offer a detailed view of social-work practice with young unaccompanied asylum seekers who are looked after by local authority social services departments in the United Kingdom under section 20 of the Children Act 1989. In doing so, the book puts forward a basic thesis – that in order to understand what goes on between social workers and unaccompanied minors, we need to see the children themselves as ordinary children, wanting ordinary lives despite the extraordinary circumstances that have propelled them many thousands of miles away from their lands of origin. Secondly, we need to see social work as a potentially valuable activity that can help them to find stability over time. Yet these aspects of the lives of unaccompanied minors and the activities of their social workers are difficult to decipher amongst the noise and heat of political opinions and policy debates concerning asylum seekers and refugees. The 'din' created by debate in this sense can obscure the quiet ways in which people resettle and are helped to resettle after forced migration. So in contexts where pressures to exclude people are applied at border crossings, as well as within the country, the book attempts to chart some of the ways that political debate affects how refugee children and their social workers manage their work together.

Key issues in working with unaccompanied minors

Media reports suggests that, like other refugees and asylum seekers, unaccompanied minors are regularly viewed as being vulnerable (MacFadyean, 2001; Valois, 2001) or as villains (Craven, 2003). More significantly within the arena of academic enquiry, Turton (2003) makes the point that research and teaching in refugee studies has tended to focus on public policy and private need, and within both these domains the predominant image is of refugees as victims. These simple polarities are, as I shall argue in this book, part of a more complex picture, where a constellation of forces have contributed in defining the position that refugee children find themselves in. For example, it is true to say that the young people themselves are far away from their families. Indeed, their families may have sent them far away to get them out from danger. Yet this combined act of protecting their offspring by making sure they get away from their homeland may leave asylum seeking children with a complex and burdensome message about what their families think about them. The families get what they want, but they risk losing what they have. The children may or may not know what they have to do for themselves, either to find their way in a stranger's country or to make a success of their lives. The stages from arrival to achieving citizenship may test their resilience in profound ways, as they integrate into new environments and disintegrate from the old. Roots and shoots may pull in differing directions. In each of these aspects of readjustment to a new life, the study that forms the basis of this book looks at how their social workers help them in practical ways to make sense of what has happened to them, so that they can, in time, begin to look back and look forward with a degree of fluency.

As another example, the young people may need to achieve more than citizenship. They may, like other migrants, have come with the message that they must succeed academically and financially. Unlike economic migrants, however, they may encounter a threat to the legitimacy of their political claims in revealing any economic sub-text to their flight, because refugees cannot risk being seen to have motivations that are financial. Particularly in contexts within which a distinction between economic and political migrants is imposed, they may choose to remain silent about any reasons for seeking sanctuary not explicitly tied to their asylum claim. The children may, in other words, be aware of the need to present the simplest, most acceptable version of their reasons for flight, in order to succeed. They may become the silent guardians of their complex stories of departure, taking care not to jeopardise their footholds within newly established territory. So the ways in which social workers manage and make sense of the stories that the young people bring, and the silences and secrets they contain, form another dimension to this book.

In some respects these young people present a fresh version of old challenges and dilemmas for social workers, and arguably there is something familiar about them, even though they come from countries far away. For example, for a profession used to working with people who risk losing their connections, the work with unaccompanied minors ought to be familiar to some degree because separation and loss, as issues brought by children entering public care, are also known to be a fundamental part of unaccompanied children's stories. As such, social workers used to working with histories of impairment and dislocation of vulnerable children from socially excluded families, ought to be particularly well placed as receptors for the bundle of experiences that these young people bring. But as yet, very little is known about the ways they transfer their understanding and experience of work with indigenous children to the needs and strengths of unaccompanied children, particularly in the provision of psychosocial care. So the study in this book tracks the ways in which workers help the young people balance 'inner' and 'outer' worlds (Schofield, 1998), allowing connections to be made between facts and feelings, and actions, events and their meanings.

In reference to the care needs of indigenous children, Utting (1997: 166) pinpoints 'their need for a continual and trusting relationship with an official of the care authority . . . who is committed to furthering [their] interests as a whole'. Given the solitary circumstances of the majority of unaccompanied minors following the rupture of networks of care and protection, the ways in which social workers provide companionship to the young people, and rebuild a sense of their belonging to a family, a social network and a community, are examined in this book. In fact, very little is known of the explanations social workers give of their own relationships with these young people, and how they use the relationship to assist in resettlement over time. Nor is their work with formal networks to secure education, health care, or immigration status mapped in any detail. Regarding the longer-term future, the ways in which social workers plan for resettlement, reunification with families of origin, or repatriation where necessary, are only dimly understood. These aspects of the redevelopment by social workers of networks that are broad and deep, and of establishing a relationship that is enduring, are examined here.

An important notion that is explored within this book is that effective social work practice with unaccompanied minors allows the young people to experience, over a period of time, a sense of belonging somewhere again, with someone, and of re-gathering material and other resources, leading to resettlement. Belonging and belongings mark the progress of resettlement. As such the term 'resettlement' is explored in detail, as both a search for and the establishment of a sense of home, where order, peace and rhythm can be re-established as a counterpoint to the messy reality of refugee life after departure. As the poet Robert Frost noted,

> Home is the place where
> when you have to go there
> they have to take you in
> > (see Garbarino and Kostelney, 1996: 3)

So what social workers do, or think they have done or could do, to make the space occupied by unaccompanied asylum seeking and refugee children less contingent, more stable and ultimately more permanent, is tracked here amongst the stories told.

The stories within the book

In designing and undertaking the study that forms the basis of this book, I asked social workers to talk about their work with one unaccompanied asylum seeking minor and, within that account, to tell me what they knew about that child or young person's life history, their current circumstances and their future aspirations. This account of the child's story was collected in the context of asking the social workers to 'set the scene' by talking a little about their own lives, experiences, skills and knowledge that they considered relevant to the work. Very much in line with Hollway and Jefferson (2000: 32), the focus of analysis for the study was designed to be

> the people who tell us stories about their lives: the stories themselves are a means to understand our subjects better. While stories are obviously not providing a transparent account through which we learn truths, story telling stays closer to actual life-events than methods that elicit explanations.

When originally designing the study, I had hoped to gather two sets of stories, one from the social workers and one from the children and young people themselves. But it became clear very early on in the initial interviews with the social workers that it would be difficult to interview the unaccompanied minors that were allocated to them, and indeed that it might be advisable not to approach them directly, even though it would have been valuable to understand their own versions of stories of resettlement. The practical difficulties of access resonated with other ethical and methodological considerations, captured in a paper by Thomas and Byford (2003). Here, these researchers focused on factors that need to be taken into account in conducting research specifically with unaccompanied minors. They suggest that there are a number of reasons for *not* involving asylum seeking and refugee children directly in research, or at least for being extremely circumspect about their participation.

> Young people with such troubled backgrounds are understandably wary of researchers asking about their past and are often resistant to discussion of experiences loaded with pain and guilt. (Thomas and Byford, 2003: 1401)

They add that 'research is a strange process for many asylum seekers', which the young people may confuse with the asylum interview (as stressful) or with getting access to services (raising false hopes). In any case, they conclude that ethically, any research designed to elicit their participation needs to be clear that it will be of benefit to the young people. They ask researchers to consider whether involving the young people is the only way to answer the research questions. Finally, they suggest that, given that the sharing of information is a complicated issue amongst refugee minors, the research should not be undertaken unless mechanisms for feedback to them are built in to the design from the start (for example, via representation on steering groups that manage research projects).

Given the ethical and practical considerations, many of the social workers in this study said that 'their' young person was unwilling to participate. This was particularly the case for those young people who had been in the UK for less than a year, and for whom interviews with officials in relation to asylum were still being conducted. Others wanted to maintain silence for a number of understandable reasons, as described in chapter 5. Overall, as it became clear that their participation was not going to go ahead, the focus of the enquiry returned to understanding the views and actions of practitioners themselves.

In interviewing social workers it was possible to address two significant issues. One was the need to look more closely at some of their discourses about refugee and asylum seeking children and practice. For example, I wanted to test out whether or not social workers really did see themselves as acting like internal border guards as reported in some of the literature. Similarly, I wanted to see whether the 'refugee child as victim or villain' discourse was prevalent in practitioners' minds, how they positioned themselves in relation to care and control, and what they felt about being on the border as the young people came towards them into care. Another issue that the interviewing strategy was able to address was the use of silence as a part of practice. Without the possibility of conversation that an interview allowed, some of the dominant themes within refugee research, such as the reluctance of people to talk about a sensitive topic, and how such reticence was used to punctuate the narrative, could have remained hidden. Kvale (1996: 4) uses the metaphor of travel in discussing research interviews as an established and important method of enquiry. He notes,

> The interviewer wanders along with the local inhabitants, asks questions that lead the subjects to tell their own stories of their lived world, and converses with them in the original Latin meaning of conversation as 'wandering together with'.

This metaphor is particularly relevant to a topic so focused on journeys and their meanings for people, and I wanted where possible to build up a companionable relationship with the social workers that allowed the migrants' stories to emerge in a context where the latter experienced the researcher as being concerned, friendly, informed and sympathetic to them (Cheetham et al., 1992: 50). Most importantly in terms of the main focus of the enquiry, collecting stories from social workers about their own practice gave me an opportunity to consider the shape that social work as a profession had taken on, in relation to unaccompanied minors. As with the deconstruction of the 'refugee as victim' approach, I did not want to weigh social work practice as good or bad, or in need of improvement through my presenting 'recommendations for practice' within a context where 'there is always something . . . wrong with social work and that practice is never (quite) good enough' (Ferguson, 2003: 1007). Rather, I hoped to study and report back on it as an uncertain phenomenon, open to interpretation in different ways. I wanted this enquiry to allow the emergence of the details of everyday practice, partly in reference to Smith's (1987: 413) observation that 'more attention should be paid [by researchers] to the process actually involved in social work activities', and partly because of knowing, through my own practice experience, that practice contained fractions of good, bad and indifferent realities, that it seldom remained consistently high or low in relation to a technical measure of effectiveness, and that research that left further questions to be asked was as valuable as research that left a residue of answers in its wake. In all, twenty-nine social workers across the four teams participated in the research and gave their accounts of thirty-four children and young people in their care. The social workers were all qualified practitioners within local authority Social Services departments, working either in specialist 'unaccompanied minors' teams, or in non-specialist 'children and families' teams.

Broadly, the interviews revealed that the social workers were guided by the young people's needs and capabilities towards three types of helping. The first of these, 'humanitarian' practice, focused on practical 'outer world' assistance. The second, described as 'witnessing', focused on 'inner world' turbulence, helping the young people to manage uncertainty and distress, related primarily to past events. The third, described as 'confederacy', focused on the development of a protective friendship with the young people that was durable, long lasting and open ended. Each of these three types of helping appeared to be carried out in a particular 'domain' of practice, referred to here as the domains of cohesion, connection, and coherence. These interwoven stories of practice and the young people's lives form the core of the book. Given this approach, the book does not lend itself easily to harvesting concrete and specific 'recommendations for practice', and is not, within the current usage of the term, 'evidence based'. However, there are some ideas inherent in the stories told by the social workers that illuminate the complexity of events and their meanings for all parties. As the pattern of what appears to be going on in the domains of practice emerges, so do some ideas about effectiveness, which may be relevant not just within the UK context, but in other industrialised nations where unaccompanied minors are currently present.

The structure of the book

The book itself is structured in a way that allows the above issues to be considered systematically in relation to social work with unaccompanied minors. What the social workers in this study knew about these strangers' children, what they did not know, what they assumed about them and feared and hoped for them, are drawn together to clarify a complex, continually shifting picture. For example, what we know is that these children are members of global communities that are on the move rather than ones that are locally based and relatively still. Membership is temporary, sometimes self-determined, sometimes legally enforced, but in any case liable to change. In this context, contemporary social work as a response to movement, particularly the ebb and flow of forced migration, can make practitioners and policy makers feel that they are knitting with water, as people, policies, laws and resources come and go. This brings demands and challenges, but also offers opportunities for intellectually and emotionally robust engagements with people on the move. In order to help these practitioners to capture the rhythm and shape of forces that they generate and are influenced by in relation to the forced migration of children, a clear and systematic picture needs to be put together that illuminates the challenges and rewards of social work in a world of change. In attempting to do this, this book offers the following frame. The first three chapters review, and offer a critique of, the existing literature related to refugees emerging within western industrialised contexts, and particularly the trajectories of unaccompanied minors within those contexts. Beyond discussing the basic legal definitions of the terms 'unaccompanied', 'asylum seeker', 'refugee' and 'minor', I offer in Chapter 1 a historical overview of the arrival of unaccompanied minors in Europe, followed by a summary of their current circumstances in the United Kingdom. The current shape and flow of policy and legal decisions that have had a major impact on the provision of services to unaccompanied minors are outlined. Then, I suggest that law, policy, and research studies that evaluate services and make recommendations for change to policy and practice within this territory are relatively impoverished in terms of theoretical frames within which the experience of becoming a refugee can be understood. Therefore in order to lay some theoretical foundations for the study, the concept of 'resettlement' is explored in reference to movement as part of forced migration. Here, the varied meanings of resettlement, both as a process and as an outcome, are examined within research studies based in a number of industrialised nations that have been used as host countries in the recent past.

These policy, legal and conceptual frameworks are then built up in Chapter 2. Here I survey and evaluate the existing research in relation to unaccompanied asylum seeking children and young people who seek resettlement in Western Europe, particularly in the United Kingdom. I examine their reasons for coming to Europe and evaluate research evidence that identifies their needs as well as their capabilities in the management of resettlement. Within this chapter I suggest that three dimensions of resettlement are worth considering. First, the type of assistance with practical and legal aspects of belonging that are known to generate a sense of cohesion for the young people in their new environments; secondly, the sense of connection they feel with other people as the psychological and emotional aspects of resettlement take shape over time; thirdly, how they use their own resilience in bedding down and re-creating a coherent sense of their own lives, so that, with the help of others, they stop being refugees and become ordinary citizens again, but this time in an unfamiliar land.

Chapter 3 focuses directly on social work with unaccompanied minors. While the literature on practice is still relatively sparse, within this chapter I synthesise key guidance documents related to raising the standards of effective practice and policy for social workers and allied professions. I then examine a series of studies carried out in the UK by Non-Governmental Organisations (NGOs) or other groups lobbying for policy change, based on advocating on behalf of unaccompanied minors. On the basis of clearly identified gaps between what the guidance suggests ought to be done, and the studies' findings, they confirm what appear to be disordered and defensive policies and practices of local authorities, the Home Office or the National Asylum Support Service (NASS). They also take a bleak view of social work practice overall and present a picture of unaccompanied minors as suffering at the hands of practitioners preoccupied with acting like border guards rather than citizen makers. In this chapter I suggest that this bleak view may not be the only one to hold, and propose that a detailed and non-advocacy-based examination of practice contains the potential to reveal a different, more complex, and perhaps a more optimistic picture of refugee children and their social workers.

From Chapter 4 onwards, the study itself takes centre stage. I begin by outlining the organisational context of the teams that took part in the study – the stage so to speak, of the play about to unfold. Here, I also describe the personal and professional characteristics of the actors, so that a sense is generated of the ways in which the social workers who took part in the study used their personal and professional knowledge and experiences of work with refugees to shape their practice with unaccompanied minors. In doing so I offer ways of seeing social work as a multi-layered activity, with practitioners' balanced 'technical knowledge' about refugee and asylum issues from legal, political, and theoretical and research perspectives, with more informal and localised 'understandings' derived from their own experiences of casework, and in some respects, their own lives. This patchwork approach to service provision can sometimes be reported as being a hasty 'cut and paste' in the absence of 'evidence-based' or 'evidence-informed' practice, and there is a tendency to say that social workers too easily 'shoot from the lip' in relation to practice. But I suggest here that multiplicity matters when dealing with the mess, speed and demands of work with unaccompanied children, and social workers can make sense of the children's lives by all available means, including reference to their own values, beliefs and experiences.

In Chapter 5 I give a detailed account of the lives of unaccompanied minors as seen through the eyes of their social workers. The chapter includes what was known to the social workers about their past, and what remained hidden, and what sense they made of why this was so. It tracks the known stories of leaving the country of origin and arriving in the UK. It also describes the young people's current circumstances, including their physical and psychological health, the type and quality of care they received, the networks they used in day-to-day living, and their social workers' perceptions of their behaviours and feelings about now living in the UK. It highlights their capabilities, as well as common difficulties they are seen to encounter. I end the chapter by examining what the social workers knew about their future aspirations including obtaining indefinite leave to remain, family contact, as well as possible repatriation. In paying close attention to the ways in which social workers could provide a narrative thread that connected these children's past, present and future lives, I wanted to see the vision and scope that practitioners held on to in their work with individual young people. What emerged were stories of the children's capabilities and vulnerabilities, their talk and silences, hopes and fears, and their endurance in the face of deep uncertainty – both building on views already within the literature, as well as extending them beyond simple formulations of victimhood for asylum seeking children.

The above elements of what social workers knew and described are used as the foundation for Chapter 6, within which I sharpen up the definition of resettlement-based social work, including stories of 'remote control' by practitioners in relation to need, of dealing with uncertainty, of the ownership of capability, optimism, humour and endurance – again, a little like the stories of the children, extending the picture of practice beyond inaptitude towards a more complex account of the workings of social work. Here, the core results of the study are laid out within the three typologies noted above – the humanitarian, the witness, and the confederate – and their impact across three 'domains' of practice, where practical help, therapeutic care and longer-term companionship co-exist, and are experienced as valuable aspects of help given to unaccompanied minors. Within this chapter I highlight the importance of establishing trust with asylum seeking children as a base for good practice, given the complex inheritance of silence and secrets that they can bring with them, and then assess the function of each typology and each domain in terms of helping the young people towards resettlement.

Chapter 7 concludes the study, and here I summarise the main findings in the context of looking back at the literature, as well as in moving towards a multi-dimensional understanding of social-work resettlement-based practice with unaccompanied minors. I suggest that in many respects social workers are attuned to complexity in their responses to the needs and capabilities of unaccompanied children and young people in ways that have not been illuminated in the literature before. In a context of asylum seekers and social workers being undervalued, the overall results of the study confirm that practitioners can show a breadth and depth of understanding of why children seek asylum, and how care can be organised to maximise their chances of resettlement. These ways of viewing social-work effectiveness also confirm that those who comment on social work in this arena need to engage with practitioners, not just as a group needing instruction for improvement, but as people whose capability can be illuminated in terms of bringing order, peace and a sense of ordinary living back into the lives of unaccompanied minors.

In a broad sense therefore the book rejects the common conceptions of unaccompanied children as victims. It displays their vulnerabilities alongside their strengths within the varied attempts they make to salvage their lives in the UK. Similarly, it seeks to establish social-work practice as varied and rich in meaning for the practitioners themselves, not as a deficit-laden activity. In reaching out for a more optimistic appraisal of refugee lives and social work practice than is currently available within the literature, the book identifies a territory where scope for solidarity exists between children and their carers as they look together for resettlement.

1 Unaccompanied asylum seeking children

As children who are seeking asylum resettle in lands that are not their own, they look for the re-emergence of order, peace and the rhythm of ordinary life. They look to a variety of skilled helpers in assisting them to find a sense of home again. This is both a complex process and a valued achievement. It relies on the capabilities of both parties to see what requires attention and repair, and when. In presenting a view of what is currently known about the resettlement of unaccompanied children and more specifically what is known about the social work responses to them, the first three chapters in this book address theoretical ideas and debates, key laws and policies, and research findings that illuminate the territory within which social workers and the young people face each other and conduct their day-to-day exchanges. This chapter lays out the contexts of resettlement-based practice, beginning with key definitions, the historical basis of forced migration for unaccompanied minors and the current picture of their presence and spread across the UK, including the impact of a number of key policy and legal decisions on the provision of care. It then considers the concept of resettlement in detail from theoretical and research perspectives, suggesting that asylum seekers and refugees play a purposeful and full part in reorganising their lives after arrival. It concludes by outlining a three-dimensional model of practice within which practical assistance, therapeutic care, and companionship have significant parts to play in shaping successful resettlement.

While the focus of this book is primarily the lives and circumstances of unaccompanied children, it must also be acknowledged that the intention of rebuilding a life that is outwardly successful and internally coherent shares its roots with many migrant stories, some of which are familiar to social workers in their day-to-day practice. To some extent the intention is part of the tales of all refugees seeking sanctuary in response to political persecution (Fadiman, 1997; Karpf, 1997; Kushner and Knox, 1999); it

1

is also part of the lives of those moving to other countries for economic reasons (Aciman, 1999); and in a more localised way, it is part of the narratives of internally displaced children and young people who enter and leave public care (see, for example, Fisher et al., 1986; Packman & Hall, 1998), or resettle into permanent substitute families (Thoburn et al., 2000). All these migrants carry hopes for progress and growth, once safety within a host culture is secured (Riley and Wood, 1996; Harding, 2000). However, while unaccompanied children share a number of characteristics associated with any of these other groups of people in transition, they also bring distinctive characteristics and sets of circumstances. I have written elsewhere that,

> When they arrive in unfamiliar contexts, they have to deal with a bewildering set of circumstances. They have to cross three psychological barriers. Firstly, as 'strangers in a strange land', they may not know the habits, rules and customs of their new territories, and have to adapt quickly and fluently in order to settle. Secondly they may be carrying memories of disintegration following war and be traumatised or haunted by ghosts from the past. They have to depend on the comfort and skills of strangers to make peace with these ghosts. Thirdly, if they are looked after by social services in the country of asylum, they have to find their way through a maze of systems of care and protection, having been through the immigration maze. . . .
>
> Given these three stressors these children often experience a series of fractures in their past, present and future lives that need to be healed. At the point of arrival, their sense of being in charge of their lives is seriously jeopardised. . . . The challenge for welfare professionals in these situations is to help the separated child find . . . a sense of direction and a safe road to travel along in their journey of belonging, in a way that allows them to take charge of their past, present and future experiences. (Kohli and Mather, 2003: 201)

In short, the suggestion is that young people who come to the UK as unaccompanied minors need help from social workers, as well as other professionals, to settle into their new environments, and that this help is both similar to and different from the help given to other groups that are seeking resettlement. In order to test whether this claim is well founded, I will initially define the term 'unaccompanied' and then consider what the term 'resettlement' means, and how it might be used in examining social-work practice with unaccompanied children and young people.

Defining 'unaccompanied'

The meaning of the term 'unaccompanied refugee child' is relatively clear, certainly within international conventions. For example, according to the 1951 United Nations Convention related to the Status of Refugees, *a refugee* is someone who makes a successful claim in a chosen country of asylum, on the basis that in the country of origin s/he has

> a well founded fear of being persecuted for reasons of race, religion, nationality, membership of a particular social group or political opinion, is outside the country of his (or her) nationality and is unable or, owing to such fear, is unwilling to avail himself (or herself) of the protection of that country. . . . (Article 1a(2))

In 1967, a Protocol Relating to the Status of Refugees widened the scope of the 1951 Convention from its original application to European nations, to be worldwide. The Convention and the Protocol together form the basis of the current universal definition. There is also agreement between international definitions and UK domestic legislation in the definition of child. According to the 1989 UN Convention on the Rights of the Child (CRC), which was ratified by the UK in 1991 (Williamson, 1999), a child is simply:

> every human being below the age of eighteen years, unless, under the law applicable to that child, majority is attained earlier.   (Article 1)

The United Nations High Commission for Refugees (UNHCR, 1994: 121) says that *unaccompanied children* are:

> those who are separated from both parents and are not being

cared for by an adult who, by law or custom, is responsible to do so.

It follows from these definitions that *unaccompanied asylum seeking children* are those below eighteen years of age who have made an application for asylum, and have gained temporary admission to the host country while their claim is considered. In the UK, the Home Office states that,

> An unaccompanied asylum seeking child is a person who, at the time of making the asylum application: is, or (if there is no proof) appears to be, under eighteen; is applying for asylum in kis or her own right; and has no adult relative or guardian to turn to in this country.
>
> (Source: www.ind.homeoffice.gov.uk)

However, these definitions are often conflated, adjusted, expanded and, in some instances, interpreted differently. As an important example of conflation, the terms 'refugee' and 'asylum seeker' are often used interchangeably, on the basis that those applying for asylum and those who have obtained asylum often have similar needs, and come from similar circumstances. It could be argued that asylum seekers are in fact living in much more uncertain circumstances than refugees who have been given indefinite leave to remain within their countries of asylum, and in terms of legal certainty, this argument is valid. However, given the many other practical, social, economic and psychological uncertainties faced by both asylum seekers and refugees, as well as the help offered to them in the form of resettlement, there are substantial similarities. It is on the basis of the major *similarities* that the terms are used interchangeably.

As an example of an adjustment and expansion of a term, the Separated Children in Europe Programme (SCEP) (Ayotte, 1999), a joint initiative of some members of the International Save the Children Alliance in Europe and UNHCR, suggests that the term *separated children* should be used instead of 'unaccompanied children' to more accurately reflect the circumstances of minors who are cared for, in transit and after arrival, by adults but not by parents or their usual primary caregivers. Instead the SCEP guidance (Ayotte, 1999: 1) notes:

> Some children are totally alone, while others . . . may be living
> with extended family members. All such children are separated
> children and entitled to international protection. . . .
> Separated children may be seeking asylum because of fear of
> persecution or lack of protection due to human rights viola-
> tions, armed conflict or disturbances in their own country.
> They may be victims of trafficking for sexual or other exploita-
> tion, or they may have travelled to Europe to escape conditions
> of serious deprivation.

Here, children are seen as vulnerable and in need of protection
for a number of reasons beyond the ones stated in the 1951 UN
Convention, and there is an explicit acknowledgement that
poverty and criminal activity can displace some minors, as well as
war. As such, the original definition of 'unaccompanied' is
subsumed under this more inclusive definition. However, the
UNHCR acknowledges that despite its endorsement of the
expanded definition, few states that are signatories to the 1951
Convention use the term (UNHCR, 2004: 1). Instead, as in the
United Kingdom, they continue to refer to 'unaccompanied
minors' in their asylum legislation and statistics.

Finally, as an example of differential interpretations, the definition of 'child' in relation to unaccompanied minors varies across
Europe. In Germany, for instance, only asylum seeking children
below the age of sixteen are considered minors. Older asylum
claimants are treated as *de facto* adults (UNHCR, 2004: 2).
Conversely, in Holland those who continue to receive government assistance after the age of eighteen are included in the
statistics returned to the UNHCR for unaccompanied minors.
Authorities in the UK have positioned themselves somewhere
between the German and Dutch interpretations of age in recent
times, as discussed in Chapter 3.

In this book it is important to note that the terms 'refugee'
and 'asylum seeker' are used interchangeably, in keeping with
general convention. In line with the 1989 Convention on the
Rights of the Child, and the Children Act 1989, a 'child' is
defined as someone under the age of eighteen years. The term
'unaccompanied' is used in preference to 'separated', although
the SCEP definition is referred to, both as it emerges within the
literature examined in Chapter 3, and in Chapter 6 when describ-

ing the circumstances of the young people as known to the social workers.

The historical context

Children displaced across borders, sometimes to countries far away from their homelands, have found their way to different parts of Western Europe (Ayotte, 2000), and to the United Kingdom in particular, for many decades (Williamson, 1995; Ayotte and Williamson, 2001; Harris and Oppenheimer, 2001). There are many records to show that the UK has allowed unaccompanied refugee children to resettle within its borders at certain moments in the twentieth century (Bell, 1996). If these records are examined within the wider frame of international refugee movements, a pattern emerges that suggests that wars can sometimes generate large numbers of displaced children, the majority of whom move to neighbouring countries. Very rarely do children flee to countries far away from their homelands. These days, relatively few come to Europe generally, or to the UK.

Ressler et al. (1988) cite numerous examples of children caught in the undertow of conflict and disorder worldwide, resulting in separation from their usual adult carers prior to seeking asylum. Depending on the nature and extent of the emergency or conflict, retrospective estimates carried out by aid agencies and researchers indicate that numbers of unaccompanied children can range from several hundred to several thousand. In the 1930s, the Spanish Civil War led at one stage to 90,000 children being reported as orphaned and abandoned. More than 20,000 of these were evacuated in an organised way to other countries, including France, Belgium, the USSR, Mexico, Switzerland and Denmark, with 4000 Basque children coming to the UK (Bell, 1996).

The 57 nations involved in the Second World War produced the biggest numbers of unaccompanied children – some 13 million, as estimated by the International Committee of the Red Cross and UNESCO. For children under threat of extermination by the Nazis, it became increasingly clear that survival depended on securing asylum away from their families and countries of origin. Particularly during 1938 and the early part of 1939, when families could not leave as units, the children within them were pushed forward as the most valuable assets by their parents, often into the care of rapidly constituted organisations and systems concerned with safety and flight. It is known that in the six years prior to the declaration of war in September 1939, 10,000 Jewish and non-Aryan children were moved to Britain in the *Kindertransport* (Harris and Oppenheimer, 2001). They came with parental consent, on the understanding that their stay would be temporary and that the countries would act as transition points for a later resettlement, and in the most optimistic forecasts, for reunification with their families after the war.

Similarly, following the Hungarian Revolt in November and December 1956, 466 unaccompanied minors are known to have arrived in Britain. The exodus of 'boat people' from Vietnam from the mid-1970s onwards resulted in some 22,000 unaccompanied children being left in Vietnam as adults fled, and the Cambodian crisis during the late 1970's generated similar numbers, either left behind, or pushed towards safety by their families, away from danger. Of these, between 1979 and 1984, about 300 unaccompanied children came to the UK as part of a group of 22,500 Vietnamese refugees under special resettlement programmes, as 'quota refugees' (Williamson, 1999).

During major conflicts in the late 1980s and early 1990s across the world, the number of unaccompanied minors coming to the UK remained small, apart from the sudden arrival of 170 young people in August and September 1990, mainly from Eritrea. For example, Blomqvist (1996) reports from the crisis in Rwanda in mid-1994, that 150,000 children were separated from their parents. The majority remained in Rwanda (100,000), and the rest moved into neighbouring countries such as Tanzania. Only 10 young Rwandan people came to the UK looking for asylum between 1994 and 1997 (Home Office, 1998). In the United Kingdom the rise in numbers arriving at ports began in earnest during the late 1990s, with the break up of the Yugoslavian Republic and the conflicts in Croatia, Bosnia and Kosovo, and also in Afghanistan, Iraq, and the Horn of Africa (Ayotte, 2000). While it appears that the worldwide refugee population fell between 2002 and 2003 (see below), the gradual increase in asylum applications from unaccompanied minors up to that time reflects the overall growth in the numbers of asylum applications in Europe between 1998 and 2002 (Zetter et al., 2003), as illustrated in Figure 1.1.

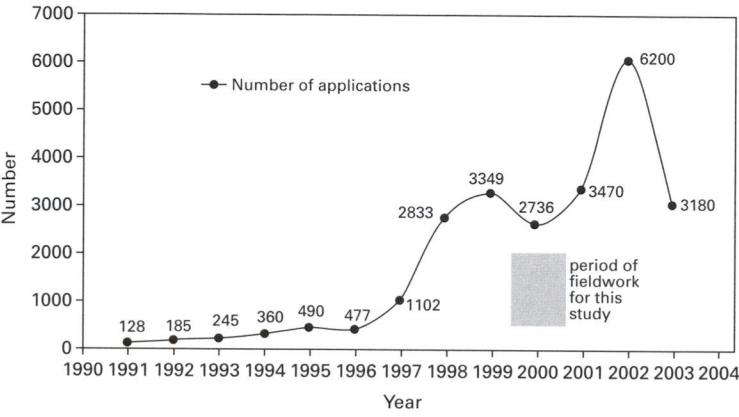

Sources: 1991 figure from Williamson (1995).
1992–2003 figures, Home Office (1998–2004).
www.homeoffice.gov.uk/rds/immigration1.html

Figure 1.1 Asylum applications by unaccompanied minors to the UK, 1991–2003

During those four years the rise in numbers can be illustrated in reference to young people arriving from various countries experiencing fragmentation. For example, in 1997 the Home Office figures show that only 119 young people from the Balkans made asylum applications. In contrast, the number of applications in 1998 had risen to 1325, an eleven-fold increase within one year. Similarly, in 2001, there were only 180 applications from young Iraqi people. In 2002, this rose to 1310, constituting 21% of all applications by young asylum seekers in the UK, with children from Afghanistan, Somalia and Kosovo also arriving in relatively large numbers. However, while the absolute numbers rose, the proportion of applications by unaccompanied minors to the UK relative to all applications remained relatively steady between 1998 and 2003, as revealed by the information compiled by UNHCR, shown in Table 1.1. Within this distribu-

Table 1.1 Applications by unaccompanied minors as a percentage of all applications for asylum in the United Kingdom and Europe

	1998	1999	2000	2001	2002	2003	Average 1998–2003
United Kingdom	6.6%	4.7%	3.4%	4.9%	7.4%	5.7%	5.45%
European average	5.8%	5.3%	4.1%	5.5%	5.2%	4.0%	4.98%

Sources: UNHCR (2000); UNHCR (2004).

tion, it can be seen that no matter how high or low the actual number seeking asylum, unaccompanied minors made up, on average, about one in twenty of all asylum applications to the UK between 1998 and 2003, slightly higher than the European average in the same period, but in overall terms, a very small proportion.

The demographic context

In 2003, the total number of people 'of concern' to the UNHCR – refugees, asylum seekers, internally displaced people, and others who are stateless – stood at 17 million worldwide, down from a figure of over 20 million in 2002. About 43% of these, over 7 million, were children (UNHCR, 2004). Of these 7 million children, 3180 made an asylum application in the UK in 2003, amounting to one child out of 2,300 displaced children worldwide, again a tiny proportion. The UK applicants' main countries of origin were Somalia, Afghanistan, Iraq, and Serbia and Montenegro.

Since 2002, the Home Office has published statistics on initial asylum decisions in relation to unaccompanied minors. These reveal that in 2002 on average about 4% were given full refugee status and about 15% had their asylum claims rejected. The majority of young people (66%) were granted Exceptional Leave to Remain (ELR) in 2002. From 1 April 2003, ELR was abolished, and replaced by Humanitarian Protection (HP) and

Discretionary Leave (DL). Figures for 2003 indicate that 32% of young people were granted ELR at the beginning of that year, and 40% were granted HP or DL, amounting in total to 72% of decisions made. Overall, the figures suggest that young people are much more likely to obtain some form of permission to remain on humanitarian grounds than their adult counterparts, but less likely to be granted refugee status (Home Office, 2004).

While figures for those making asylum applications, and latterly, asylum decisions, have been available for some time, statistics about those already in the UK were seldom available prior to 2002 (BAAF, 2001). Certainly at the time of conducting the fieldwork for this study in 2000, it was not possible to ascertain with any certainty how many unaccompanied young people there were in the UK altogether. Figures were fragmented and localised. However, since 2001 the Department of Health (DH) and Department for Education and Skills (DfES) have included unaccompanied minors within the annual statistics for 'looked after children' in England, as well as the more occasional Children in Need Surveys. These reveal the following picture.

The Children in Need surveys of September/October 2001 and of February 2003 indicate that there were between 12,500 and 12,600 asylum seeking children in England, representing 6% of all Children in Need (DH & National Statistics, 2002; DfES and National Statistics, 2004). The vast majority of these children and young people – between 10,000 and 11,000 – were living in families or independently, according to the surveys. What the surveys do not reveal is how this group was constituted between those living independently and those in families. Nor do they give any detail of how they were supported as 'children in need' within the terms of section 17 of the Children Act 1989. Instead the figures, as well as the commentaries attached to them, simply confirm that the majority of asylum seeking children and young people remained outside the provisions of care under section 20 of the Children Act 1989. However, as indicated in Table 1.2, a much clearer picture is available of children looked after by local authorities in England in 2002 and 2003 (DH, 2003a; DfES & National Statistics, 2003a; DfES & National Statistics, 2003b). The statistics overall show that:

- In 2002, 3.6% of children looked after were asylum seekers (2,200 out of a total of 59,700).
- In 2003, 3.9% of children looked after were asylum seekers (2,400 out of a total of 60,800).
- 9 out of 10 were living in London and South-East England.
- Boys outnumbered girls by 4:1 in both years.
- About half the looked after young people were over 16, and half were younger (DfES & National Statistics, 2003b).

Table 1.2 Unaccompanied asylum seeking children looked after at 31 March 2002 and at 31 March 2003 by region in England

	2002			2003		
	Total	Boys	Girls	Total	Boys	Girls
All children	2,200	1,700	500	2,400	1,900	580
North	50	50	–	100	70	30
Midlands	160	140	20	190	180	10
London	1,600	1,200	390	1,700	1,200	470
South-East (exc. London)	410	330	80	430	370	60

Source: DfES & National Statistics (2003a: 11).

In addition, Table 1.3 provides a comparative picture of the types of placements made available to unaccompanied minors and indigenous children. This shows that foster care was provided at the same percentage rate for unaccompanied minors as for indigenous children. However, proportionally more were living in children's homes and hostels or living independently than their indigenous peers. No unaccompanied minors were placed for adoption, in comparison with a consistent rate of 6% for indigenous children. The reasons for these similarities and differences are, however, not yet apparent.

None the less, the figures offer a clear backdrop for this study, particularly in attempting to understand the types of decisions social workers make in the provision of assistance and care. From the facts as they are known to UNHCR, the Home Office, the

Table 1.3 Comparing placement rates by types of placements for unaccompanied minors and indigenous children

	2002				2003			
	Unaccompanied children		Indigenous children		Unaccompanied children		Indigenous children	
	Number	%	Number	%	Number	%	Number	%
Foster care	1,300	60	37,900	66	1,600	68	39,400	68
Children's homes and hostels	550	25	6,200	11	480	20	6,200	11
Living independently	250	12	860	1	240	10	980	2
Placed for adoption	0	0	3,600	6	0	0	3,400	6
Other	70	3	8,900	15	70	3	8,400	14
All placements	**2,200**	100	**57,500**	100	**2,400**	100	**58,400**	100

Sources: DfES & National Statistics (2003b) (for 2003 figures).
Department of Health (2003a) (for 2002 figures).

Department of Health, and more recently the Department for Education and Skills, we can conclude that only a tiny fraction of children who need protection, worldwide, manage to enter the UK. Of the ones who enter, a few thousand are perceived to be 'children in need'. They are the ones who are in need of resettlement, requiring the expertise of social workers to rebuild their lives.

The UK policy context

Like many industrialised nations making a response to the presence of refugees, the United Kingdom appears to have chosen to narrow the straits through which refugees enter (Harding, 2000; Kushner and Knox, 1999). In relation to unaccompanied minors, evidence has built up for some time that the standards of care they receive after arrival are poorer than those offered to indigenous children in need. For example, the Audit Commission (2000) has noted that,

> Many unaccompanied children have multiple needs because of their experiences of separation, loss and social dislocation. . . . Yet in many cases they do not receive the same standard of care routinely afforded to indigenous children in need, even though their legal rights are identical. (Audit Commission, 2000: 66)

In some important research studies within the United Kingdom, which are reviewed in detail in chapter 3, the equation is presented in quite simple ways – the children's and young people's needs are said to be ignored or misunderstood by service providers, who act defensively in creating restrictions in the ways resources can be accessed to help them resettle, particularly for those deemed to be on the threshold of adulthood. In addition, in lobbying for change to these restrictive policies and practices, many commentators recommend that social workers ought to practise in ways that are based on open access to services for children in need. For example, there is an emergent consensus between these lobbyists and central government in insisting that in the case of unaccompanied children needing assistance there should be a 'presumption' that they should be treated on a par with all children in need, and where necessary looked after under section 20 of the Children Act 1989 unless there are clear reasons related to the child's well-being for not doing so (Department of Health, 2003b). This view also has judicial support, through what has come to be referred to as 'the Hillingdon judgement'. In August 2003, in conducting a judicial review, the High Court determined that four unaccompanied young people, who had been supported by Hillingdon Social Services under section 17 of the Children Act 1989, were entitled to after-care services as they would have been had they been looked after under section 20. The local authority had argued that it did <u>not</u> owe them a duty of care under the Children (Leaving Care) Act 2000, because it had not accommodated them under section 20 of the Children Act 1989, although it had provided them with accommodation under section 17. The judge found that this distinction was 'mere sophistry' on the part of the local authority, and the children were 'relevant children' under the Children Act 1989 and were owed the same level of support as all children who were looked after under section 20. Yet a recent evaluation by the British Refugee Council (Dennis, 2005) has highlighted that local authorities have thus far been inconsistent in responding to government guidance and 'the Hillingdon judgement' effectively, in that the standards of care provided by social workers to unaccompanied minors require further improvement. In all, social work services and practices have been, and continue to be, viewed within this arena in a dystopian frame.

In some respects, this frame is a familiar one for social work practitioners and policy makers, who are seldom appraised as valuable contributors to the provision of welfare, often being judged by people who do not know, or want to know, the details of the way practitioners think about and do their work (Davidson and King, 2005). It is in this context that the next two chapters consider whether there are any ways of representing social work with unaccompanied minors that illuminate a different view of the profession apart from one where there are gaps, defences and instructions for improvement. With this spirit of enquiry in mind, how do social workers, given their experiences of creating and sustaining networks of care and protection for vulnerable children, view resettlement-based practice as it already exists? In order to address this question I will first consider what the term 'resettlement' means from a theoretical and research-based perspective, and the ways a fresh conceptualisation of the term can act as a foundation for understanding practice in a refreshed way.

Resettlement: theoretical and research contexts

Resettlement can mean many things to many people. In its simplest formulation within the field of refugee studies it refers to the mechanism by which some governments allow refugees to remain within their territories via a planned 'quota refugee' entry, mainly in cooperation with the United Nations High Commission for Refugees (UNHCR, 2002). While the United Kingdom has until recently generally only accepted refugees on an *ad hoc* basis (Zetter et al., 2003), several industrialised nations have run resettlement programmes for many decades designed to offer durable solutions to those defined as refugees (UNHCR, 2001). As Newland observes (2002:1),

> Refugee resettlement is the process by which some refugees are allowed to leave a country of (initial) asylum and start life anew in a third country that is willing to receive and protect them on a permanent basis. Resettling refugees are, in this way, distinct from asylum seekers, who arrive without prior authorization to seek refugee status.

But this relatively clear definition of resettlement, relating strictly to quota refugees, has become indistinct in the literature in a way that parallels the refugee experience itself. In the same vein as the labels 'refugee' and 'asylum seeker', which are used interchangeably (Russell, 1999; Harding, 2000), the term 'resettlement' has come to have a diffuse rather than distinctive definition. Starting from the UNHCR definition, the term has seeped out of the worlds of NGOs, and spread into different arena as refugees have become a topic of study by many disciplines. As Stein (1986) notes,

> Refugee research does not fit neatly into disciplinary categories. The breadth of the problems and subject demands an

> inter-, cross-, multi-disciplinary approach. Sociology, psychology, anthropology, law, political science, linguistics, medicine, social work, history, and (the many) subdivisions of these disciplines all impinge on refugee studies. (Stein, 1986: 1)

Within these divisions and subdivisions, commentators have used the term 'resettlement' in varying ways. For example, in a review conducted on behalf of the New Zealand Immigration Service, Gray and Elliott (2001) suggest that the term now has an adaptable meaning that relates, amongst other things, to notions of acculturation, assimilation, integration and settlement, all used within the literature to describe processes and outcomes that help refugees <u>and</u> asylum seekers to arrive and become part of the host community over time. Lifting the term out in this way from the strictures of the UNHCR definition, and spreading it across disciplines, allows a diverse yet coherent picture to emerge of people on the move as a consequence of forced migration, needing different sorts or remedies in order to manage a successful transition to a new land. Berry (1991) offers a schema that outlines some of the precursors to and consequences of forced migrations that take into account not just key phases in the journey of resettlement, but also events and experiences that refugees and asylum seekers commonly encounter. While he is careful not to make a case for the schema being universally applicable, Berry's (1991: 30) exposition exemplifies an attempt to deal with the notion of resettlement from a multi-faceted perspective, containing psychological and social perspectives, and a time frame that describes a protracted period of dislocation before these migrants come face to face with service providers in their chosen country of sanctuary.

What it illustrates is that contact with helping agencies comes towards the tail end of the resettlement journey, and that the roots of movement are fairly well established before the refugee arrives at the social services' duty desk. Within the schema (see Figure 1.2) the pulse of movement is generated during the pre-departure phase, either as a major event, or in a series of deepening crises involving violence, conflict and persecution. Life dramatically or slowly becomes untenable, and people have to resort to flight. During the flight phase, risk of capture (or recapture), loss of people, valuables and status, all combine with a

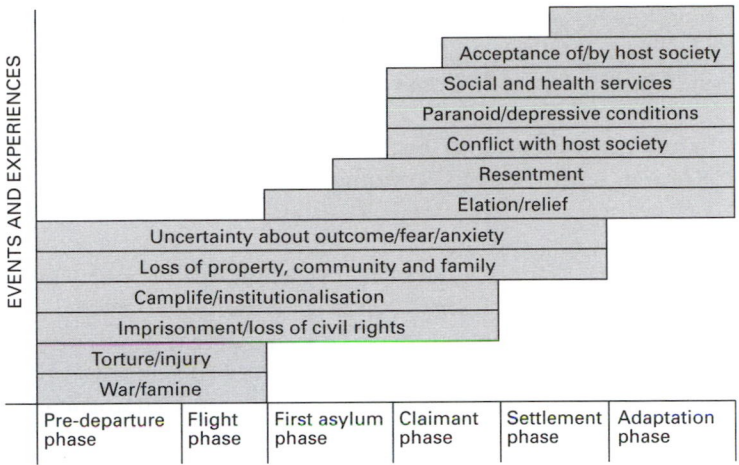

Source: Berry (1991: 130).

Figure 1.2   Phases, events and experiences during a refugee career

growing sense of uncertainty about the future. As people cross borders from their own homelands, perhaps to a neighbouring country, they experience a sense of relief, followed by hope that their asylum claim will one day succeed. But as they begin to realise that adjudication on their claim may be delayed in their country of asylum, or that they may be rejected and subject to deportation, a worsening uncertainty can, in some cases, lead to the emergence of resentment and hostility, leading to

> conflict with officials and hostile citizens of the host society. In extreme cases, paranoid conditions and depression become common during this phase.   (Berry, 1991: 32)

During the settlement phase, fresh challenges arise. Berry (1991) notes, for example that dispersal as a policy aim has seldom been effective in resettlement, because it can wipe out the seed bed of support that many refugees use to re-root themselves in their new environments. Yet over time, in the final phases of settlement and adaptation, which Berry (1991) maintains are open ended, most refugee populations do succeed in fitting into their new environments, and developing 'routine lives'. It is this establishment of ordinary living that is used in the European Council on Refugees and Exiles (ECRE) definition of integration, which suggests that resettlement occurs as

> A refugee becomes an *active* member of the [host] society from a legal, social, economic, educational and cultural perspective. (ECRE, 2002: 4)

In the ECRE definition, as in many definitions of resettlement (see, for example, Canadian Council for Refugees, 1998), two elements are discernible. One is a focus on the psychological processes that resettlers go through in order to succeed in their new environments. Another element contains a humanitarian focus on the practicalities of bedding down in an alien land.

For example, Hulewat (1996) writing from the perspective of clinical social work with Soviet Jews coming to America, refers to resettlement as a 'cultural and psychological crisis', that requires refugees to maximise opportunities and minimise risks in successfully replanting themselves. Working within an explicitly psychoanalytic frame of reference, she suggests that these risks and opportunities exist at several stages, from the preparation for departure, through migration and transition, to arrival, to slowly beginning to adjust, unravel and finally belong. Within the latter stages, she identifies three sub-groups of resettlers, adjusting in three different ways. The first she refers to as the *help me get started* group, which in her experience represents the largest group of refugee resettlers. The second largest group is referred to as the *take care of me* group, which Hulewat (1996) describes as people for whom dependency is high, because they have lost their capacities for self-maintenance. The third and smallest group is referred to as the *you must do it my way*, consisting of *people who deal with fear and anxiety by trying to control and be manipulative* (Hulewat, 1996: 134). Recommendations for effective practice range from a general call for social workers to be trustworthy, authoritative and supportive, to ways in which dependency and resistance can be minimised in order to allow the refugees to move beyond the cultural and psychological crisis to a state of relative calm. Within this type of approach, the distinctions between those who are helped and their helpers are strictly drawn and a rather simple view is exposed to suggest that needs associated with resettlement occur as a consequence of unfavourable exposure to traumatic events, and that the impact of such events can be alleviated by the kindness and skills of professional helpers.

Spake (2001), in a conference report on the integration and resettlement of refugees, looks on the other hand at the practicalities of resettlement and offers a list of ten types of provisions and services that can be made available to refugees in countries with existing resources and infrastructures designed to provide comprehensive support.

1 Financial assistance
2 Grants for clothing and household items
3 Housing
4 Child care services
5 Special educational support, including language training
6 Medical services
7 Education and skills training
8 Vocational and employment assistance
9 Cultural orientation
10 Psychological care   (Spake, 2001: 4)

Here again the hosts and the newcomers maintain their separate roles and as with Hulewat's (1996) exposition, refugees and asylum seekers as active participants in the co-creation of resettlement are not as visible as the benign helpers who are offered guidance about what to do when faced with resettlement issues. A simple matching equation is presented between refugee need and community resources. However, research in the UK, both nationally (Carey-Wood et al., 1995; Bloch and Schuster, 2002) and locally (Centre for Inner City Studies, 1992; Coate and Kamasa, 1997), shows that far from being passive recipients, refugee communities value and use their own energies in the reconstruction of their lives in reference to many of the items on the above list. For example, in developing a detailed sense of how 'cultural orientation' and 'psychological care' interact with the more material aspects of resettlement, Valtonen (1994) and Joly (1996), amongst others, put forward the proposition that refugees, like other migrant groups, go through a series of adjustments in their new contexts over time. First, they acclimatise, learning or attempting to learn the language, norms, roles and customs of the host community, while confronting what they have lost as a consequence of forced migration. Secondly, they adapt, learning to deal with new roles and customs as they drive to rebuild their lives. Thirdly they make attempts – often arduous and with mixed success – to participate in host societies, at least at the level of employment and income, education and training, and living in contexts that are safe and comfortable (Carey-Wood et al., 1995). Fourthly, resettlement takes place at the level of shifts and absorption of cultures of belonging, within which looking back to a time and a place that are no longer retrievable is made to fit with a context that contains its own opportunities and limitations. Even within a simple, linear exposition of stages such as this, reciprocity is highlighted as part of resettlement. Members of refugee communities and host-community members are seen to work towards a mutual construction of outcomes that are positive for all – a sort of common philanthropic endeavour with a belief in a cooperative future.

Yet Berry (1997) notes that this hoped-for outcome carries complexities for members of refugee communities. For example, while opportunities to progress materially might be eagerly grasped, people adjust at differing rates, and no standard rate of resettlement can be used to predict the type, range and quality of outcomes. Similarly, integration and disintegration are processes that happen together, and knitting the present together can sometimes mean becoming unravelled from the past. In this respect, refugee families are known to struggle with making sense of changes, especially if different generations are facing in differing directions – some looking forward, others looking back – when trying to find meaning in their lives. Papadopoulous and Hildebrand's (1997) clinical work leads them to conclude that refugees can sometimes experience a constant underlying tension between these two orientations:

> On the one hand to privilege and remain loyal to the past, not to forget the home country and its ways, to honour the home culture and its belief systems, to value the old, the pre-war relationships and their connections, and to emphasise the previous styles and modes of being with their corresponding perceptions, values and aspirations; and on the other hand to focus

on the benefits of their current place of safety, to value their adjustment to their new life, to emphasise their new modes of being, to ensure maximum gain from new relationships and connections, to explore and benefit from the new lifestyles found in the receiving country, and to look towards the future ensuring that they make the best of their new opportunities. (Papadopoulous and Hildebrand, 1997: 218)

These tensions are heightened in a context of ambivalence or hostility from the host communities, adding to a sense of being unsettled about the present, as well as about the past and future. In a review of major longitudinal studies looking at resettlement for quota refugees in North America and Australia, Silove and Ekblad (2002) comment on two significant findings. First, it can take up to a decade for people to recover and resettle in host communities. Secondly, the climate of distrust and hostility towards refugees generally and asylum seekers in particular, has worsened substantially since the late 1980s. They say,

> These long term studies are based in an epoch in which [refugees] were offered favourable resettlement conditions, including permanent residency and full access to work and educational opportunities. In contrast asylum seekers arriving in many Western countries now face daunting challenges. Temporary residency, detention, restrictions on rights to work, to study, to language classes, and to health care, as well as administrative obstacles to family reunion, all generate insecurity and fear, anxieties already provoked by past trauma experiences. At a communal level, the insecurities suffered by refugees are intensified by the upsurge in hostility towards immigrants, a tendency that has been fuelled by fears of global terrorism. (Silove and Ekblad, 2002: 2)

Their conclusion is that the new territories that the asylum seekers and refugees encounter are shifting, unpredictable and uncertain and that the task of refugee resettlement, which was complex but navigable a generation ago is much more fragmented and unpredictable now. Bihi (1999), as a refugee himself, confirms the view that resettlement is about a 'recovery of meaning and a sense of belonging' in a context of increasing levels of uncertainty (Bihi, 1999: 12), and that it involves the *restoration* of livelihoods and health, the *maintenance* of habits and customs from the past, and the *transformation* of life chances through making the best of opportunities for advancement offered within the new environment. In each aspect of this process the refugee can be seen to resettle through a reconfiguration of individual and social factors associated with the past, present and future. Joly's (1996) research in relation to the ways in which particular ethnic and national groups reconfigure their lives provides some evidence of this. Moreover, she argues that the resolution to the tensions described by Papadopoulous and Hildebrand's (1997) study can happen at group levels, as well as in families. In a comparative analysis of Chilean and Vietnamese refugees in the UK and France, Joly (1996) found two distinctive patterns in the way these communities dealt with their circumstances. She found that for the Chileans resettlement was substantially influenced by constantly looking back towards Chile, and wanting to, 'regain their power as social actors in the society of origin, albeit from a distance', whereas the Vietnamese spent much of their time and energy looking forward.

> Their main orientation is that of the society of reception . . . [and] all their efforts tend to address adaptation and settlement in the host society. . . . Their aim is to gain social power in the host society. . . . The concrete desire for return is not part of their strategy. (Joly, 1996: 185)

In identifying these sought-after connections, and the tensions and resolutions associated with them, these writers and others establish a relatively under-researched aspect of resettlement – the ways in which refugees and asylum seekers use their own capabilities to resettle in their new contexts. While much has been written about refugee suffering, resilience in the face of adversity, so far as research within the refugee field is concerned, has received less attention. As Muecke (1992) observed over a decade ago, new paradigms for understanding refugee health and capability – as opposed to pathology and need – could be used to understand how people in adversity retain some power and influence in the ways their lives are constructed.

> Refugees present perhaps the maximum example of the human capacity to survive despite the greatest of losses and assaults on human identity and dignity. The concept of resilience has been examined among a variety of populations who have been exposed to major life stressors and could be of use in the study of healthy refugees. (Muecke, 1992: 520)

These paradigms have begun to develop, and as Punamäki (2000) notes in a volume related to researching the psychosocial *wellness* of refugees (Ahern, 2000),

> As a researcher, my task is to reveal the phenomenon in all its richness and to document and crystallize the human conflict of suffering *and* endurance [emphasis added]. (Punamäki, 2000: 106)

So, another important part of resettlement becomes the way in which displaced people can act as agents of resettlement, not just recipients of expert aid. The emphasis on agency and the capacity that refugees have to create and sustain durable solutions receives some support from therapeutic literature related to recovery from loss. In brief, the message is that endurance has always been a part of the refugee experience, and now researchers have both seen it for what it is, and valued it in relation to a process of self-healing that occurs naturally over time, particularly as communities of friendship and support are rebuilt during the resettlement period (Loizos, 2002).

Summary

To summarise, 'resettlement' at its core is an NGO term, particularly used in reference to the relationship between the UNHCR and those countries that receive quota refugees, when people cannot return to their countries of origin, nor remain in the country of first asylum. It is also used in a much more malleable way to denote a process of bedding down in a new country for refugees and asylum seekers, with or without the benefit of organised systems of help. Where organised systems exist, resettlement has been closely tied to the provision of resources and opportunities and the settlement of inner-world turbulence through 'cultural orientation' and 'psychological care'. People appear to go through *stages* (Berry, 1991) or *types* of resettlement (Hulewat, 1996); differing aspects of life adjust at different rates, and whether people look back or look forward appears to depend on their cultures and individual and group preferences. Finally, people resettle themselves, and are seen to be resilient in the face of vicissitudes, including hostility from host communities, when they can rebuild networks of support and care over time. In the various usages of the term, resettlement relates to what is done, as well as the consequence of what is done. In other words, it is defined both as process and as an outcome, and in both instances relates to re-establishing a home in a stranger's land, and becoming an ordinary citizen within it.

Given these considerations, we can see that resettlement practice with unaccompanied asylum seeking minors can be characterised in three different ways, all of which may already be familiar to social workers offering a service to looked after children more generally:

- First, as a **humanitarian activity**, designed to offer practical, authoritative help to young people who are disorientated after flight and need sanctuary. Particularly in reference to Davies's (1994: 40) idea of social work as a 'humanist endeavour' that maintains the bridge between those who need and those who provide resources, the details of what refugees and asylum seeking children are seen to need in their 'outer worlds', and what is known about how these needs are met by social workers, can be examined in more detail by understanding what social workers do to be practically helpful to children in need.

- Secondly, as a psychosocial **intervention** addressing inner-world turbulence, particularly for those who have been directly or indirectly badly affected by war, and carry ghosts from the past with them into their new territories. Again, what research tells us about the needs of unaccompanied minors for psychosocial care can be placed within the frame of linking inner and outer worlds as part of effective child and family social work (Schofield, 1998).

Within this frame, a focus can be maintained on the ways in which social workers address the impact of past experiences on the reality of everyday life as they tune in to joining the inner and outer worlds to help vulnerable children (Goldstein, 1992).

- Thirdly, as an attempt to provide **companionship-based practice** that optimises the use of resilience in order to assist in the reconstruction of a safe and durable context over an extensive period of time. In comparison with research focusing on humanitarian activity, or psychosocial care of refugee and asylum seeking children, research that takes their resilience into account or examines what social workers might do over a period of time in the reconstruction of natural networks of care and support for them, is rarer. Yet there are messages from social work with looked after children (for example, Gilligan, 2001; Bilton, 2003) that are relevant here both in keeping resilience in mind, and in social workers being companions for those children for whom companionship is a rare commodity after having lost family and friends. These aspects of practice are discussed below in relation to working with unaccompanied minors.

An important thing to say about these ways of conceptualising resettlement practice is that they overlap – they do not exist as distinct entities or as a menu of that which workers must utilise in order to maximise their personal effectiveness. The invitation here is to consider them as differing aspects of a coherent whole rather than placing them in hierarchically differentiated positions in reference to each other. As a counterpoint to the fragmented and polarised debate about asylum itself, an attempt is made to find out what is worthwhile for the young people in *each* of these ways of working. The second thing to say is that an attempt is made here to steer away from accounts of refugee lives as spectral and bleak. Important as these aspects are, they miss something. As Papadopoulos and Hildebrand (1997) observe,

Becoming a refugee engenders stressful experiences which may lead to temporary or permanent psychological dysfunction in individuals, families and communities. However, such experiences, despite their painful nature, may also have positive consequences in so far as they may lead to the development of more appropriate coping mechanisms, deepen a sense of identity in individuals, strengthen cohesion among family members, and offer an opportunity for a more fundamental re-evaluation of one's life. (Papadopoulos and Hildebrand, 1997: 206)

Thirdly, related to this second point, social work and social workers are held in mind as optimistic contributors to the care and well-being of refugee and asylum seeking children. As I have said, the litany of woe, or of help given being insufficient or flawed, is pervasive in the refugee literature, directed at social work and many other professions. While many contributors base their concerns on a type of humanitarianism that social workers would feel a binding sympathy towards, their glum appraisals 'often fail to appreciate either the breadth or the subtlety of social work practice' (Davies, 1994: 44). So some attempt is made to locate literature that differentiates simple complaints about social workers from more complex and balanced appraisals in relation to those offering 'recommendations for good practice' about resettlement of unaccompanied minors. With these *caveats* in mind, Chapter 2 considers what the literature shows about what the concept of resettlement means to unaccompanied children. Then Chapter 3 describes and appraises views of resettlement practice by social workers as portrayed within several research-based studies in the United Kingdom.

2 The meaning of resettlement for unaccompanied asylum seeking children and young people

There is no indication when examining the existing literature that a great deal is known about the pre-departure histories of the asylum seeking children and young people now living in the UK or in other parts of Europe. There is a tendency for researchers not to look back, as if the stories only begin when they become visible as asylum seekers. By only beginning a story from the point of departure, the chance to see unaccompanied minors as 'ordinary people driven by ordinary desires (such as wanting to live in peace in a democracy that allows free speech', (Robinson and Segrott, 2002: 64) has not yet been grasped by researchers. At present, just a few of their stories of ordinary living are gathered up, and presented as small illustrative vignettes from a generation ago (Bell, 1996; Harris and Oppenheimer, 2001) or the more recent past (Minority Rights Group International, 1998). Some of them are linked with a heartfelt sense of bewilderment when transmitting the loss of ordinariness in becoming a refugee. Within these accounts children speak of simple and mundane events with affection. For example, Zacharia Wurie, a child in exile in the Netherlands says,

> In Sierra Leone, my school days were the best period of my life. Every morning all the classes got together, we swam and then we each went to our different classes. At break time we went cycling, or played football, or we told each other stories about long ago while sitting in the sun. There were lots of nice things that I cannot write about now, but I think they were just like everybody else's school day. On holidays . . . people

ate at their neighbours' houses in order to watch the matches between the two best football teams of Sierra Leone, the Eastern Lions and Black Pool. I was an Eastern Lions fan. When we won, we danced in the street. (Minority Rights Group International, 1998: 13)

In a similar vein, Lorraine Allard who grew up in Fürth, Bavaria, and left on the *Kindertransport* when the Nazis came to power, reflects on a family life that has a universal appeal,

> My parents had an extremely happy marriage. My mother sitting on my father's knee for a cuddle was an everyday occurrence. I had to join in because otherwise I would have been jealous. He had to have both of us on his lap. . . . I remember doing lots of nonsense with him, like Sunday morning playtime, tickling and acrobatics, things like that. I was the apple of his eye. (Harris and Oppenheimer, 2001: 21)

For some of those in exile looking back as adults to the landscape of childhood, the powerful impact of a primary attachment, not just to a parent, but to a country, lives on:

> The country of my childhood lives within me with a primacy that is a form of love. . . . It has given me language, perceptions, sounds . . . the colours and furrows of reality, my first loves. The absoluteness of those loves can never be recaptured: no geometry of the landscape, no haze in the air will live with us as intensely as the landscapes that we saw as the first. (Hoffmann, 1989: 74)

However, these vignettes and reflections, describing habits, people and landscapes, are not yet part of a broad and systematic understanding related to reliable research-based enquiries about what life was like before the decision to leave was made. Instead, what some research studies provide is a steady view of suffering, and to a more limited extent, endurance in the face of harm, and these studies are presented below.

Why leave?

While a considerable body of literature exists that describes what happens to refugee children once they arrive in industrialised nations, only one study has considered *why* children who had to move away from danger or harm, seek sanctuary in Europe (Ayotte, 2000). This study can be framed within a broader discussion prompted by Home Office commissioned research (Koser and Pinkerton, 2002; Robinson and Segrott, 2002; Zetter et al., 2003), which has begun to look at why forced migrants choose particular countries to move to, and what the response within those countries has been to being chosen in this way. For example, Robinson and Segrott's (2002) study focusing on the decision making of asylum seekers shows that when people seek asylum, a number of factors guide them ultimately towards particular destinations. They interviewed 65 asylum seekers living in the UK, 5 per cent of whom were aged 16 or below at the point of arrival, roughly equivalent to the proportion of asylum seekers internationally who are unaccompanied children (UNHCR, 1997). While making no claims to be representative of asylum seekers' behaviour as a whole, the study makes a number of points pertinent to unaccompanied children. According to the respondents, the first-stage decision to leave was made on the balance of the *political* 'push' forces, not economic 'pull' factors, although money was an important factor for those with resources, for whom staying put or internal displacement were not viable options – having money bought the choice of how far one could afford to travel from the homeland. At the second stage, decisions were made to use or not use agents depending on the ability to pay, the available networks of re-routing and escape, and any knowledge about particular destinations held within those networks. If agents were used, then a number of options opened up at stage 3 – specific countries were identified, depending on choice and availability, and on the agent's own networks and resources. They note,

> Agents play a key role in channelling asylum seekers. Some agents facilitated travel to a destination chosen by the asylum seeker. Some asylum seekers had no choice and were directed to particular countries by agents. Other agents provided a

'menu' of destinations from which asylum seekers chose . . . agents often offer the only means of escaping the country of origin and reaching a destination where asylum can be sought. (Robinson and Segrott, 2002: 2)

Within such a scenario, agents were experienced as protective people who could help the asylum seeker to get to safety, at a price. The provision of travel documents, including tickets, visas and passports, organising and facilitating the journey, and giving advice about which country to choose at any particular moment, were part of the agent's repertoire of services. Furthermore, the respondents in this study reported that they felt as if they were equal partners with the agents, that the eventual destination was a joint decision, and that they chose the country that they did if they perceived it as relatively safe, rich and containing opportunities for advancement, particularly in relation to education. For example, the UK was consistently described by the respondents as offering high quality education, and this was a main reason for choosing to come here. While knowledge of asylum policies or welfare benefits and housing, employment rights and opportunities were vaguely known and were relatively weak determinants of deciding to choose a particular country, having family or friends made a strong impact on their choices. This finding reflects an earlier EU-funded study by Böcker and Havinga (1998), which confirms that having friends, relatives or compatriots in a destination country substantially outweighed any other factors in deciding to head for that country. In reference to the UK, Robinson and Segrott (2002) note,

Family and friends shaped the migration decisions of respondents in two distinct ways. First, family and friends acted either as the primary reason for choosing the UK or as a factor that tipped the balance in favour of migrating here. Even when asylum seekers had only vague connections with distant relatives in the UK, the knowledge that they would know someone made it more attractive than other possible destinations where they would be completely alone. Second, relatives and friends in the UK passed information about life in this country back to potential asylum seekers, either before or during the latter's journey. This information was often generalised in nature and very scant. The presence of a very distant relative (perhaps not known personally by the asylum seeker) or a family friend in the UK might seem an inadequate explanation for choice of destination but for asylum seekers faced with a choice of countries about which they know little, the presence of such a person in the UK can be extremely important. At the very least it provides someone who can be approached when they first arrive. (Robinson and Segrott, 2002: 3)

Ayotte's (2000) study confirms that these considerations and reasons also apply to separated children coming to Europe, including unaccompanied minors. In this study 218 case studies were compiled of separated children, gathered from 67 interviews with young people from 28 countries, as well as 'officials, professionals, and NGOs' (Ayotte, 2000: 9). Of the 218 cases, 67% were boys, and 33% girls. The whole sample yielded 449 '*movement reasons*' that had led them to Europe, because some of the children cited multiple factors that influenced their decisions, or the decisions made on their behalf by their families. These are illustrated in Table 2.1.

There are a number of reasons to be cautious about accepting the results of Ayotte's study at face value, while noting some of its valuable yet unusual features. First, 424 of the 449 are accounted for in the above categories but no explanation is given for the missing 25 'movement reasons'. Some of these 'movement reasons' are less clearly defined than others. For example, 'refugees in orbit' is a term that remains unexplained, whereas cases that the authorities found hard to believe have very specific rationales attached.

Some cases in the study involved children from West African countries who claimed to be from Sierra Leone, and others from Albania who claimed to be Kosovar in order to be recognised as refugees. Several Guineans appeared to have been provided with the same stories of political repression, imprisonment and escape. . . . All of these children had applied for asylum and it was in this context that doubts or uncertainty arose. (Ayotte, 2000: 61)

Table 2.1 The reason separated children leave their homelands

Movement reason	Frequency of reasons
The homeland was undergoing armed conflict or serious disturbances that had led to the flight.	104
1951 Convention-based reason (i.e. the children themselves were subject to persecution in relation to political opinion, ethnic origin, religion, nationality or social group).	94
Separation from parents because they were missing, imprisoned or dead or had abandoned the children	77
Serious deprivation in the homeland including living as street children and escape from 'brutal conditions' in orphanages	30
Trafficking related to prostitution, illegal drugs, petty crime, begging, or cheap labour, and 'debt bondage', primarily involving Nigeria, Albania, and China.	26
Torture by state authorities	25
Lack of educational opportunities	16
Abuse and neglect by family or 'problems within the family'	16
Medical condition needing treatment	15
Unknown, unclear reasons, or reasons given to authorities that were considered 'hard to believe' because the stories were repetitive. Some children were coached, stories were rehearsed.	6
'harmful traditional practices' including escape from ritualised murder, shamanism, voodoo, or coercion into ritual abuse or servitude	6
'Refugees in orbit' – probably children moving from one asylum country to another	5
Refusal of or desertion from state military service	4
Total number of reasons discussed in the study	**424**

Source: Ayotte (2000: 25–6)

Even so, no account is given of how the categories were devised, and weighted for relative importance to the young person or to the authorities, or how many of the children gave multiple reasons. In other words, the categories read very much as a series of poorly constructed researcher ratings, with no clear methodological justifications. Therefore a simple numerical presentation of the data as above is difficult to interpret in terms of the cluster and spread of reasons across the whole group, how many children there were per category, their ages, origins, or other defining characteristics.

Yet there are a number of important aspects of the study that are worth summarising. For example – and this is unsurprising given the entry criteria for many European countries that allow children to enter at least on a temporary basis – the major reasons given for leaving and seeking sanctuary are related to war and its impact on the fragmentation of day-to-day living. Some children are on the move before a war-related crisis hits them, and others suffer persecution within the terms of the 1951 Convention. Around the periphery of these main reasons, other reasons emerge. These are linked to pre-migration circumstances of deprivation, or conditions that generated abuse (from outside as well as within the family) or criminal activity resulting in a decision to move into contexts that could offer safety and opportunity, both for orthodox economic and educational gain for the children themselves, and for some, further involvement in criminal activity. While it does not identify whether people from the children's homelands were also present in receiving countries, Ayotte's (2000) report contains many vignettes illustrating a broad range of suffering according to the main elements of each of the above categories, and is a concerted attempt to view the dangers that may befall children that cannot be strictly contained within the narrowness of the 1951 Convention's definition of 'refugee'. It is this broad sweep that allows their many and wide-ranging needs to be specified as they come face to face with the authorities in their chosen country of refuge; in these circumstances social workers familiar with indigenous children needing care and protection can begin to understand the complex set of circumstances that lead these children towards them, related to three areas of special significance:

- War and vulnerability
- Resilience and overcoming the odds
- Silence that brings bothprotection and heightened risk

War and vulnerability

The many adverse impacts of local explosions on indigenous children entering local authority care are well documented, and well researched (for example, Howe et al., 1999; Jones, 2003). While there are many similarities of suffering between refugee children and indigenous children who are vulnerable, it is the degree of exposure to harm, and the subsequent degree to which refugee children are perceived as 'victims' by researchers and clinicians, that could be said to stand in contrast to the ways in which indigenous children are described. For children and young people who become refugees, the effects of war or natural disasters are seen as punishing in various ways. They may, as Petty and Jareg (1998) note, have witnessed the deaths of close family members, or torture and sexual assault of parents, siblings and friends. They may themselves have participated in acts of violence. Whatever has held them in place in their homelands becomes unravelled. In these circumstances, Summerfield (1998: 16) emphasises that they are forced into exile and experience 'a rupture in the narrative threads running through their lives'. In these circumstances, unaccompanied minors may have lost not just the narrative threads, but the whole collective plot by living through 'total war', where

> mass terror becomes a deliberate strategy. Destruction of schools, houses, religious buildings, fields and crops as well as torture, rape and internment become commonplace. Modern warfare is concerned not only to destroy life, but also ways of life. It targets social and cultural institutions and deliberately aims to undermine the means whereby people endure and recover from the suffering of war. (Bracken and Petty, 1998: 3)

Yule's research (1992) into the impact of such events on refugee children, both accompanied by family members and unaccompanied, can be summarised in the following ways:

- Children are troubled by repetitive, intrusive thoughts about the traumatic event or events, particularly at times when they are quiet or reflective. Flashbacks, sleep disturbance, recurring nightmares, and other symptoms of stress related to the events, are regular occurrences.

- Difficulties in concentration are reported, especially in schoolwork, as well as memory problems in grasping new material and remembering old skills.

- They carry a sense of a foreshortened future, finding it difficult to plan, or survivor's guilt, being disorientated by their own good fortune in comparison with those who were left behind or killed. Life is experienced as fragile.

Montgomery (1998) reviews the literature in relation to age-specific responses to war, and suggests that pre-school children may act regressively, with clingy behaviour and heightened anxiety when left alone or with strangers, and that their adolescent counterparts may act aggressively, towards themselves and others, or take on the responsibilities of adulthood before their time, particularly in coping with younger siblings. In noting that 'the central character of trauma is that of disconnection', Melzak (1995a) confirms that refugee children can show uneven development, in that some of them appear to have the strengths characteristic of older children and vulnerability characteristic of younger children so that the chronological age is at variance with the child's developmental age. Girls and boys appear to differ in their responses to trauma, with some studies showing higher rates of depression and anxiety amongst girls caught up in 'single event' natural disasters (Lonigan et al., 1991; Yule, 1992), and boys responding to 'multiple event' stressors such as war with greater anxiety than girls (Milgram and Milgram, 1976). Despite some controversy surrounding the application of Post Traumatic Stress Disorder (PTSD) to refugee children (Bracken, 1998; Summerfield, 2000), Thomas and Lau (2002) confirm, via a review of 130 major international research studies conducted between 1992 and 2002, that exposure to highly stressful events at the pre-migration stage, during flight, and during the period of unsettlement in the host country, create clusters of disorders and deep unhappiness. Fazel and Stein (2003) and Hodes (2004) suggest that prevalence rates for mental ill health amongst refugee children in Britain are comparable to those in other industrialised nations, and higher than in comparison with the general population in the UK.

In some instances, higher cognitive abilities and a track record of achievement at school are associated with lesser degrees of trauma for children (Yule and Gold, 1993). It is worth noting that the presence or absence of adult caregivers for children during trauma and flight is strongly associated with their capacities to adjust. In some instances, when family members have fled together, caregivers act as buffers against adversity (Montgomery, 1998: 193), and provide continuity of roots. But in situations where the caregivers are themselves traumatised, children carry a multiple awareness – of needing to represent the adult in the asylum context, of caring for them, and of remaining sensitised to ways in which the caregivers may re-enact their own abuse by becoming passive or aggressive within the new family home (Pynoos et al., 1995).

When unaccompanied children leave their homelands, and are brought over by agents into a new country, the psychological effects of leaving are also complex. In examining their clinical work with unaccompanied minors in Denmark, Christiansen and Foighel (1990) consider that unaccompanied children are packed up and sent, not only with the bundle of fears associated with war and suffering, but with a series of messages that may be paradoxical and difficult to comprehend:

- In being sent away to safety *because they are loved and treasured*, they may feel discarded. For a parent to say to a child that the child is loved enough for the percent to risk losing them in a bid for their survival is hard for a child to grasp, particularly if the child is very young.

- In being told that he or she must move away from a situation of danger, whilst the family remains exposed to it, can leave the child preoccupied with worry for the family's well-being.

- The child may have been seen within the family as its best, most adaptive member, able to fulfil potentials that the parents were not able to realise for themselves. Becoming the carrier of hope for the family as a delegate in this way may be experienced by him or her as an honour as well as a punishment.

- On the other hand, being involved in political activity at home, and being seen by the family as a saboteur and a risk prior to leaving, may mean that the child carries a self-image of turbulence or dangerousness into exile.

- The family's funding the flight may result in the children expecting to give the family a return on the investment. An economic sub-text to exile is generated which the child may try to live up to by carrying all the expectations of the economic migrant, on top of the particular pressures of being an asylum seeker.

- Finally, the child may have been sent away with a promise of reunification, which may remain unfulfilled. He or she may grow up within a culture so different from the culture of origin that resettlement results in a desiccation of roots and connections with families left behind.

Anderson (2001) observes that these experiences create varying levels of complexity for each child, depending on his or her capabilities and circumstances. The departure to another country far away is, in a sense, an attempt to cut a Gordian knot, literally 'to get out of a difficult position by one decisive step; to resolve a situation by force or by evasive action' (Kirkpatrick, 1992), yet the attempted severance in itself may generate other knots that cannot easily be understood or undone. Furthermore, in the absence of research linking the experiences of indigenous children to those who seek asylum, it could be cautiously asserted that unaccompanied minors searching for citizenship in a new land, new networks of care and protection, a new family, and a new language may be in the same boat as indigenous vulnerable children seeking sanctuary, but perhaps they are on different decks, with an uncertain journey towards resettlement and finding a new home. Their needs may be deeper, and the things they have to do in order to belong may be more numerous than those of their indigenous counterparts (Kohli, 2001).

Resilience and overcoming the odds

Having said this, it is also worth considering the evidence in relation to the ways in which refugee children are said to be resilient, and how they sustain resilience based strategies in their new contexts. While the overwhelming focus in research terms is on refugees as victims, the aspects of vulnerability described above are beginning to be reappraised in light of other paradigms within research with refugee communities that emphasise survival, not just victimhood (UNHCR, 1994). One aspect of refugee children's lives that is under-reported in clinical and research literature, in comparison with the emphasis on vulnerability, is their capacity to respond robustly to the stresses that surround them, confirming an increasingly held view that becoming a refugee is a purposeful act of strength and capability (Muecke, 1992; Ahern, 2000), and even though there is evidence that a minority are deeply troubled and need psychiatric intervention, the vast majority do not appear to be as psychologically dishevelled as one would expect, given the nature of some of their experiences. Indeed, the willingness that unaccompanied minors show to succeed and overcome the challenges of resettlement has become an important part of the characteristics welfare professions encounter when they work with them (Richman, 1998a). In short, many demonstrate resilience in conducting their day-to-day lives. In considering the fluidity of the concept of resilience, Gilligan (2001) offers the following version of three important dimensions, initially identified by Fraser, Richman and Galinsky (1999). Resilience is:

- Overcoming the odds – being successful despite exposure to high risk
- Sustaining competence under pressure – adapting to high risk
- Recovering from trauma – adjusting successfully to negative life events

In examining the proposition that 'a resilient youngster is one who adapts successfully to risky circumstances' (Gilligan, 2001: 5), we can enter a territory shared by researchers in social work in the United Kingdom and Ireland (Howe, 1995; Daniel et al.,

1999; Cairns, 2002; Gilligan, 2004) and their counterparts who study the lives of refugees worldwide (Barudy, 1990; McCallin, 1996; Ahern et al., 1998; Ahern, 2000; MacMullin and Loughry, 2000; Mann, 2000; Loughry and Eyber, 2003). For example, Howe (1995) groups together a range of responses under the terms 'understanding', 'support' and 'psychotherapy', which can be used as building blocks to promote well-being:

- Understanding from people around the child, including workers, who demonstrate a capacity to be kind, compassionate, steady and reliable.

- Support that is practical, nurturing, status building, clear and informative, companionship – group and community based – that weaves people back into the social fabric of the society and context they live within. It generates and sustains a sense of belonging. Gilligan's (1999) valuable exposition of the role of mentors who enhance resilience clarifies and specifies the practicalities of such support.

- Psychotherapy, within which understanding the self leads to reformulations of patterns of connection in the inside and outside worlds in a way that makes peace with demons and ghosts, and allows a safer passage into a liveable life.

The emphasis in these responses is in sympathy with the notion of helping people to relocate, pick up and re-weave the lost *narrative threads* referred to by Summerfield (1998), so that knowing where they have been, where they are, and where they need to get to, become part of the broad (re)construction of their lives in contexts that offer them opportunities to thrive. Blackwell and Melzak (2000) make a similar point in reference to refugee children when they say that the following factors help in ameliorating distressing experiences:

- **Belonging**: feeling they belong to at least one adult who is emotionally attuned to their feelings, and that they belong to a family, to a community, to a school, to a social group.

- **Thinking**: being able to think about their experiences in safe relationships with adults and peers.

- **Agency**: feeling they can make some active choices in their lives that help to shift a sense of helplessness. Apfel and Simon (1996) extend this notion to allowing the child or young person to experience a sense of *learned helpfulness*, by moving on to helping not just themselves, but others in similar circumstances. Sen (1993) confirms that well-being is closely associated with this *ability to do valuable acts or reach valuable states of being.*

- **Cultural integration**: finding a sense of continuity between the culture of their own country and that of their new one. Being able to mourn aspects of their culture, which is now inaccessible (Eisenbruch, 1992, refers to a process of *cultural bereavement*), while continuing to explore their own niche within their host culture.

These processes are built upon in other aspects of refugee research by linking well-being to material and practical resources and opportunities. For example, refugee children are known for their hunger for education (Rutter and Jones, 1998; Williamson, 1998), refugee status (Russell, 1999), for citizenship (Stanley, 2001), and for a determination to succeed by aiming for high social status and wealth (Armstrong, 1988).

There is also some evidence in the literature that the pre-departure circumstances of children who wish to become refugees and can afford to seek asylum in western industrialised nations may not be ones of impoverishment, but of relative privilege and wealth, confirming to a degree Robinson and Segrott's (2002) hypothesis that those with the most money tend to travel the furthest. As has been noted, very little is yet known about the ordinary life of asylum seeking children before they sought asylum, but some authors comment on refugee children coming from backgrounds of relative emotional and material affluence. For example, Summerfield (1993) in considering the arrival of Somali and Bangladeshi refugees in the UK confirms their middle-income status prior to entry. Finlay and Reynolds (1987: 96), in referring to the compound losses experienced by refugees, also list loss of social status, financial self-sufficiency and emotional security as common features of new asylum seekers. Rutter and Jones (1998), whilst cautioning against making generalisations, assert that children who have fled the world's poorest countries are primarily the urban middle classes, and Williamson (1998: 58), in reference to unaccompanied children from Ethiopia and Eritrea, notes that these children have generally experienced secure and intact family life before their flight. These views are confirmed in the Department of Health Guide on unaccompanied asylum seeking children, (Department of Health, 1995a), which says to social workers:

> It is important to remember that despite the often traumatic circumstances surrounding the flight from their homeland the majority of these children are likely to have come from otherwise secure, stable family backgrounds. They will have quite different care experiences, and consequently carry different expectations and assumptions about relationships, to those of the majority of indigenous children accommodated or cared for by local authorities. (Department of Health, 1995a: 2.54: 17)

However, these anecdotal observations of material and emotional wealth are few and far between in the literature, and in the absence of more empirical investigations of pre-departure circumstances, can only be accepted tentatively. Yet there are examples of the existence of 'supportive, affectionate and reliable relationships' (Parker et al., 1991: 95) in the networks left behind that may illuminate and explain how some refugee children use their childhood experiences of safety and care to make safe transitions into resettlement countries. For example, Mann (2001) reviews the evidence in relation to the nature and quality of care arrangements in a wide variety of cultures. She suggests that our thinking about refugee children as victims, who have lost their primary adult caregivers, is too narrow a perspective. Instead, her review cites a number of anthropological observational studies that confirm that many children are raised in ways that develop helpfully widespread attachments with a number of carers, including other children, especially siblings. She notes (Mann, 2001: 6) that,

> Children who act as caregivers to younger children tend to transfer the nurturing behaviour they learn to other relationships in their lives, and especially to peers. In this way child–child relationships may be an important protective factor for separated children.

One of her main points is that attachments happen across the horizontal plane of relationships as well as the vertical, and that they are more diffuse in nature than the traditional conceptualisations of attachment within a western paradigm of the bond of the mother/child dyad in a nuclear family. This diffusion and spread is purposeful in many communities that make intensive multiple demands on adults. Within these communities the responsibility of care-giving tends to spread across a number of people, including older children from an extended social and familial network.

> Children in this context typically have multiple caregivers, and experience exclusive maternal care only in the first few months of life. From the time of weaning, and often before, socialisation takes place within the multi-age peer and sibling group. In some societies, parents may employ a deliberate strategy for training their children to cope effectively for periods of time with minimal or no adult involvement. (Mann, 2001: 19)

Weisner (1987) argues that in places where there are significant threats to community safety linked to communal violence and war, siblings are more likely to look to each other for protection. Rousseau et al.'s (1998) study of northern Somali boys living in exile in Canada emphasises that these patterns of shared care of each other, and emergent self-sufficiency, are valued attributes. In this study, in establishing extensive autonomy by early adolescence within their communities of origin, as well as living together through adverse circumstances, the boys had reframed seeking asylum together as a valuable life experience that brought wisdom and knowledge. In other words, as a contrast to the notion of victimhood, they saw their sojourner status within Canada as a deliberate and purposeful creation that they had engaged in, in order to enhance their life chances.

Given that this capacity to reconstruct positive meanings out of bleak experiences fits well with current thinking in relation to resilience, one would think that it would be resolutely grasped in the design of optimistic resettlement strategies. However this does not appear to be the case; on the contrary, it is worth noting that in order to succeed within an asylum country, the opposite of optimism needs to be presented to the authorities. The way immigration regulations and laws radiate outwards from the notion of a refugee as sufferer within the terms of the 1951 Convention, means that victimhood trumps survival. No matter how individuals construct personal meanings for themselves within their new environments, the publicly broadcast meaning of their position as recipients of aid holds them in a static caricature of need (or greed, if one includes the broader preoccupations with 'bogus' refugees in the media). Craven (2003), for example, writes in impassioned terms in reference to greed and bogus asylum seekers:

> A devoted Christian [who] took in what he was told were two 16-year-old orphans from war-torn Kosovo. In fact they were Albanian Crooks, aged 20 and 21, who fleeced him and tried to seduce his daughter. Astonishingly, social services told him this happens all the time. . . . (Craven, 2003: 16–17, *Daily Mail*)

In any case, the dynamics of capability seem to be occluded while so much space is occupied by bleaker explanations. This process of hiding aspects that could be more visible than they are is also apparent in another aspect of unaccompanied children's lives – the maintenance of silence. This issue, which is rarely addressed in the literature, is not about vulnerability or resilience; rather, it is about both, because silence appears to offer protection, as well as risk.

Silence that is protective and risky

An important emergent issue in the lives of children seeking asylum concerns the ways in which they maintain silence, or remain economical with the truth, in reference to their flight. To some extent they are similar to the 'closed book' indigenous children in Schofield et al. (2000) and Beek and Schofield (2004), who worry about safely talking to others, or have been instructed by their families of origin not to reveal facts, feelings and thoughts to those who are caring for them, and can appear compliant and polite yet troubled – but the reasons for unaccompanied children not talking are perhaps more complex than those ascribed to indigenous children, in the same way that their circumstances are more shocking in terms of the collapse of order in their original worlds.

Melzak's (1992) hypothesis from a psychotherapeutic perspective is that war silences children, and that the silence is a way of dealing with deep disturbance – in some ways an attempt to survive intolerable loss. Similarly, Papadopoulos (2002) asserts that forced migration leaves people temporarily disorientated, as if they were frozen – a type of *psychological hypothermia* (Papadopoulos, 2002: 33) – and they need to thaw out in order to proceed with ordinary living again. Sometimes, Melzak (1992) notes, it is not just that they do not talk about their experiences, but they actually forget them – wipe them out of conscious memory – or become confused about what happened and when, and lose the capacity to tell a story as a sequence of events. If their lives become jumbled in this way, then the stories about their lives become jumbled as well. For example, as noted by Green (2000) in her research with unaccompanied minors at the Danish Refugee Council, at times the children carry 'unclear losses' (Green, 2000: 4), in that they may not know how the people they have left behind are living their lives, or whether there is any point in hoping that reunion may happen one day. Yet, as noted above in reference to Ayotte's (2000) study, sometimes the children try and squeeze stories into the narrow channels acceptable to asylum givers in their chosen country of refuge, and there is some evidence that these stories are rehearsed with parents or agents prior to departure in order to maximise the chances of acceptance, no matter where in Europe they appear (Anderson, 2001). To borrow a phrase from Meyerhoff's (1982) study of a Jewish community in America that developed strategies for being visible and invisible in particular ways within the host society in order to survive,

> They 'make' themselves, sometimes even 'make themselves up,' an activity which is not inevitable or automatic but

reserved for special people in special circumstances. (Meyerhoff, 1982: 100, quoted in White, 1995: 177)

Anderson's (2001) study in Germany recognises these special circumstances for unaccompanied minors and takes into account that all the children who have left their homelands – for whatever reason – have to wear silence as a protective carapace, or that they carry a complicated legacy of confusion that has an outer layer consisting of a simple asylum story, in order to arrive relatively safely:

> they have been told that only a particular version of the truth will enable them to remain, 'because that is what the interrogators want to hear'. Regardless of whether this conforms to the exact truth or not, the young persons are therefore under enormous pressure always to get the details exactly right and keep them consistent – otherwise they will fail.   (Anderson, 2001: 196)

The children's experiences, according to these expositions, are complex – in a sense one could say that they have what White (1997) would call 'thick stories' (the stories of multiple motives and an ordinary wish to succeed in the world), which are presented to the receiving authorities as 'thin stories' in order to succeed (the extraordinary stories of a particular sort of suffering). While the thick stories might be more real, it is the thin stories that are perceived as being admissible to the receiving authorities. The thin stories are therefore purposefully constructed as an acceptable amalgam of honesty and compliance with criteria in the 1951 Convention definition. They act as the key to entry into the country of choice, and may reappear in the stories told to social workers at the point of entry into care, particularly if the workers are identified with 'the authorities' and mistrusted.

Summary

In summary, very little is known about the ordinary pre-departure lives of children who become refugees. What is increasingly clear is that amongst children seeking political protection and care there are a few for whom deep poverty may be a driver towards asylum providing countries, including children who are trafficked. Yet for the majority of those able to head towards western industrialised nations, indications are that political rather than economic impulses dictate the primary decision, and that sufficient wealth exists to fund departure. Money for agents is found from somewhere. For unaccompanied children, at least from the Horn of Africa, some anecdotal evidence exists of economically robust families, who send their children away with good intentions.

The pre-departure crises they face are confirmed in a number of studies as vivid in the sense of civic society breaking down. In these circumstances families of origin appear to 'volunteer' their children into the care of others in a different country. They want their children looked after, because they cannot offer them protection themselves. This jettisoning of the children, and the experiences they go through before departure and during the flight, make them vulnerable in specific ways; they also test their resilience and capacity to survive the transition.

There is some evidence to suggest that, for a number of reasons, they experience a high degree of vulnerability due to war, and also that they may be more capable of managing their new environments than we suppose. For a number of complex reasons, while the children are sent to the 'arms of strangers', like their *Kindertransport* counterparts two generations ago (Harris and Oppenheimer, 2001) they are warned not to talk to these strangers apart from telling them thin stories. At the point of entering an unfamiliar territory, particularly in seeking care, these children may therefore present the carers with specific challenges in resettlement, determined by the carers' understanding of their special circumstances, needs and capabilities. The next chapter considers how those receiving unaccompanied children respond in such circumstances.

3 Social work with unaccompanied asylum seeking children and young people

What do unaccompanied minors say they want from their lives, and what is known about social work practice with them? Williamson (1998) gives a glimpse in a summary of a study she conducted in the early 1990s in the UK. She reports that she asked twenty-three asylum seeking young people to tell her about their experiences, wishes and feelings. Her report suggests that they wanted caring adults who kept them safe, who understood the complexity of their experience and connected them to networks that were meaningful for them, as key aspects of support. In addition, the young people wanted opportunities to eat 'home food', or keep up with cultural affiliations; teachers who were strict but fair, and recognised that failing in education would be 'a disaster'. They wanted good legal representation in the asylum process, sympathetic welfare workers, careers advice, learning about 'the British way of life', and plenty of social activity to keep their minds off their problems. To an extent, this brief report by Williamson (1998) summarises key aspects of the resettlement task for unaccompanied children. It represents some of the types of issues that social workers could consider in practice to take account of the children's memories, present needs and future hopes. To have a remembered history, an unremarkable sense of enjoyment in the present, and aspirations that secure status – both legal and social – and make past sacrifices worth it, are part of individual testimonies within the literature (Minority Rights Group International, 1998). They also encapsulate the three elements described by Bihi (1999), referred to in Chapter 1 as being central to the recovery of stability and equilibrium for refugees generally, namely:

- the **restoration** of livelihoods and health;
- the **maintenance** of habits and customs;
- the **transformation** of life chances through making the best of opportunities for advancement offered within the new environment.

The first element focuses on the practicalities of daily living, the second on the continuation of rituals and rhythms from the past, and the third on success in the future. Furthermore, Bihi (1999) emphasises that these should be viewed as different working parts of a whole that is simultaneously delivered as part of resettlement practice, rather than as a sequence of events. In considering how contemporary social-work practice has been evaluated in reference to these aspects of the resettlement, the literature can be further considered by asking two questions.

1. What should be done to make resettlement for unaccompanied minors effective?
2. What is being done, as seen in a number of UK-based research studies?

In answering the first question three guidance documents are discussed here that have been issued over the last decade to practitioners offering a service to unaccompanied minors. These appear to set the template by which services for unaccompanied minors should be designed. Addressing the second question leads to a presentation of a number of research studies conducted into the lives and circumstances of unaccompanied minors which evaluate welfare services and practices, including social work. Beyond summarising and describing the key studies, this chapter appraises them in terms of their worth and limitations within the broader picture of refugee children presented earlier.

What should be done? Guidance in relation to unaccompanied minors

Altogether, the guidance stems from national and European sources and consists of the following, listed in order of date of publication:

1   The Social Services Inspectorate's *Unaccompanied Asylum-Seeking Children: A Practice Guide* (Department of Health, 1995a), issued alongside a training pack for social workers.

2   The *Statement of Good Practice*, issued by the Separated Children in Europe Programme (SCEP), under the aegis of UNHCR and Save the Children (Ayotte, 1999; SCEP, 2000).

3   *Food, Shelter and Half a Chance: Assessing the needs of unaccompanied asylum seeking and refugee children*, issued by the British Agencies for Adoption and Fostering (BAAF), as a Department of Health endorsed document (Kidane, 2001).

Together, they endorse the point that refugee children are credible and needy, that practically helpful things can be done to protect them, and that they deserve and have a right to fair and open-handed treatment in the reconstruction of their lives. The dominant theme within the guidance documents is one of seeing them as 'children in need' first and as asylum claimants second. In establishing the broad ethical tone of the guidance, the Social Services Inspectorate reiterates the position that unaccompanied children have

> An absolute right to be protected from neglect and/or abuse of any kind and this must be the primary consideration. (Department of Health, 1995a: 10, section 2.22)

The SCEP statement is firmly founded on the UN Convention on the Rights of the Child, 1989, and related international instruments for the protection and care of refugees, and establishes some basic principles for resettlement practice with children who are separated, including unaccompanied children. These assert, *inter alia*, that:

- The *best interests* of separated children should be used to guide policy and practice.
- They should be treated similarly to indigenous vulnerable children, as *children first and foremost* rather than immigrants or asylum seekers.

- Their wishes and feelings must be sought and taken into account in any decisions that affect them, and they should participate in decision making if their age and understanding allows.
- They should maintain their mother tongue and links to their culture, and be encouraged to do so by those meeting their care, educational and health needs.
- Information they disclose should not be shared without their permission with others, in case it jeopardises the family left behind. Confidentiality should be maintained at all costs.
- Information for the children themselves should be in a form that is absorbable by them, and should let them know what their entitlements are, what services are available, what the asylum process involves, any family-tracing facilities they can use, and what is happening in their country of origin.
- Decisions should be based on a long-term view of the children's interests and welfare, and taken in a timely fashion with minimal delay.

For social workers used to referring to the welfare checklist in the Children Act 1989 (section 1:1), these principles are familiar, particularly when contextualised within the principles at the heart of the volumes of guidance and regulations related to the Act itself (Department of Health, 1990). The Social Services Inspectorate's view at the time of publishing the practice guide for working with unaccompanied asylum seeking children, in 1995, echoes this child centred focus, in noting that its own recommendations are 'firmly rooted in the Children Act 1989' (Department of Health, 1995a: 1). Similarly the *Framework for the Assessment of Children in Need and their Families* (DH, DfEE, HO, 2000), in discussing the assessment of children in special circumstances, advises social workers responding to the needs of unaccompanied minors to turn to the SCEP statement,

> which provides a straightforward account of the policies and practice required to protect the rights of [separated] children. (DH, DfEE, HO, 2000: 48, section 3.58)

Further Government endorsement is given to the BAAF guide (Kidane, 2001), which refers explicitly to the Assessment Framework and encourages social workers to use its ecological approach to guide their practice with unaccompanied minors. The recommendations for good practice that coalesce from the principles that connect all these guidance documents again echo established good standards of humanitarian child-care practice. They support Ayotte's (2000) position, confirming that no matter how the children appear on the doorsteps of the authorities in Europe, those authorities have a responsibility to offer them care and protection where possible, given their age and potential vulnerability as unaccompanied minors. While the SCEP guide is designed to be used by many officials, from health, education, immigration and social care, the BAAF and Department of Health (DH) guides focus more explicitly on social-work practice. Some differences of emphasis and points of view exist between the three guides yet overall, in framing good practice for social workers, they appear to confirm, and arguably predict, the UK Government's position in three respects. First, they appear to anticipate and reflect the Government's emphasis on improving the care and resettlement of unaccompanied minors as stated in the Green Paper *Every Child Matters* (DfES, 2003), which describes them as 'some of the children in greatest need' in the UK (para 2.30). In posing the question of how unaccompanied minors are best supported, the results of the consultation on the Green Paper carried out between September and December 2003 show the need for 'a guardian/mentor who could act as advocate and protector' for all unaccompanied minors (DfES, 2004:47), possibly mirroring the role of the personal advisor as defined in the Children (Leaving Care) Act 2000, which came into force in October 2001. Secondly they reflect Government advice to local authorities issued via a Local Authority Circular (Department of Health, 2003b) no. 13, issued on 2 June 2003, which confirms that

> where a child has no parent or guardian in this country, perhaps because he has arrived alone seeking asylum, the presumption should be that he would fall within the scope of section 20 and become looked after, unless the needs assessment reveals particular factors which would suggest that an

alternative response would be more appropriate. (Department of Health, 2003b: 3)

Thirdly, they recommend that all children and young people seeking asylum are accommodated under section 20 on the basis of need, and that those who have been looked after under section 20 or under a care order of the Children Act 1989 should be entitled to benefit by the provisions contained in the Children (Leaving Care) Act 2000 in the same way as indigenous children. This exactly mirrors the 'Hillingdon ruling' of 29 August 2003 (see chapter 1). Overall, the European and national guidance seems to fit well with what appears to be the UK Government's specific commitment to unaccompanied minors, and the broad confirmation that the provisions in the Children Act 1989 are there for the use of all vulnerable children, from home or abroad. But many recent commentators note that in reality there appear to be gaps between what is said and what is done, no matter how large the degree of coincidence between policy, guidance and laws, as illustrated by the studies below.

What is (or is not) being done? The evaluation of care for unaccompanied minors

Within the UK, as in other industrialised nations receiving unaccompanied minors, concern has been expressed by many writers that the road back to ordinary living is long and unjustifiably complicated for them and that the context of care is turbulent, insufficient or ineffective in many important respects. In other words, there is an implicit and explicit presentation of a case that the policies and practices that have an impact on these children are faulty, resulting in the systems of care and protection failing them over time. The criticisms extend to national and international immigration law (Russell, 1999), the health-care needs of refugee children (Gosling, 2000; BMA, 2002), and their educational needs (Rutter, 2003). In relation to social work, they are articulated in broad terms by the Audit Commission (2000), noting that,

Many unaccompanied children have multiple needs because of their experiences of separation, loss and social dislocation.

> Their development may be accelerated in some areas and arrested in others, and they may need additional support to make the transition to adulthood. Yet in many cases they do not receive the same standard of care routinely afforded to indigenous children in need, even though their legal rights are identical. (Audit Commission, 2000: 66)

This is seen not as an accidental emergence of unfortunate circumstances but as an expression of organisational ambivalence towards the presence of unaccompanied minors, reflecting a broader culture of ambivalence towards refugees and asylum seekers (Macaskill and Petrie, 2000; Hamilton et al., 2003; GLA Policy Support Unit, 2004). Furthermore, the chain of ambivalence is extended in such a way that it links national policies with local procedures and practices. So, for example, Ayotte and Williamson (2001:18), in questioning whether the UK is applying the standards demanded by the SCEP guidance, find that,

> In many respects UK governments have sought to place immigration considerations above those of children's best interests.

The proposition is that no matter what the UK Government says about its specific commitment to the care and resettlement of unaccompanied children, in practice the reality they experience is impoverished, and far removed from the standards set in the guidance. This perspective cascades down through criticisms of local government, a number of professional groups including immigration officers, lawyers, teachers, doctors and social workers, to a point where it meets a sea of similar criticism in the studies cited above. For example, Stone's (2000: 11) survey of policies and practices in relation to unaccompanied minors in 103 English, Welsh and Scottish local authorities finds

> variable levels of political commitment to service these young people, seemingly as a result of their refugee status and within the context of the general political climate for asylum seekers.

The concerns that are expressed are deep and serious. Broadly it is alleged that service provision fails to measure up to the standards of care stipulated by the national and European practice guidance. In some respects, there is a re-creation of a disappointing performance in reference to some basic standards of humanitarian care, familiar in other contexts related to the protection and care of indigenous children (Jordan, 2000). In relation to describing practice generally, Stanley's (2001) study of the views and experiences of 125 unaccompanied young asylum seekers, and 125 professionals working with them throughout England, is perhaps the widest ranging in its scope and content. Within it, the ways in which they were dealt with by many professions is described as 'a lottery', with many 'chaotic experiences' and little or no support. Young people were reported as being reticent about asking for help, either because they were grateful for whatever they received, or because they were unused to seeking professional assistance in their countries of origin and did not have the repertoire to seek assistance from helpers. In any case, in reference to the need for professionals to establish a trusting relationship with the young people, the evidence is at best equivocal in a context where they saw their social worker 'only if they had a problem', and had a

> mixed experience of support from social workers, [from] a sense of resignation that they did not have either the will or the power to do much, to a deep sense of appreciation. (Stanley, 2001: 56)

They were lonely, and isolated, particularly from communities of origin that had settled elsewhere in the country; they were suffering from racism (not just from indigenous white people, but also from black people as well as from other refugee groups) and,

> It [was] common for young people to be placed in locations where there is no knowledge or appreciation of their culture, food or language'. (Stanley 2001: 40)

These aspects of feeling friction, tension and 'unbelonging' are very well supported by, for example, Ayotte and Williamson (2001). Their study, based on interviews with 126 young people and their professional helpers, found 'prejudicial attitudes among social services staff', insufficiently skilled interpreters, and young people who could not buy the homeland food that they wanted, or go to a mosque or church of their choice. Whilst noting individual exceptions, nothing in either of the studies suggests that the standards set within the guidance in relation to social workers assisting them to feel less isolated, more connected with communities of origin, and supported in dealing with racism, were met in any consistent, broad-ranging manner.

Health

In relation to health, while most of the young people were noted as being physically healthy, various studies confirm a consistent pattern of emotional vulnerability, yet none offer a more complex account, either of the range of psychological difficulties that the young people may encounter or of their resilience in the face of adversity. For example, the Barnardo's study asserts that 'unaccompanied young people are vulnerable young people' (Stone, 2000: 10) and others say that

> their psychological needs are not catered for and they may continue to suffer in silence or act out their grief and pain inappropriately.   (Ayotte and Williamson, 2001: 21)

The Greater London Authority (GLA Policy Support Unit, 2004) cites evidence from, amongst others, Fazel and Stein's (2003) study of 101 refugee children in Oxford who were rated by their teachers using the 'strengths and difficulties questionnaire' (SDQ) as having 'large and unmet mental health needs that need to be tackled'. While finding that counselling is seen to be unappealing to many young refugees, Stanley (2001: 111) also notes that the respondents in her study had difficulties in asking for help with the management of painful feelings,

> because in their country of origin, emotional or mental health problems are not discussed or are even equated with madness.

No specific evidence is presented in this study regarding the ways in which social workers took account of the young people's physical and emotional health, either through direct practice or in making sure they had access to safe, trusting relationships within which they could talk about their experiences, as recommended in the guidance. Yet the studies imply that by and large, providers failed to notice, and the young people themselves failed to say, what troubled them. This situation became worse, the studies suggest, in the absence of culturally appropriate services in localities where the young people lived, and by specialist therapeutic resources such as the Medical Foundation for the Care of Victims of Torture being often hard to reach, and too much in demand.

Education

These clusters of concern also carry over into educational provisions, so that Stanley (2001: 71) concludes:

> it is clear from our research that social workers and education professionals do not always work together to ensure a young person has a place on a suitable educational course . . . [and] that those placed 'out of area' in independent and semi-independent accommodation suffered from the failure of either social services and/or private providers to facilitate access to education. (Stanley, 2001: 75)

In the Refugee Council survey (Dennis, 2002) only 62 of the 118 children were accessing some form of education, and 56 were not in education at all. When they were able to obtain a school place, they experienced delays in beginning a programme of study, had no money for school uniforms, or for travel to and from education providers. In many cases, as with Stanley's (2001) cohort, there was insufficient English language support in a context where the children were seen as unwanted strangers whose experiences and contributions were marginal to the wellbeing of the school. And yet, there were also persistent concerns about their high expectations of themselves, as expressed by this teacher in the Stanley (2001: 82) study,

> The problem is they come with a dream, maybe that their parents told them when they left, like be a doctor or an engineer. It is a dream they hold on to. It is hard enough for anyone to fulfil those dreams, but it is three or four years

before they have the level of English language [needed] for University.

While difficulties in access to education are highlighted in this way, there is no information on whether social workers are following the practice guidance in gathering information about the young people's educational histories, coaching them about aspects of British life, or connecting with educators from the communities of origin. The studies do, however, confirm the generally well established picture of the young people prioritising learning English, and working hard in school, and looking for and sometimes finding teachers helpful at many levels. Stanley (2001: 83), for example, reports that the researchers in her study identified teachers and education support workers as a key source of care for the young people who were in education. A number of students explained how, in their eyes, a teacher had taken on the role of a surrogate parent:

> My dad's not here, my mum's not here, but actually . . . I can clearly say that [the teacher] is like my dad here in this country.

This role of the surrogate parent is generally not ascribed to social workers within the studies. In a sense, to use Harris's (1993) vivid metaphor, some teachers within these studies are given a good press. They are like the 'milk van' offering help that is low key, unobtrusive, nurturing, regular, reliable, long term, whereas social workers, by and large, are presented as 'the fire brigade', and associated with practice that is sudden, invasive, and crisis driven (Gilligan, 2004: 97).

Immigration

In reference to immigration, criticism is limited within the studies to a number of factors. First, the asylum process itself is blamed for being so restrictive that it compels people to lie in order to gain entry into countries as well as access to systems of protection and care. It is said to not recognise the tense reality of people sometimes needing to travel with falsified papers in order to cross borders, or of children often not knowing their precise age, or being unable to report back on the facts related to the asylum application in ways that are consistent and non-contradictory (Ayotte and Williamson, 2001: 54ff.). In its own way, this is an exposition of the management of 'thick' and 'thin' stories referred to earlier, with thin stories, which can be posted through the narrow channels of acceptance as defined by the immigration rules, being told in order to placate the authorities. Once the stories are told, delays in the young people receiving initial asylum decisions are noted as 'extensive' (Stanley, 2001: 4), and she quotes one young person who made a heartfelt plea, to illustrate the cost of waiting:

> I think the Government helps us a lot but people [applied for asylum] two years ago, for children it's not good. You gonna go mad. . . . It's hard. You remain empty. (Stanley, 2001: 105)

Of the 125 young people in this study, just 19 (15%) had received an initial asylum decision, after an average wait of 11 months, and a survey by the Prince's Trust of life in the UK for refugee children reports average waiting periods of 13 months between the screening interview and the initial decision (Chapman and Calder, 2003). Only 1–2% of the young people ever achieved refugee status, with the majority being granted some form of time-limited leave to remain on humanitarian grounds (Stanley, 2001: 105), and none in this study being forcibly returned to the country of origin. There is a call to protect the young people from unskilled, negligent or unscrupulous immigration advisors (mainly lawyers), and for asylum caseworkers within the Immigration and Nationality Department at the Home Office to be trained in sensitively interviewing children 'who may have particular difficulties recounting painful histories' (Ayotte and Williamson, 2001: 54).

While these important aspects of the young people's lives are revealed in the studies, they have very little to say about how social workers interact with others in securing clarity about immigration status for the young people, as outlined in the practice guidance. So they do not, for example, routinely reveal whether social workers accompany the young people to asylum-related interviews, whether they filter the quality of legal assistance by finding a reputable lawyer, or if they keep their eyes on the speed at which the asylum application is dealt with by the Home Office.

Social work – direct practice with unaccompanied minors

While these concerns about shortfalls in education, health provision, and immigration practices are outlined across a number of studies, stringent criticism is reserved for social work policies, procedures and practices that directly impinge on the lives of unaccompanied minors. It begins with the simple declaration that local authority Social Services departments, in providing cheaper services to young people via accommodation and financial assistance under section 17 of the Children Act 1989, are failing in their legal obligations to them as children who are manifestly 'in need' within the terms of the legislation, and indeed that the legislation has been interpreted and applied incorrectly (Dennis, 2002; GLA Policy Support Unit, 2004). Perhaps the most controversial aspect of this interpretation is related to age. For example, the Refugee Council's report asserts that,

> Many social services departments provide services according to age rather than the assessed needs of a young person, which is contrary to government policy. It says more about resources than need, and can have a very detrimental effect on a young person. Some local authorities deny access to children's services to anyone they believe to be 16 or over. (Dennis, 2002: 18)

At the heart of this exposition is the charge that Social Services departments have set up what are in effect internal borders that keep the majority of unaccompanied children aged 16–18 out of their territories (Humphries, 2004). Social workers within these systems have become preoccupied with trying to assess age as a factor in determining the response to individual applicants, and many of the studies suggest that it is a crude exercise, based on an individual social worker trying to guess age by appearance, without the benefit of advice from the Royal College of Paediatricians that

> The determination of age is a complex and often inexact set of skills, where various types of physical, social and cultural factors all play their part, although none provide a wholly exact or reliable indication of age, especially for older children. (Levenson and Sharma, 1999: 14)

Instead, the studies report their concerns over a 'growing culture of disbelief in respect of the age of those claiming to be under 18' (Ayotte and Williamson, 2001: 70), and the treatment of anyone over 16 as a *de facto* adult, getting access to food and shelter, but little else. As layer upon layer of concern is built up about a 'hardening of practice and attitudes in this area' (Mitchell, 2003: 182), the broader strategic picture that is painted is rather bleak. Stanley (2001) notes the lack of 'strategic preparedness' for the arrival and long-term resettlement of unaccompanied minors, citing as evidence the lack of any mention of asylum seeking children in the Management Action Plans submitted by local authorities to the Department of Health under the 'Quality Protects' initiative. Ayotte and Williamson (2001) observe that two-thirds of local authorities have no policies related to unaccompanied minors. Some authorities, it is alleged, worry that if their provisions are seen as generous, more unaccompanied minors will be attracted to their area, and these authorities appear to avoid having an attractive reputation (Stanley, 2001: 25) because their services are unable to deal with increasing numbers (Ayotte and Williamson, 2001: 34).

As these failings in policy are listed, the fault lines in procedure and practice become apparent. Stone (2000: 10) reports that 'there is no proper assessment of need', and the young people are not often allocated a named social worker, particularly for those supported via section 17 of the Children Act 1989, echoing the finding that 'assessments are being compromised in order to make them fit practical circumstances, such as the availability and cost of placements' (Stanley, 2001: 33) and that 'they saw a social worker when they went to the office to collect money or when they had a problem. It was rare for a young person to report that social workers visited them in their accommodation' (Stanley, 2001: 57)

In these circumstances, there are reports of a distanced relationship between the social worker and the young person, filled with hesitance and disengagement, as in this young man's view:

> As an asylum seeker I feel I shouldn't say 'I want this'. . . .
> When I say I want something, I am not demanding it. The
> social worker should listen to how you feel properly, not just
> writing all the time. . . . I can't complain, who am I to
> complain, [I'm] not asking for more help – just the right kind
> of help.   (Stanley, 2001: 110)

The studies cite many instances of the young people being
housed in hostels and Bed & Breakfast establishments outside
the responsible local authority's area, therefore limiting contact
with social workers (Ayotte and Williamson, 2001: 31). Some
local authorities are accused of covertly placing unaccompanied
minors far away, without letting the receiving authorities know
(for example, Ayotte and Williamson, 2001: 38; Stanley, 2001:
55), and setting up a type of unofficial dispersal scheme. The
implication in some of the reports is that these attempts to push
the young people away have resulted in lowered standards of care
in comparison with indigenous children (Stanley, 2001: 40).

> Given the needs of these young people, serious questions must
> be asked about the appropriateness of arranging the provision
> of care from a distance of as much as 300 miles from the phys-
> ical location of the local authority with responsibility for that
> care'.   (Stanley, 2001: 59)

The concerns are compounded by reports of the young people
living in unsupervised contexts with adults who were strangers to
them – private landlords who were unresponsive to their needs to
access health and education services; of their not having enough
money for food and bus fares, being far away from places of
worship, not being skilled enough to manage budgets or to cook
and eat, and being confounded by noisy accommodation and
lack of privacy.

   Young people allocated to social workers in some child and
family social-work teams were reportedly 'lost' in the chaos of
competing demands, perhaps echoing the Victoria Climbié case
in terms of the lesser visibility of transient children who are relatively quiet, as opposed to those embedded within the locality
who are relatively loud enough to require a response (Laming,
2003). As one social worker observed,

> My experience tells me that in a busy caseload when you've got court deadlines, where you have got a lot of very demanding, damaged children and you have got an asylum seeker, the asylum seeker will take very much second place because they are not making any demands. They are going to school, they are not causing you problems, they are not demanding and they are just a case. (Stanley, 2001: 60)

In the meantime, a constant absence of independent visitors is noted, even for those who are looked after under section 20 of the Children Act 1989. For example, Stanley (2001: 40) reports that 'none of the local authorities [within which the research took place] ran an independent visitors scheme'. The Greater London Authority (GLA) Policy Support Unit also observes that most refugee children have little or no access to an independent advisor or guardian, despite the UN Committee on the Rights of the Child recommending that the UK Government should 'consider a system of independent guardians' (GLA Policy Support Unit, 2004: 19). Ayotte and Williamson (2001: 67) note that in the UK there is no system of guardianship (*qua* legal guardian as well as someone able to act with parental responsibility) 'who ensures that a separated child's entitlements are respected and their needs are met', as exists in many other European countries. Some of the studies point to the clear benefits derived by asylum seeking young people from the Panel of Advisors scheme run by the Refugee Council, but also note the severe strains the scheme operates within given the demands placed on it by an increasing number of young people seeking assistance. The GLA report further suggests that in the absence of a guardian the children are denied two things. First, assistance through the legal process via instructing legal representatives, a little like the current role adopted by members of the Refugee Council Panel of Advisors; secondly, as an advocate and befriending and companionable person, a little like the traditional model of an independent visitor or mentor.

The studies also report a considerable confusion and anxiety amongst the young people at the time, about what would happen to them once they reached their 18th birthday. As Dennis (2002: 15) comments,

For unaccompanied asylum seeking children particularly those whose immigration status has yet to be decided, this threshold to adulthood may be something to fear more than to celebrate.

In this study, 35 of the 118 young people were on this threshold, and conveyed several worries, including not having leave to remain after 18 and being returned to the country of origin, being expected to cope independently especially if they were dispersed, and being confused about changes in systems of support between childhood and adulthood. A number of vignettes are presented to highlight the point as a genuine and deeply felt concern, including this one, a tale of almost Dickensian suffering:

> Artur arrived as an unaccompanied minor and was placed by social services with an accommodation provider in the Midlands. Although Artur began to settle in, social services did not discuss the future with him, and did not visit him after he had been housed. The rent payments to his landlord by social services ended on Artur's 18th birthday. As a result Artur was evicted on the same day. (Dennis, 2002: 16)

In these circumstances the studies suggest, young people living outside the protection offered by indefinite leave to remain on humanitarian grounds face 'the very real threat of removal' (GLA Policy Support Unit, 2004: 21). However, while rumours and reports continue to circulate about the Home Office establishing a 'tough' returns policy (Taylor, 2004), there is no evidence of unaccompanied minors being forcibly returned without safety being assured in their countries of origin .

The studies focus instead on social work practice in relation to reunification between the young people and their families. Ayotte and Williamson (2001) make the point that adults who achieve refugee status can apply for their families to join them in the UK, and their descendants and dependants can benefit by this, whereas similar rules for unaccompanied children do not exist – adults in the family on whom they have depended before departure cannot join them, and that this is in contravention of Article 10 of the UN Convention on the Rights of the Child, to which the UK is signatory. Furthermore, they say that their study confirms that in general practitioners have no guidelines to follow in relation to family tracing, and that this absence of a standardised approach has in some instances led to social workers thoughtlessly leaking or seeking information without the child's knowledge or consent.

> There have been instances in the past where, for example, inexperienced social workers have approached foreign embassies to request information about a child's family, or have passed information to the Home Office without consultation with a child's legal representative. . . . Professionals need to be aware that the relationship between a child and his or her legal representative is a confidential one: social services caring for a child have no right to view the child's asylum application.   (Ayotte and Williamson, 2001: 26)

In making this type of observation, the studies appear to remain flat and unenthusiastic about social work practice, largely falling into a portrayal of ineptitude, having described failing organisational contexts. The organisations also appear to fail their employees' needs for training in this complex area. Both Stone (2000) and Ayotte and Williamson (2001) note the absence of training for professionals, and the poor usage by social work agencies of the training pack for working with unaccompanied children that was published by the Department of Health at the time of issuing the practice guidance in 1995 (Department of Health, 1995b). For example, one of Stone's (2000: 61) respondents, a social work manager, suggests a way of working informed by localised responses rather than national guidelines, and generates an impression of practice evolving as a reaction to whatever the social workers face on a day-to-day basis rather than a more comprehensive understanding of the fuller picture that includes laws, regulations, guidance, and messages from research.

> I've got very little information or guidelines; we create our own guidelines and we've kind of sussed out what other people's ideas were and then formed a position within those.

Overall, in relation to the thresholds of acceptable practice set by the guidance, the studies appear to confirm that the young people face a range of adverse experiences when seeking assistance that can leave them feeling disconnected and uncared for. From the humanitarian perspective maintained by many of the studies, this type of fragmentation is seen as avoidable. However, there is some recognition that the territory within which the young people and their social workers live also contains complexity and indeed that there are some positives amongst the general gloom. For example, Ayotte and Williamson (2001: 42), despite their deep concerns, quote an un-named Department of Health official who clearly wants to portray a world beyond the 'isn't it all awful' story:

> Separated children have varying degrees of vulnerability. There are children who are completely on their own, those with older siblings, and those with adults where the relationship is not at all certain. You must assess the level of vulnerability that the child has in its own right and also as part of the refugee experience. Then you have to assess [his or her] vulnerability in relation to that of all other children that social services comes into contact with such as abused children and disabled children. In a world with unlimited financial, placement and staffing resources this wouldn't be a problem, but it is very hard to weigh up the conflicting priorities when there is only so much to go around.

The study by Stone (2000: 28) is perhaps the most consistently sympathetic to social work. She notes that,

> Authorities recognise that they are experiencing difficulties in delivering services to these young people *and many of them are trying to improve their service provision*. Several authorities are actively looking for support and guidance on these issues and would welcome ideas and suggestions from other authorities or the voluntary sector with greater expertise in this area [emphasis added].

Furthermore, Stone is quick to acknowledge that many unaccompanied minors are in authorities that already have high levels of need, and where the demand for services is considerable. In these circumstances, local authorities are providing services to them in competition with indigenous demand. In addition, substantial difficulties in recruiting qualified social workers, foster carers and interpreters, or finding good-quality placements in residential care or in semi-independent and independent accommodation, all add to a sense of unmanageability, despite good intentions. Similarly, Government special grants to local authorities to assist with the care and resettlement costs of unaccompanied minors are seen as insufficient in meeting demand, even if they are a necessary step in the right direction. Finally, adding to a sense of complexity is a concern voiced, within many of the studies, of ineffective 'joined up' working between social services, and education and health services (Stone, 2000: 11; Ayotte and Williamson, 2001: 28; Stanley 2001: 55), so that unaccompanied minors have to re-negotiate entries into these systems separately. Many instances are cited of the young people waiting for leave to enter and remain at local levels – for schools, for registration with GPs – reflecting their experiences in terms of their immigration status, and their relationships with social services.

In light of the detailed concerns, and in recognition of some of the disconnections and gaps that emerge from the studies, it is perhaps unsurprising that the positives which occasionally light up the gloom are focused on strategies and practices that help the young people to feel embedded in networks of care and protection. In so far as fragmentation and movement are issues of deep concern in the young people's lives as refugees, it is connections and the possibilities of coherence emerging over time that act as a contrast. In their own way, they signal attempts at resettlement.

The studies note, for example, that the young people, even in dire circumstances, were often 'very grateful for the shelter and support offered to them – no matter how limited' (Stanley, 2001: 6), and that some strategic and operational responses had emerged over time that could be identified as exemplars of effective resettlement policy and practice. For example, Ayotte and Williamson (2001: 32) report that despite the concerns about extensive uncertainty, the Home Office was trying to ensure that there was minimum delay in processing asylum applications from children, thus minimising planning blight in relation to resettlement. There were some instances of local authorities providing 'good to excellent' care (Ayotte and Williamson, 2001: 31), including ensuring that all unaccompanied minors were accommodated under section 20 provisions in the first six weeks of being in the UK, during which time a full assessment of need was carried out. Others were using money made available under the 'Quality Protects' initiative to fund educational support workers linked to residential units as well as a specialist health visitor to create a 'health action plan' for unaccompanied minors who are looked after (Stanley, 2001). There was an example of one local authority working in partnership with the Refugee Council to provide a hostel staffed by reliable, knowledgeable and skilled workers, which the young people said was like a 'safe haven' for the first few weeks after arrival. Another local authority had developed specialist housing for its young people, comprising a bathroom/kitchen/bedroom unit for each young person in a house, with 24-hour support-worker cover (Stanley, 2001: 51). There was one instance of a Social Services department using volunteers from a local university to help the young people with their schoolwork, and engage them in leisure activities. There are several reports of leisure activities being valued by the young people, as an antidote to loneliness. One young person in the Stanley (2001) study had this to say:

> Last month I was very depressed and I used anti-depression tablets and my doctor told me 'You need to do some more swimming'. I didn't have enough money to go swimming and I told my social worker and he help me a little bit to be able to go swimming. (Stanley, 2001: 112)

A voluntary sector organisation, in conjunction with a local Social Services department, ran an activities group for new arrivals, and there were a few befriending and mentoring schemes described within the studies that the young people were said to benefit by. One such scheme, run by the Medical Foundation for the Care of Victims of Torture, was highlighted as an example of innovative practice, linking individual young people to an adult befriender. A recent evaluation of the scheme (Thurlow et al., 2004: 1) comes to the following conclusion, reflecting both the presence of valuable practice, as well as the absence of more general provision.

The team identified the need of these young people for strong individual relationships with a protective adult who can act as their advocate – the kind of relationship that was envisaged by the Children Act's independent visitor concept but which is all too often not part of the package of state provision. Our evaluation found that the young people considered that they gained enormously from their supportive relationships with a protective adult, regarding them as trusted adults and establishing what they hope will be a 'lifelong relationship'.

These examples were supplemented by two more general findings. First, that specialist teams for unaccompanied asylum seekers appeared to offer good models of organisational response to growing demand. Stanley's (2001: 55) enquiry indicates,

A strong link between young people reporting a positive and fruitful relationship with their social worker and the existence of a specialist asylum team within children's services.

Similarly – but on the basis of little further evidence – Ayotte and Williamson (2001: 37) confirm that their preferred model of practice includes 'a dedicated social services team for separated children'. Secondly, across all the studies, young people who were able to access provisions via section 20 of the Children Act 1989, fared better than their counterparts supported via section 17. So, for example, they were more likely to have an allocated social worker, with whom they had regular contact, and were more satisfied with the level of financial support they received. They were more likely to be registered with a GP. In the Stanley (2001) study, all were in full-time education, even if sometimes the responsibility of finding a school fell to the foster parent, particularly in cases where out-of-borough placements were arranged. Those living in foster care reported the fewest problems with placements (Dennis, 2002: 12), and being cared for in a family was good according to some of the young people, who listed the following beneficial elements:

learning another language, getting advice and support, people were nice, holidays and going to school, support with homework and 'protection'. (Stanley, 2001: 42)

These were the children and young people who were in effect in calmer surroundings; at least until their immigration status was determined. They were the ones social workers were most likely to know well and assist over time, and who were provided with a 'supportive and companionable relationship' with their social worker (Bilton, 2003: 18). In some ways, they were the ones who were at the eye of the storm, having experienced the flight to sanctuary, and been allowed to enter the same systems of care and protection as vulnerable indigenous children. Yet, like their counterparts being supported under section 17 of the Children Act 1989, they were still unclear about whether they would achieve citizenship in the future. It is the lives and circumstances of these children that are now considered in greater detail in the rest of this study. But before that is done, there are a number of threads that need to be pulled together by reflecting on the literature as a whole in order to explain the frame within which the detail is being considered, particularly in relation to social-work practice.

Summarising the literature

The literature that has been reviewed across the first three chapters reveals a complex picture. Within the more general literature reviewed in chapter 1, resettlement appears as a process and an outcome. It is a phenomenon that requires adjustments over time, in inner and outer worlds, for refugees as well as the host community. Ultimately, a test of effective resettlement appears to be the re-establishment of routine lives for refugees, which include the continuation of the heritage they have brought with them, as well as a lessening of the material disadvantages and psychological burdens they have carried with them into their new contexts. Refugees are seen to be active participants in resettlement, so long as they are allowed to be, and prefer to put down roots in territory that already has some 'home community' representation, so long as members of those communities are friction free, safe, trustworthy and reliable. Dispersal appears to lead to isolation and an intensified struggle for resettlement, especially if there is continued hostility from the host community. Sometimes the struggles to adjust are brought 'home', with different generations within one family integrating in differing ways, resulting in tensions that require resolution. There is some good-quality research evidence to show that resettlement takes time, and that in a worsening climate of fear and distrust of asylum seekers, resettlement has become more difficult than was the case a decade ago.

In Chapter 2, the review established that very little is known about the histories and backgrounds of the children and young people who come to industrialised nations seeking asylum. However, their reasons for leaving and their trajectories towards these nations are beginning to be more clearly understood via research. This shows that the children and their families are motivated by a number of factors associated with the need to preserve a family member in the face of political violence or poverty and the collapse of civic structures in the home country. Those children who come to richer countries do so with the assistance of couriers and agents who are paid for their services, and at least some of whom appear to be seen as protective. In entering the country of sanctuary, and particularly when they turn to social workers, they can be seen to share some characteristics with indigenous children needing protection and public care following a rupture from the family. But they also carry some exceptionally complex messages of being 'volunteered' to the care of a public service – being the one the family chooses to save and invest in through funding the departure is a difficult process to manage for many of them. Yet the children are also thought to be resilient in the face of adversity, a resilience attributable in part to their upbringing in their contexts of origin. In any case, when they arrive, and as they begin to interact with the authorities in their asylum countries, they maintain their guard, telling 'thin stories' in ways that are likely to maximise their purchase on the new territories.

One of the striking aspects of the studies reviewed in this chapter is the way that this complexity of the young people's lives is contained within quite simple constructs. In their simplicity, these constructs are both helpful and problematic. For example, they bring to light urgent issues about practical matters that need a resolution in order for the young people to begin to experience resettlement. They also confirm the real and heartfelt importance of not letting these young people drift into the margins of concern in debates about the public care of vulnerable children.

They criticise policies and practices that disenfranchise them, or endanger them further, or see them as asylum seekers first rather than children in need of care and protection. Instead they look for ways in which they can be helped to combine different parts of their bids for citizenship in a way that is cohesive and functional. In these circumstances this form of humanitarian action is seen by the young people themselves as an expression of a valuable commitment to their well-being (Minority Rights Group International, 1998; Chapman and Calder, 2003), very much reflecting Bilton's (2003) view that practical help from social workers who are reliable, persistent and committed is highly valued by indigenous looked after children. Yet this humanitarianism is seldom attributed to social workers in any explicit way in the studies themselves.

If we follow the links between the principles for practice, the practice guidance and the results of the studies as delineated above, then it would be reasonable to conclude on the basis of the gaps identified between what ought to happen and what is seen to happen, that social-work practice is viewed as rather shallow overall, and local authority policies are seen as defensive or reactive. Even the very general findings within the studies confirm this view.

Apart from the absence of detail, there are many areas of the young peoples' experiences, as well as social workers' practice, that are not clearly defined. For example, although trust and distrust are clearly important issues for unaccompanied minors, as they are for many refugees, they are scarcely mentioned in the studies, even if they are more visible within the wider refugee literature. So, for example, no links are made between the statement by Zivic (1993) that 'trusting a close adult is a very important source of support for a child [who is] exposed to the terror of war' (quoted in Ahern et al., 1998: 221) and the observation by Utting (2003: i), in reference to all looked after children, that

> Children to whom the local authority acts as a parent . . . need a human intermediary, a known and trusted adult, who is responsible for regarding them as a whole person.

Clearly this is an issue that requires further examination in order to see whether social workers recognise and respond to the young people's need to establish safe, trustworthy relationships, where they present the human face of corporate parenting (Bilton, 2003). Similarly, issues such as silence are hardly addressed, and this fits within the frame of the maintenance of simple stories (as opposed to complex realities). While the young people's 'thin' stories are used to illuminate their vulnerability, the 'thick' stories remain unseen and unheard. As part of the promotion of a vulnerability perspective, their resilience and willingness to prosper in adverse circumstances are underplayed and remain relatively underexamined. The humanitarian helper remains clearly to the fore as a key reconstructor of refugee lives, and we see very little of the way in which young people manage their own lives effectively. Trust, silence, and the promotion of resilience-based strategies in the young people's lives therefore also require closer examination, if a direct link is to be tested between key messages about resettlement in the broader refugee literature, and contemporary social-work practice.

Issues about race, culture and belonging are similarly simplified. While open attention is given to experiences of racism by the young people – and only Stanley (2001) alludes to the source of racism being wider than the white indigenous community – how the young people feel they fit with communities that they left behind is appraised in a way which perhaps sentimentalises communities of origin as protectors and care providers, when the situation may be far more complex. As I have said elsewhere,

> An unaccompanied young person may well experience integration into the host community alongside disintegration from the community of origin. The pace, focus and pattern of these shifting and fluid affiliations will vary according to individuals' personal choices and their capacities to manage changes that are thrust upon them. The choices may be mediated, for example, by sensing safety in the anonymity of an unfamiliar culture and locality, or they may, conversely, be signalled by re-creating a strong affiliation with others from similar cultural backgrounds. Both similarity and difference may offer dangers and opportunities in relation to belonging, but neither will in itself provide a complete 'one size fits all' guide to the well-being of each individual. Promoting cultural integration . . . may mean taking account, in a non-colonising way, of an indi-

vidual's story and its current re-enactment in the UK context, without reducing the culture of origin, the processes of reintegration, or the powerful impact of the host community into good and bad ciphers added blandly to the delicate, rich and personal equation of resettlement. (Kohli and Mather, 2003: 205)

How social workers make sense of what the young people say they want in terms of similarity and difference, and ultimately what sense the young people make of where they feel they belong and who they belong with, therefore requires further investigation.

Furthermore, there are seldom any accounts of social workers taking the psychosocial needs of unaccompanied children into account in practice, or of working with them with 'therapeutic care', defined by Papadopoulos (2002) as, 'the wider application of psychotherapeutic principles to any form of assistance to refugees'. As Howe (1996) would say, the studies make no clear link between 'surface' and 'depth' issues, and the psychosocial elements of resettlement receive very little attention, particularly in relation to what social workers might do to assist the young people in helping them to voice and make sense of their experiences and feelings. As Stanley (2001) has noted above, they do not want 'therapy'. Richman (1998a) and Burnett (2002) also suggest that many of them do not need it, or understand what it is. Similarly they may not have time to attend to feelings of loss at a time when they are trying to manage the practicalities of life in the initial period of resettlement (Richman, 1998b: 179). Yet as we have seen, the well of complex feelings can be very deep for children who have been sent far away from (and sometimes by) their families of origin, and there may be times when social workers need to help them by connecting events in their lives with what meanings they give to the events, particularly the experiences of leaving their homelands. In this respect, further exploration of how social workers connect to the young people needs to take place, either to confirm the studies' general findings in greater detail, or to qualify or challenge them.

Finally, the studies tell us very little about any longitudinal aspect of the care and resettlement of unaccompanied minors. Given the importance of time as a factor in the resettlement process, they contain few ideas about how social workers might work collaboratively or companionably with them to reconstruct their lives, as they get to know the young people, over time, as ordinary individuals rather than as asylum seekers.

In signalling these areas of further enquiry, this study will now examine social work with unaccompanied minors along three dimensions. First, in relation to the **breadth** of 'outer world' activity, to look at social work more closely as a 'humanist endeavour' (Davies, 1994). Secondly, in relation to **depth**, particularly as practice that connects inner and outer worlds. Thirdly, **over time**, as practice within which the young people can reconstruct their lives, tell their 'thick stories', and embed themselves in safe communities of belonging.

4 The social workers, their backgrounds and their work contexts

The social workers who took part in the study came from a variety of backgrounds to this area of practice. Some were veterans, some relative novices in relation to the work. They represented many perspectives and experiences of providing a service for the young people in their care. This chapter describes their backgrounds and contexts, and identifies the ways they used their knowledge and skills to navigate across what was at times conflicted territory. So this chapter focuses on two major issues. First, it gives a picture of the social workers themselves, in terms of personal characteristics including the ways their own histories and backgrounds influenced their practice with unaccompanied minors. Secondly, it details their professional characteristics, including the ways in which experiences of working with refugees since qualifying, building up a knowledge base for practice, and refugee-related guidance within their agencies, provided the frame within which they acted. The intention within this chapter is to present the 'stage' where the action took place, before moving on in Chapters 5 and 6 to look at the parts played by the young people and their social workers in the 'drama' of resettlement.

The teams

The social workers belonged to either specialist Unaccompanied Minors teams, or generic Children and Families teams within four Social Services departments.

Team A

An Inner London Children and Families team, within which workers undertook a broad spectrum of child and family social work. The representation of unaccompanied minors within the borough in which the team was located was below average in comparison with the distribution across the whole city. At any one time approximately 35 asylum seeking young people were allocated to the child and family social workers as part of their caseloads, compared with the city average of 107 per borough. Unaccompanied minors had been present within the locality for a decade prior to the research taking place, mostly from the Horn of Africa, and more recently from parts of Europe and Asia, primarily Kosovo and Afghanistan. Nine social workers were interviewed and they described their work with nine young people.

Team B

Another Inner London Children and Families team within a borough where the numbers of unaccompanied minors, at 120, was slightly higher than the city average, and demand for a service was heavy. A major railway terminal was located within the borough. Apart from children who had arrived from various parts of Africa during the late 1980s and early 1990s, the most recent arrivals were from Europe – ethnic Albanians from Kosovo. Eleven interviews were conducted with eleven social workers.

Team C

An Inner London Unaccompanied Minors team, holding specialist responsibility for the Social Services Department in relation to the young people. Demand for services was heavier than in Team A, and similar to Team B. Here the team dealt with about 140 young people at any one time, with a worker carrying an average of 25 cases. The team had been established for one year, following organisational recognition that increasing demand required a specialist response. The vast majority of its work was with young Albanian men, some from Kosovo and some known to be from Albania. Four interviews were conducted with four social workers within the team.

Team D

A specialist Unaccompanied Minors team in a rural location, linked to a major port of entry. At any one time the team was likely to be dealing with 200 to 220 young people from Africa (75%), Europe (12%) and Asia (12%), with 1% from other parts of the world. Demand for services was significantly higher than in any of the inner city teams and the team had been established specifically on the basis that this level of demand was best responded to via a specialist team. Each worker carried a caseload of about 40 on average. Some of the young people were known to be trafficked children (about 10%, mostly from West Africa). Ten interviews were conducted with five social workers, each worker offering two cases for discussion.

Overall, the teams presented some contrasts amongst their similarities. All contained at least some staff with lengthy experience of looking after unaccompanied minors, and across all teams there were workers who had followed the lives of these children for years as the allocated social workers. Casework with refugee families was familiar to many. The contrasts existed primarily in relation to demand for services by unaccompanied minors and the organisation of the services themselves. The senior managers responsible for the specialist teams, Teams C and D, interviewed as key informants within this study, were clear that creation of these teams had been driven by a steady increase in numbers and a wish by the organisation to provide a consistent, coherent and receptive service to the young people. Whilst Teams A and B retained their generic child and family social-work focus, within their agencies these existed alongside specialist asylum teams for those over 16 years of age.

The social workers: personal characteristics

In the initial and concluding parts of the research interview, workers were asked to talk about themselves and their backgrounds, particularly in relation to personal and professional experiences that they felt had an impact on their work with unaccompanied minors generally. So in telling their stories of working with the young people, many of the participants in this study made some effort to think back to their own childhoods, and compare and contrast their own lives with the disruptions and opportunities that the young people faced. They brought their own histories with them to the casework with the young people – of migration and settlement, of difficult childhoods and of being cared for by extended family members and kind strangers. The retracing of childhood memories appeared to prepare the ground for them to enter the young people's worlds with empathy. They appeared to use their own childhood reflections as ballast in attempting to stay still enough to listen to the young people's stories.

In some instances, social workers told brief stories of surviving childhood adversity themselves, and seeing something in the young people that reminded them of themselves, either through an expression of vulnerability or through resilience.

> *I think that if you look into your own past, anybody who's had difficult experiences especially in childhood can always find a connection with our clients, and sometimes you have to use that connection to build a rapport. My own childhood was quite horrific. My family was horrible to me.*

For many social workers who themselves had been migrants, in childhood or as adults, the narratives of their own stories were woven into their understanding of the young people's lives. Clear similarities and differences were visible to many of them, as in the following example, where a social worker who had been born in the Caribbean and been sent to England as a child, talked about a boy from Eritrea.

> *I think I am similar to him in the sense of 'Why me?' I had lack of contact with my parents, because I was sent here to be looked after by friends. Also there was uncertainty – you know, how long I was going to stay there, when I was going to see my brother again, and anger, a bit of hatred about why I was being sent away, and not my brother, who carried on being looked after by my parents. But I had to leave.*
>
> *The difference is that I didn't have the anxiety about having to return home. Although I wanted to return, it wasn't a case of 'Oh, if I go back it will be detrimental' and I always felt that I*

could come and go, and more choice. My immigration status wasn't under threat in the same way. I didn't come from a war torn region.

For indigenous social workers, connections with their own childhoods could sometimes yield important ways of seeing and holding on to the young people's experiences, even when the going was tough, with the young person being demanding, belligerent and insisting that more could and should be done to make his or her life in the UK more tolerable.

And I just feel, oh, this child, what am I going to do with him? And then I just think, I'd probably did exactly the same when I talked to my parents, and they would probably say I was just as bad and I understand exactly what he's going through. I have a great deal of sympathy for him, but I just think at times he's his own worst enemy and then that's part of growing up isn't it. It's only after a while that you look back and you realise, God, was I that bad? Did I do that? How the hell did I survive into adulthood?

In any of these types of responses, the maintenance of clear and firm links between the past and present, particularly in the 'survival through adversity' stories that the social workers told about themselves and the young people, helped to form a foundation to the relationship that made the social workers empathic, prepared to see surface and depth in the young people's behaviour.

I mean, I put myself in a position of not knowing where my family were, you know. I didn't have a good family, but I know where they all are and I choose not to have contact with them, you know. It's a very, very different thing but actually not knowing where somebody is or not being able to contact them I just can't imagine, for a child, you know.

Gender of the social workers

The majority of social workers interviewed were women (22/29). Gender and its impact on the lives of the young people was generally articulated in terms of a mothering role for some of the female workers, as noted by one who was very experienced and had seen many of the young people through from the time of admission to care, to adulthood.

> *Older young people who may be in a hostel and going to independent living, they call me 'mum'. And I say, 'Well I'm not', but . . . in a way it's fine. I went to a young person's wedding. She got married and it was all black people at the wedding and she kept introducing me, 'This is my mother, this is Mum,' and they were going . . . oh!! I'm her adopted mother and I'm small and white!*

Male participants on the other hand were less likely to link gender and practice in the same way, apart from one participant who saw a 'father figure' role as significant and meaningful to young people who would not necessarily have a concept of 'social work', but would have experienced the management of authority and care within a patrilineal context in their lives before departure.

> *And I suppose particularly with the girls I work with, I am a safe male for them. In fact, at a recent review S. said, 'Oh,' she said, 'so you're like my daddy aren't you.' And I said, 'Well not really.' I said, 'A better word is your legal guardian in your father's absence' . . . The way I operate is as a good parent would do, and I'm a parent and had sons, and I've paid for swimming lessons, paid for football kit. I've bought them a squash racket or tennis racket and these young people should have those things because their parents aren't there to get them. I want to be a guide for them, a guide to get them through their adolescence and into their independence.*

Race of the social workers

Most of the social workers were white (22/29), with almost half the group (14/29) being 'white UK' in origin. But across all teams, diversity of some sort was present – if not in race, then in nationality, and hence in self-definitions of roots of belonging, experiences of migration and integration. In terms of a simple self-categorisation of race, workers added detail to the 'white' and 'black' denomination by adding locality, region, nation, ethnicity, or personal histories that told of familial choices in moving on from one region or country to another. As one worker originally from a Scandinavian country, married to an Englishman, noted, sometimes the bureaucratisation of race into Equal Opportunities categories hid a more complex personal response.

RK: *Race?*

SW: *I find this question really difficult. I ask our young people this all the time, and then I think . . . White. And I would see myself as white, Scandinavian rather than white European, but if you tick on these forms, it's usually white European. I see myself more [country of birth]. It's not an easy question sometimes, is it? To me my cultural background is Scandinavian. I feel very much Scandinavian for some reason. This is something I started thinking about since I looked at the questions for this interview. I hadn't really thought about it before and it's interesting. I've learnt so much more about my country and the way I think and the way my people tend to think. I've become more aware of that here, living in England, working with people from all over the world, than you would do if you were just in [my country].*

Languages spoken by the social workers

All spoke English as the main language, but individuals also spoke Dutch, Swedish, Hebrew, Urdu, Hindi and Yoruba as birth languages. One of the workers spoke Albanian, and was able to communicate with the young people from Albania in their mother tongue. Others had sufficient grasp of modern European languages, particularly French and Italian, to communicate in a basic fashion with those young people who had learnt these languages in their countries of origin, as part of a colonial legacy. All others communicated with the young people using English-only, and sometimes used interpreters to cross language gaps between themselves and the young people. Being monolingual was a frustration amongst the majority of English only speakers, because entering into a fluent relationship with the young person was often difficult, and they felt they only caught a glimpse of the complex and precarious lives that the young people led. These frustrations grew less as the young people developed a grasp of English.

Religion of social workers

Two-thirds of the social workers had been born into Christian families and 10 of them were practising now, with regular church attendance a feature of ordinary life. Altogether, nearly half of them described themselves as practising their religion of birth. Very few of those that claimed a faith were confident in expressing its practical worth to them, almost as if they were shy or apologetic about it. Typically, neither those who practised their faith, nor their secular colleagues made any direct connection between their own personal faiths and their professional work. However, many of them were able to recognise the centrality and importance of religioun for many of the young people, as discussed in the next chapter.

Culture

The term 'culture' meant different things to different people, some tying it to the idea of nationality, or religion, or race, or nation and region of origin (see above). Accordingly they used these wider-ranging categories to describe their own and the young people's cultural backgrounds. Most felt concerned about not being able to offer a simple response to the question of their own culture of origin, and a minority remained confidently puzzled, reflecting on the inherent complexity of giving a definitive response, particularly within heterogeneous work and (for some) home contexts. One worker described her own origins as African Caribbean, and said the following:

> **RK:** *How would you describe your own cultural origin?*
> **SW:** *I would say Caribbean because I used to live in Guyana for*

the first five years of my life. I was born in England and then I went there when I was three months old and I stayed there until I was over five or six. So I would say that a lot of my values have come from my young upbringing in Guyana and also I would say that my stepfather is from Jamaica, my mother was Guyanese – so I would say that the upbringing I had from them was Caribbean.

But I have noticed that I've also mixed that in with the British way of life, so I would say that cultural origin ... originally would be Caribbean African. But it's a blend. The perfect word is blend in. Blend in, take on a bit of this, but keep what I've got, that's my foundation.

Diversity had been a personal choice for some (8/29) in establishing mixed-race relationships, and was seen as a part of their ordinary lives, rather than an extraordinary encounter in 'working with difference'. One worker was herself a migrant from another European country and was married to a black African husband. She noted that,

I think the experience of migration – even though I wasn't a refugee – the fact that English was my second language and I didn't have as much English then as I have now, made you feel very patronised. People talk to you as though you are a child ... they shout at you because you can't understand the language.

Also the isolation in a sense, and being married to a black person and then when our children were born and the first racism that I encountered. I can sort of put myself in their shoes a bit and remind myself what it's like for them. I think that has helped, those experiences have helped me to understand more.

One in three (10/29) social workers had personal experiences of migration into the UK, though none had experience of being a refugee. For some their own journeys of migration created rhythms and patterns that were used by the workers in developing an understanding of the experiences of the young people, particularly as new entrants into the UK. Here is the response from a female worker, born in the UK, raised in another country and now working in a specialist inner city team, dealing day-to-day with ethnic Albanian adolescent boys from Kosovo.

> RK: *Have your own experiences had an impact on this work?*
> SW: *I think in lots of ways. The biggest one is that I'm not from here, that I experienced being an outsider here. I identify with the boys, that they don't really know anyone, they're still on the periphery. Although in both countries English is the main language, we're worlds apart, miles apart. The culture is different, the understanding is different, the systems are different. Everything about it is different. My partner and I were born here, we have British citizenship, yet we're on the periphery and always will be for everything. We'll always think differently, we'll always do things differently, we'll always understand the world differently. I think I work with these personal experiences of being in England, and shifting countries and moving away from family and all of those things, and trying to settle myself even years later.*

In all, these workers formed a heterogeneous group in relation to race, culture, language and religion. As they talked about their individual orientations towards the young person they had chosen to discuss during the research interview, or about the lives of the young people in general, glimpses of the workers' own histories, characteristics and current circumstances were made visible as interwoven parts of the whole story that was told. The cues many of the workers gained from making connections between who they were and what they did, led on to understanding the position of the young people as anxious strangers in the UK, as they themselves had been, or their family members had been, in the past and now.

The social workers: professional characteristics

In terms of experience in social work practice after qualifying, the sample divided into three sub-groups. About one-third of the workers were relatively newly qualified – within the 2 years preceding the interview. About one-third had been qualified for 3–4 years, and the rest had been in practice for five or more years. Although each team contained its share of what one could broadly term 'novices' and 'veterans', the workers in the non-specialist inner city teams – Teams A and B – contained the majority of novices in the sample, including six who had been qualified for less than 12 months. To a degree, these newly qualified workers represented a familiar pattern of rapid change in personnel in child and family social work within the agencies. Workers came and went at some speed, and fractured continuity was part of the experience noted by those workers who remained core members of these teams as the new peripheral members passed through. In contrast, workers in Team D, the rural specialist team, formed a relatively stable and coherent grouping, as did two of the four workers interviewed in the specialist inner city team, Team C. The tendency within the specialist teams was for workers to stay for longer after arrival than their peers in non-specialist teams. The post-qualifying journeys of the workers towards the specialist teams included substantial lengths of time in other areas of child and family social work. Child protection of indigenous children had, for example, alerted this worker to the possibilities of a different sort of protection work associated with vulnerability following asylum applications.

> *I'd been working in child protection for about ten years. And although I'm quite good at that and I enjoyed it, I wanted to do something different. And H. and I, who's another social worker in this team, we worked together before, so she arranged for us to meet up and talk a lot about this team, about the work they were doing. I used to think it was so interesting. I think in this rural area you just do not get any experience of working with people from different cultures . . . and I really had a real interest in it. I just thought it was such an interesting job. So when a vacancy came up, I was really pleased and I applied. It's something that I've been planning for quite a long time probably about two years.*

This route of entry into the specialist team – in some ways reflecting the planning of the asylum journey itself, as well as the use of contacts to establish a claim in the country of asylum – was supplemented by the experiences others, who had been worried at arrival about the territory they were entering, and its languages, rules and customs, before finding that they could offer skills that were portable.

I think that one of the things that worried me slightly was going into a team where I hadn't got any experience, whereas normally when you move on somewhere else, you're taking all your experience with you. You're developing it, you go into a different role and you think I'm here and I know that and I can do this and I'm building on that, whereas I came here thinking this is a totally new area for me. But actually it's quite interesting how you can transfer the skills that you've learnt and it isn't really different, there's just a lot of interesting things to learn. So it's quite nice.

It wasn't like a new worker having to learn all the different procedures. So that was lovely and I could just get on with the work, but at the same time I could spend a lot of time getting to know the young people, finding out where they come from, meeting all the new agencies and there are so many, so it was good. A good combination of old skills and new knowledge.

For some of the workers in specialist teams, there had been an opportunity to escape from the pressures of child-protection work, and the chance of working with unaccompanied young people offered the possibility of escape from indigenous families harming their children.

There was also a selfish angle about it, ah look, here's a great opportunity to get away from all this really heavy child protection work and court reports and great long difficulties with the Children Act. I thought this could be quite refreshing and different, and easy.

These forms of migration towards working with unaccompanied children were also reflected in the accounts of foreign social workers who had come to the UK looking for employment. Transitions involved searching for the right context, and the establishment of safe and durable connections with trustworthy people.

When I came to England I went to a social work agency. They told me some of the groups they worked with and I asked specifically if I could work with asylum seekers. In some ways I'm not exactly sure why. I thought it would be a good opportunity because I knew

in my own country it would be difficult for me to get to work with
asylum seekers without being bilingual. But I was nearly put off
at the start because I went for an interview to a group home for
unaccompanied minors in [County X], *which frightened me a*
bit because it looked like a prison. And then I came for the inter-
view here and I was really impressed with the team leader. She was
so welcoming and confident . . . and so I took it on the spot.

There appeared to be no obvious relationship between length
of post-qualifying experience and thinking about the complexity
of work in relation to unaccompanied minors. Novices and veterans were as likely as each other to both notice and ignore
complexity, depending on their own orientation towards the
young people. Rather, a complex grasp of the issues facing unaccompanied minors was a feature of those that had made an active
choice of working within the specialist teams, or with groups of
these young people within their local work contexts.

Experience of refugee-related work

Amongst the whole group of participants, experience of refugee-
related work ranged from those who were dealing with their first
case of an unaccompanied minor, to those carrying up to 40
cases of asylum-related work with unaccompanied young people.
But experiences in relation to other aspects of refugee work, and
other areas of social work, were brought to bear on their contemporary demands. Some of the participants had experience of
working as residential social workers before qualifying, or in day
units, hospitals and family resource centres.

I've worked with refugee women, particularly African mothers,
who were diagnosed HIV positive, who were delivering their
babies in the local hospital. I had a lot on my caseload and post-
birth of the child I worked with them when the mother died. So I
suppose they were unaccompanied in a sense. I've had five years as
a manager of a juvenile justice centre and a lot of troubled and
troublesome boys who, I believe, were unaccompanied by a father.
There's a lack of father in their life. Throughout my social work,
I've always thoroughly enjoyed working with adolescents. I work

with young people all the time, they keep me young and I still think young.

Others had experienced a rapid turnover of asylum-related work, with destitute families coming to the duty desk for financial and practical support. Whilst family support featured large in the workers' responses to questions of experience related to their work with unaccompanied young people, one worker told the story of a previous involvement in child-protection work with a refugee family (Box 1), with a view to clarifying how complicated separation and reunification can be in protecting children from harm in refugee families.

For workers in Teams A and B, the work with unaccompanied minors was held alongside child protection work with asylum seeking and refugee families, predominantly from different countries in West Africa. So rather than making a choice between leaving child protection and moving on to asylum-related work, these workers carried on at the interface between the generic demands of child and family social work and the particular pressures of understanding the nature and extent of the refugee experience related to adults as well as children. As they came across refugee families within their localities, new types of work came to light, in some instances throwing the work with unaccompanied children into a sharp relief. Workers told stories of children who were orphaned through parental terminal illness, and lacked any extended family support network. These children had become 'in-country' unaccompanied, and unlike their counterparts arriving alone at the ports of entry, had originally made the flight as members of whole families seeking asylum. There were children who had clearly come to the UK disguised as family members, but in effect used as servants by the families that had brought them here. These children had fled from the 'harsh regimes' imposed on them, and turned up at the duty desk seeking care and protection.

Broadly, therefore, the workers carried between them a breadth of experiences ranging from family support, to child protection, to the care of looked after children as part of residential social work provisions. These experiences informed their work with unaccompanied minors across all teams, and added to their knowledge and skills in an incremental, casework basis.

Box 1 Working with child protection concerns in refugee communities

The social worker was newly qualified and working in an urban child and family social-work team. On duty, the team received a referral of a burn to a child. The assessment worker gathered the following information:

> The family consisted of father, mother and three children, the eldest boy being an adult, an adolescent girl, and the youngest a 10-year-old boy. The family was from Iraq. The father was still in prison in Iraq and was a known opponent of Saddam Hussein's regime. The mother fled with the children from Iraq but had become separated from them. The children had come to the UK without the parents, and the oldest child was responsible for the day-to-day care of the younger two. The 10-year-old had been burnt with the tip of an iron by his older brother for not going to school '. . . because there was that feeling that, well, here we are in a safe country, school is there, everything is there, everybody is here to help us and he doesn't want to go to school. So he needed to be severely punished he felt.'

The injured boy was removed from the care of the family and the court granted an interim care order. The boy was returned when the mother was able to join the others in the UK. The father died in Iraq. A decision was taken by Social Services not to pursue the matter further via court proceedings; however, the family 'got together and fell apart again' after the boy was returned. The social worker noted that

> . . . in the whole picture of them as refugees who had been separated from each other for so long, we couldn't possibly separate them again, it did not feel like the right thing to do . . . he had to be safe, but there had to be other ways and I think we looked at that very creatively. And I can only say that thanks to the managers that we had at the time . . . because, I mean, they could have looked at it in a very different light, taking the child away rather than trying to get the family together. So that was a good . . .

Knowledge of refugee issues

The workers in this study did not lay claims to having any extensive research-based knowledge about refugees. They tended to refer to media stories of circumstances related to unaccompanied minors, within the broader context of a hostile coverage of refugee issues, but very little else. As people who were pressed for time, learning appeared to be a matter of quick absorption of some facts 'through the skin', rather than a more detailed appraisal of research relevant to practice. In almost every instance, knowledge derived via theoretical frameworks (for example, around attachment or loss) was associated with qualifying training, sometimes applied in attempts to explain some moments of distress in the young person, associated with missing family members, or to help them understand their current lives and circumstances. Similarly, research related to substitute care that might have informed practitioners, not so much of the specific needs of their refugee charges, but of the more universal aspects of providing stability for looked after children, also remained largely unaccessed. In broad terms these workers appeared to have made a choice about working in a manner eloquently described by Schön (1995: 42) as follows:

> In the varied topography of professional practice, there is a high, hard ground where practitioners can make effective use of research-based theory and technique, and there is a swampy lowland where situations are confusing 'messes' incapable of technical solution. The difficulty is that the problems of the high ground, however great their technical interest, are often relatively unimportant to clients or to the larger society, while in the swamp are the problems of the greatest human concern. Shall the practitioner stay on the high, hard ground where he can practise rigorously . . . but where he is constrained to deal with problems of relatively little social importance? Or shall he descend to the swamp where he can engage the most important and challenging problems if he is willing to forsake technical rigour?

Schön (1995: 43) further explains that within these *swampy lowlands* of practice, professionals deliberately involve themselves in messy but crucially important problems and, when asked to describe their methods of inquiry, they speak of experience, trial and error, intuition, and muddling through.

The large majority of these workers appeared to behave exactly in this manner when asked to explain their ways of working in reference to specific knowledge or skills. This muddling through was sometimes presented during the research interviews in a slightly apologetic manner, as if technical expertise ought to have existed, but somehow remained out of reach. However, when they felt confident about working with the messy reality, what they showed was that they had some localised ways of learning about their work. For example, knowledge appeared to be layered, with the inner core consisting of knowledge derived from the day-to-day work with the young people. Each case deposited a film of experience that built up over time to offer depth of understanding and reflected Teoh et al.'s (2003: 160) contention about everyday social-work practice that 'Knowledge is created interactionally, rather than being absolute and being given from on high.' This understanding was then supplemented by the pooling of experiences with peers. Here, workers held together a sort of patchwork of stories, depending on each other to confirm similarities and illuminate differences between them, comparing what they knew and did not know. This *ebb and flow of narratives* laid down the foundations for receiving and understanding new referrals and their stories over time.

A second layer followed this layer of stories, consisting of laws, regulations, and general information available via links with specialist legal, therapeutic and educational resources. Press releases, articles in professional magazines, newsletters from refugee organisations, and legal updates were readily shared, particularly in the specialist teams.

> *If there's anything interesting then people will photocopy it and we'll send different things we've read around at team meetings. We actually get information from the Refugee Council, they send us different publications and they'll pass the information round. I try and keep up with the press, but I haven't read anything else, I just read articles. I haven't actively looked for anything else.*

No library of written materials related to working with refugees existed in any of the agencies. In response, some of the workers had tried to put together 'best practice' guides. For instance, two of the participants in the study had experience of writing practice guidelines for working with unaccompanied young people, and rather exceptionally, one was a co-author of a report discussing European policy perspectives in the care of unaccompanied minors. Each of them had attended a Department of Health special interest group concerned with social work with unaccompanied children, and each was keen to push the idea of informed practice across their agency's internal borders. For these workers, these initiatives were based on needing a clear protocol that could stabilise and improve their collective responses to the work, particularly when the young people could be needlessly 'pinballed' between different parts of the service, particularly in the context of 'screaming caseloads'.

> SW: *What became apparent to me when I came into post was that there was a complete lack of communication between area offices and the asylum seekers-team. So, for example, when a client was referred between different offices, there wasn't a clear understanding about what exactly the referral criteria were, there wasn't a clear understanding about what documentation was needed, about finance and what budget it comes out of, and that in turn caused a number of things. One, it caused – I saw tensions between different teams and hostility, and also it meant that clients were getting what I summarise as a pinball approach. So in essence it wasn't doing the clients any favours and it was causing big tensions in social services. This could have been so easily avoided and that's why I put this little booklet together to try and smooth that path because at the end of the day we were getting wound up and it meant that the clients weren't getting the service.*
>
> RK: **What impact has your production of this booklet had so far?**
>
> SW: *I don't quite know. Within the department itself I would say very little because ... I'm not getting feedback ... because people are too busy to read. If you've got a caseload screaming at you, it's very hard to read, but at least you*

know if you need to know something you can refer to it. So I don't think it's had a huge impact as yet. Colleagues need to be involved and use their own brains because your demands are so high and free time to read a booklet may not be a priority.

The notion of not being able to absorb sufficient knowledge was linked clearly and directly to lack of time across all teams. More time meant more permeability between the different layers of learning, but the absence of sufficient time meant that connections between the different layers were dry and patchy. None of the participants in this study dismissed the need for having time to absorb each layer in order to work more efficiently and effectively, although some were clearly more at ease with the messy and emotionally charged business of working in the swampy lowlands, and others longed for the hard high ground, at least for some of the time, so that they could analyse the patterns and shapes of their involvements in the work more clearly.

Some workers had attained a different type of high ground – not technical but ethical – through a pursuit of what they described as universal humanitarian objectives associated with the care of vulnerable children. From this vantage point, the first thing the workers claimed to see was not a refugee making a claim for asylum, but a young person far from their homeland for whatever reason, political or economic, needing the shelter offered through social services. As one noted in reference to young Albanian people claiming to be political refugees from Kosovo,

My job is there to promote the safety and well-being of that young person and that's it. Whoever they are, wherever they come from they're still young people, they're still fleeing from something, they're in need, they happen to be claiming that they're Kosovan because they have to, because they're forced into that position and they're not any less or more deserving than anybody else.

So, in all, knowledge was gathered in a piecemeal and functional fashion dependent on the needs and demands of particular cases. Pressure of work hindered the gathering and application of technical knowledge. However, a robustly articulate ethical position helped many of the workers orientate themselves towards the complexity they faced in their work with the young people.

Learning through training

Training in working with asylum seeking minors across all teams appeared to be haphazardly organised and poorly accessed, exactly as noted in the UK studies (Stone, 2000; Ayotte and Williamson, 2001). Nineteen of the participants claimed to have received no training in relation to any aspect of working with unaccompanied young people. Specifically, in Team A, social workers had been offered no training within their agencies, and had no information related to intended training events in the future. Typically their responses to questions in reference to training were brief.

> RK: *Have you had any training in working with unaccompanied children?*
>
> SW: *No. I have not had any direct training with refugee children. I've learnt through working with them directly.*
>
> RK: *You're not aware of this agency having provided or purchasing any?*
>
> SW: *No.*
>
> RK: *Do you know of any training that the agency intends to provide?*
>
> SW: *Not that I know of. They may have in the new training booklet that was out last week, but I haven't had a chance . . . there may well be something in there.*

Team B social workers were in a more varied position, with some having advocated on their own behalf for the external purchase of relevant training. Some, through pressure of other work commitments, had not been able to access the limited training provided by their agencies. This combination of some workers drawing in expertise from the outside, and other workers not being able to find the time to take advantage of this provision, had led to a patchy experience of training overall, as noted by this interviewee working in one of the children and families teams.

I have attended different conferences and I can't remember all of them, they were very interesting. Just recently, I attended a three-day course that was working with refugee families which was very interesting. I am hoping to go on a ten-week course on the same thing. And it's not a problem from the department's point of view in terms of supporting me to do that training. I think the three-day course must have been bought in by this agency, but it was very disappointing that there were only about five people from the whole of the department who attended the course, so that maybe that says something as well. I thought it was a real shame because it was a very good course and I just thought it was a shame that not more people attended; there was nobody from the asylum team, there was nobody from the area offices, I think that was a real shame.

The workers in specialist teams fared little better in relation to the experience of regular training in differing aspects of this work, but had a clearer idea of what training might focus on and how it might improve practice. They had a clear idea of what they did not have. Workers in these teams wanted someone to help them keep track of fast-changing immigration legislation, particularly in relation to the impact of the National Asylum Support Service (NASS) on the lives and livelihoods of the young people as they became adults whilst still waiting for their asylum claims to be determined. They wanted updated information about welfare rights and entitlements for the young people, again in reference to asylum legislation, and its weight of influence on practice in comparison with the duties and responsibilities specified within the Children Act 1989. They wanted digestible 'messages from research' training events, looking at the impact of forced migration on the health and well-being of children across the world, particularly unaccompanied minors. They wanted psychotherapists to lead them towards understanding the emotional complexities that they could see the children and young people carried. Finally, they wanted skilled facilitators – 'team builders' – who would help them work in a coherent way, and recognise that the stories that some of the young people told were hard to bear and that the numbers of young people they cared for were hard to carry, pushing them to the edges of their capacities to care. Some, in a more diffuse and hopeful way within a homogenous rural context, wanted cultural awareness training, to help them as indigenous white people carry through a sensitive responsibility on behalf of the young people from non-European contexts. In the meantime, within these teams, the more experienced workers shared a responsibility with the team leaders in inducting new workers into the systems they used, in ways that allowed entry to be experienced as manageable.

> RK: *Have you done any training in working with unaccompanied young people?*
>
> SW: *All I have done is I had an induction which went on for about a month. All I did was I shadowed different workers, all the different people from the Refugee Council, immigration, all the placements. I met lots of different young people, went to reviews to get to know where they come from, how the process works, shadowed duty, did a lot of work going to the port of entry, so I did all that. But in terms of formal training, no.*

The ethos in the specialist teams was one of replicating some of the processes of resettlement for any new arrival, whether a young person or a new team member. The 'veteran' workers acted as the guardian gatekeepers, making sure that new information, new links, and new methodologies of working had a chance to be absorbed, while at the same time, established skills could be transferred and embedded within the new contexts. While pressure of work for new entrants was expected to build up, there were, within the first few weeks of arrival in the new teams, opportunities to connect with the different layers of the work and the culture of the teams. So acculturation acted as a substitute for formal training, replicating the ways in which learning by experience acted as a substitute for technical learning. Pressure of time and the demands of the work may have held back the workers' capacities to absorb and apply skills gained via structured learning opportunities.

Knowing and using networks

To the extent that the social workers reached out beyond the boundaries of the team to facilitate their work, there was evidence across all contexts that refugee-specific networks influenced them. One-third of them had built a store of information for themselves that they used extensively. Such links and resources were either national NGOs, like the Refugee Council, or regional resources such as specialist educational, legal and therapeutic services, or local community groups and associations, or projects funded via their local authorities. Instances of workers not knowing about these networks, or using them rarely, were in the minority, no matter how geographically close or distant the teams were in relation to them. The majority of workers could offer concrete examples of using such resources, for general information gathering, advice and assistance, as well as in referring the young people to specialist therapeutic help.

However, there was little evidence that links were systematically sustained and developed within the generalist child and family social work teams. Here, workers tended to go where a child or young person's background, immigration status, and practical needs led them, so their own knowledge flowered within the furrows made by their own case, or those cases that their immediate colleagues discussed. Such was the beneficial effect of the cross-pollination of information amongst busy workers, as indicated by the example below.

> *With this case, I've had to get information from my colleagues that would help him. When I work, I like to know what I'm doing, so I asked for information, I read everything I could read on Ethiopia, Eritrea, on the war, just to find out exactly what's going on. I try to educate myself and I found information for others if they wanted to take up training courses etc.*

But this form of cross-pollination appeared to be anecdotal and accidental in comparison with those working in specialist teams. Workers in the specialist teams reported that links were wide ranging, and knowing about them helped them feel more certain of their ground in response to specific cases. In contrast to their generalist colleagues, their knowledge was patterned rather than incidental, where a web of connections was used to guide the young person towards settlement. Workers could nominate therapeutic and educational services, lawyers and immigration advisors, and community contacts that they could use. The quantity of contacts they nominated was allied to an appraisal of their quality, so that each part of the formal and informal networks was discussed in relation to both the type and standard of support available to the young people. Good lawyers, safe community contacts, sympathetic teachers and understanding therapists were brought forward as exemplars of effective containment and care. In addition, the links that the specialist workers valued helped them to feel as if they were gathering knowledge which lay beyond their immediate experiences as social work practitioners. They said that a little legal expertise, some general information related to the young people's contexts of origin, a little practical advice from therapists and teachers that helped them see the young person's hidden world and intellectual capability, all contributed to their own capacity to make sense of the work. The multi-disciplinarity that they were part of, offered its own organic layer of understanding, which helped them see a young person multi-dimensionally.

Summary

In summary, the four teams were dealing with different numbers of unaccompanied minors, ranging from 35 for Team A to over 200 for Team D. Increasing demand for services had led to the establishment of the specialist teams. With regard to the social workers' personal characteristics, there was a strong sense that many of the workers across all teams could draw on who they were to explain, clarify, and contextualise their responses. Some aspects such as their gender (or more specifically, motherhood and fatherhood) and their history of migration were signalled by them as important. The salience of personal familial experiences and their influence on professional practice was commented on in various ways, as they tried to make sense of the young people being here without family members. There was a high proportion of migrants within the group, and their journey to the UK was at times compared with the young people's journey, to find similarities and differences. Other aspects, such as personal religious faith, appeared to have a relatively less important bearing on practice. Some found self-definitions of race and culture quite difficult to grasp and explain, and dealt with this challenge by being brief. Others responded by using the research interview to reflect on the meaning for themselves, and subsequently for the young people. Only speaking English was a frustrating fact, for the monolingual workers, because it sometimes made it more difficult to communicate fluently and quickly with the young people sometimes.

In relation to professional characteristics, there was some evidence to suggest that the social workers, particularly in the specialist teams, wanted to work with unaccompanied minors in preference to looked after indigenous children. Experience of working with refugees varied extensively, but the participants brought more general experience in child and family social work to this specialist area, and used it as a foundation for building specialist knowledge. However, this knowledge was, in most instances, locally derived, stemming from casework experience, and a cross-pollination of useful information, links, and shared advice amongst team members. This was then framed within a broad understanding of laws and regulations pertinent to asylum seekers and children in care. 'Technical knowledge' via research and theory was harder to reach and use, partly because the organisations appeared to offer very little in the way of specialist training or learning resources. The lack of access was compounded by a shortage of time. It was in these conditions, with these sorts of personal and professional histories and experiences, that the workers offered their accounts of the young people's lives and circumstances.

5 The unaccompanied minors and their circumstances

This chapter relates the stories of the young people that the social workers discussed in the research interviews. Here, the lives and circumstances of the thirty-four young people are laid out in the following way. Initially, some of their basic characteristics are briefly described and linked to what the social workers knew about their ordinary lives before departure, the people who looked after them and the places where they grew up, as part of the background information needed to understand the genesis to their stories of movement. Also, their stories of leaving their countries of origin and arriving in the UK are presented, to give a flavour of the type and extent of biographical information available to the social workers. Secondly, there is an exposition of their experiences in the UK after arrival, including what the social workers knew about the process of making an asylum application, producing passports, being referred to Social Services, and being looked after in relation to the number and types of placements made available to them. Thirdly, their current circumstances are described, including major issues related to physical and psychological health, and the quality of day-to-day care, including self-care. Within this picture their attitudes to and use of educational provisions and of networks of support are discussed, as well as their behaviour and feelings as perceived by the social workers. Finally, the social workers' descriptions of their hopes and wishes for the future are discussed in reference to achieving refugee status or indefinite leave to remain in the UK, repatriation, family contact, and independent living. All of these aspects of the young people – the past, present and future – are then carried forward to the next chapter, to give an account of social work practice.

Basic characteristics

There were twenty two boys/young men and twelve girls/young women, in part reflecting a general trend of more males than females coming to the UK as unaccompanied minors (UNHCR, 2004). At the time of the research interview, the young people were said to range in age from 11 to 19 years, with an average age of 16 years and 5 months. This sample is also reflected in the age trends in the data maintained by UNHCR (2004), which suggest that the majority of unaccompanied minors are likely to be older adolescents at the time of arrival in the United Kingdom. However, as with many aspects of their lives, reliable evidence of their ages was hard to establish. The ages given by the young people were approximate, for a variety of reasons that the social workers offered in the research interviews. First, the young people did not appear to know their dates of birth, and had come from cultures and countries where no formal record is kept of precise dates. Some of them were known to be worried about being 'found out' to be younger or older than they claimed to be. Their social workers said that they knew that the young people had probably lied about their age in order to add legitimacy to their asylum claims, and to be accepted within the 'looked after' systems run within the agency – an acknowledgement of the existence of 'thin stories' was often advanced by the workers in reference to age in the first instance, before their accounts broadened out into other areas of the young peoples' lives. In some instances the youngsters appeared to be more mature psychologically than their years, leaving workers wondering about the legitimacy of their chronological age. In any case, there was seldom any documentary evidence to support the age claim made.

The young people came primarily from Africa and Europe. Between them they represented twelve countries – Afghanistan, Algeria, Cameroon, Eritrea, Ethiopia, Kosovo, Liberia, Rwanda, Sierra Leone, Somalia, Sri Lanka, and Tanzania. Eritrea and Kosovo accounted for eighteen of the thirty-four in the sample, reflecting to an extent the legacy of past conflicts in the Horn of Africa, and the aftermath of war in the Balkans. However, they came into the UK like individual *tabula rasa*. Only two of the thirty-four young people had a passport, or any other form of identification to show who they were or where they were from. In several of the cases where an agent had brought the children into the UK, the travel documents had disappeared with the agent at the port of entry, leaving them as anonymised individuals. All bar one had made an application for asylum, and each of them was looked after by a local authority Social Services department under section 20 of the Children Act 1989. Four had recently been moved to section 24, and two had recently been discharged from care, but were being provided with support and assistance under section 17 of the Children Act 1989. However, this grouping proved to be a simple representation of the types of young people the social workers discussed. Within the wider group there were three types, broadly reflecting the types of young people described in Ayotte's (2000) study:

- Forming the largest sub-group were those that were known to have a 'well founded fear of persecution'. These were the ones most easily classified as 'genuine' asylum seekers, who had given credible and detailed accounts of reasons for seeking sanctuary in the United Kingdom. Twenty-one of the young people could be ascribed to this category.
- Forming the second largest sub-group were those that had made similar claims to the first group, but for whom the claim was problematic in the sense that an economic sub-text was at least partially visible to the authorities, and suspicions about the credibility of the asylum claim were under close scrutiny by immigration officials. Ten of the young people were in this category.
- The third group consisted of those that had entered as part of a cohort of trafficked children, about whom there was grave concern within the police, immigration and Social Services in relation to potential sexual exploitation, or drug and fraud-related crimes. Three of the young people were confirmed as belonging to this category by their social workers.

However, these types of distinctions between the groups proved at times to be very unclear, and supported the argument put forward by the Separated Children in Europe Programme that it is very difficult to make the varied circumstances of minors seeking asylum fit the narrow definitions of 'refugee' within international conventions. For example, the social workers said that most of the young people had said to them that they wanted to improve themselves educationally or materially, no matter how their claim was received. In other words, all were seen to have an economic reason for flight. The social workers also noted that a few had said that they had fled from abusive families, not just abusive regimes, and needed the care and protection offered by Social Services. In all, however, what appeared similar about them to the social workers, despite the differences, was that many of them appeared to be vulnerable because of the distress of departure and as strangers in a strange land. Confusion, opportunity and danger were noted as existing for them here, making them cautious about establishing trusting relationships in their new environments. The majority were relatively new arrivals to the United Kingdom, just as they were within the systems of care and protection offered by Social Services. Most of them had come to the attention of Social Services within hours and days of arrival, so the time between getting through the port of entry and coming to the duty desk appeared to be brief. At the time of the research interviews, twenty-two of the thirty-four had been in the UK for less than a year, and were still in the throes of practical 'outer world' resettlement, allied to sorting out their immigration status, finding a school and a good GP, learning English, and establishing a network of care and support. These new settlers were spread evenly across all teams, ranging from 50% of the cases discussed in Team C, to 80% of the cases discussed in Team D.

Twelve had been in the UK for longer than a year and just three for longer than five years. All these longer stayers were people either from the Horn of Africa, or from West African countries. The European young people or those from Asian countries were entirely within the new entrants group. To an extent, this bias in relation to the region of origin reflects the history of post conflict flight to Europe, where children from various parts of Africa had come for sanctuary during the late 1980's and early 1990's (Williamson, 1995) and the ebb and flow of conflict in various parts of the world had deposited them on UK soil at different times. Two-thirds of them had been

Table 5.1   Immigration status

	Frequency	Per cent
Temporary Admission (TA)	22	64.7
Exceptional Leave to Remain (ELR)	10	29.4
Indefinite Leave to Remain (ILR)	1	2.9
No application made	1	2.9
Total	**34**	**100.0**

granted Temporary Admission while their initial claims were assessed. One-third had been granted Exceptional Leave to Remain (ELR) (replaced by Discretionary Leave (DL) and Humanitarian Protection (HP) from April 2003) on humanitarian grounds. One had achieved Indefinite Leave to Remain (ILR) on humanitarian grounds (see Table 5.1). None therefore had full refugee status. All except one child, who was a new arrival, had claimed political asylum, citing civil war as a major reason for propulsion to the UK. About half the group had already made 'in country' asylum claims before they came to the Social Services department, and had found a solicitor to represent them, particularly those who turned up at the duty desk in the inner city teams. For them, a network unknown to the social workers appeared to be working effectively to ensure that their claim was in order. For 'port of entry' applicants, primarily related to Team D, a standardised approach was for social workers to alert the Panel of Advisors at the Refugee Council to incoming young people, and ask for a Panel member to guide them through the initial stages of application, and where necessary to find a solicitor to act on their behalf. The pursuit of certainty in relation to immigration had left them anxious. Social workers described many instances of 'planning blight', with some young people waiting for up to two years from the time of the application to hear the outcome. In that period, not knowing whether there was a future in the UK, not travelling abroad, not contacting family members, compounded a sense of being only on the fringes of calling anywhere home.

Histories: ordinary lives and fragmenting events

All the young people were reported to carry a sense of mystery about their origins, within which only fragments of the everyday lives left behind were known to the social workers. A consistent pattern described by the social workers was of a reluctance to talk openly about their past lives. Some never talked at all. Others talked only when prompted by the workers. Silence about the past was an organising feature for many of them. '*They focus on the present first, the future next, and the past last,*' said one of the workers. They gave reasons for the existence of silence which resonate with the ones noted in the literature.

- First, that the young people had been told to be quiet by those who had sent them – 'closed where possible and open where necessary' – so that their applications for asylum were not jeopardised by revealing fragments which might have undermined their formal claim.
- Secondly, some of them were too shocked to talk, and had squashed their experiences into boxes in their minds which they would not, or could not, unlock at the time. This particular silence, like any other silence associated with grief, had its own viscosity that slowed the young people down in their acts of ordinary living and was the most worrying of silences for the social workers.
- Thirdly, despite everything, they wanted to get on with the practicalities of resettlement, and in many instances were occupied, like any other teenager, in dealing with their day-to-day lives and not so concerned with looking backwards or forwards in detail. They wished to be ordinary, not extraordinary.
- Fourthly, fear about the future meant they were too unsettled in the present to reflect on the past.
- Fifthly, they were never quite sure about what impact the disclosure of details of their past lives would have on the lives of those left behind. They worried that their families would be traced and put at risk in some way, if their whereabouts were known.
- Finally, for a minority, whom the social workers thought had left behind abusive families, there was a sense of

closing doors behind them, and not opening them up again. Moving on was part of a search for healing.

From the varied accounts given by the workers, there was a clear sense of the young people carrying their version of Pandora's Box, with hope wrapped in silence. Particularly for those who had come to the UK several years ago, extensive silence appeared to have eroded the capacity to remember anything much beyond the story given to the Home Office, as if this learning by rote of thin stories had obliterated other experiences and memories. But some thicker stories had emerged over time. From these, the social workers noted that material circumstances prior to flight were varied. Twenty-two of the young people from Africa, Europe and Asia were described as coming from prosperous family backgrounds, five were from backgrounds where the family had been sufficiently viable financially to fund the flight, and seven from poor, mostly rural backgrounds. There was evidence to suggest that the Europeans in this group were more likely to be from families with middling incomes, or from humbler financial backgrounds, often in rural settings. Those from Asia or Africa appeared to come from prosperous backgrounds on the whole, apart from the trafficked children.

I recently worked with an Afghani interpreter. We had two Afghani brothers come into the office and he was very helpful to the brothers; he got them to a solicitor and we managed to get them into a placement. He was saying these Afghan boys: you're talking the crème de la crème of Afghan society. Not even middle class and forget the poor, these boys' parents have got American dollars and that's how they get here.

Comments made by the young people themselves about financial privilege and educational achievements in pre-flight life were used as crude measures to define power and position in the country of origin. When family life consisted of maids, cars, private education, tutors, big houses, refined political awareness, business contacts, and parents in esteemed professions, workers surmised that they had accrued advantages not usually associated with children entering local authority care. For workers used to caring for disadvantaged indigenous children, there was a spark of resentment if these young people carried over some aspects of their relationship with servants to their relationship with public servants in the UK. In some instances, their regal expectations were resented by the workers.

> *I guess my personal impression about people who flee the war, they seem a bit more sophisticated as a family and that they were very important in their own country. They dressed in their best clothes, they knew what they wanted and appeared to be a lot more sophisticated, but that's my personal impression. I remember I felt they thought I was their servant and therefore they would tell me to do things rather than ask which made me very uneasy. I rather think it was a cultural thing and they probably felt that because we were working, that we were lower than them. Maybe if you have people look after you and cooking, perhaps they just didn't understand the ways of working here. It could be that they were quite used to that, used to having people doing things for them and therefore they accepted it, but I didn't . . .*

For a small minority, their parents were known to run small businesses, be self-employed as artisans, cooks, hairdressers, labourers, and servants; again this is based on fragments of information volunteered by the young people. There appeared to be a relatively strong link between wealth and distance travelled, with the Africans and Asians in this group needing and using robust financial resources offered by relatively wealthy urban backgrounds to come to airports as ports of entry to Europe, in comparison with the Kosovan Albanians entering through sea ports, after shorter, relatively less costly journeys by lorry.

In sketching out their material circumstances prior to departure, social workers also made guesses about the emotional environments the young people had grown up in. These – like many of the informed guesses made by the social workers – were based primarily on their observations of behaviour, in the absence of meeting the parents and in the absence of any form of corroborating evidence. One set of hypotheses generated by the participants in the study was that the parents had invested something of themselves in the young people in the past, both materially and emotionally. They had loved them enough to give them up to authorities in a far away country and had had the intention at some stage to project their children into a safer, more secure world than the one that could be offered in the home country, as noted by the following, describing a boy whose mother had been killed just before his departure:

> SW: *He describes his family life as very loving, happy, good relationship with his parents. I suppose the only other thing he's talked about is that they had a very good life. They had opportunity, they had money, which is obviously difficult for him now because he has no money and his life changed in every way. I think he had a very close relationship with his mother because he talks about her, about going out shopping, what she did in the day. He's always quite animated when he talks about her.*

Yet amongst the general impressions, few of the social workers had detailed knowledge of the young people's ordinary experiences of childhood prior to departure. In over half the cases, basic information such as a family tree was missing, either because the social workers had not approached the young person to do it, or more frequently, when they had asked the young person had refused to engage with the task. Information about exact geographical location was either not known, or vague. Few records existed within the social workers' files of the people or places remembered by the young people, nor of important events prior to separation from their families of origin. Little was known about their medical history – of major illnesses, immunisation records, needs for a special diet etc., nor any details of their schooling or educational history prior to departure.

Stories of leaving home

In comparison with this lack of detail about the ordinary aspects of their past lives, social workers knew comparatively more about the extraordinary nature of events leading to the flight from home. About one in five of the young people's stories were recorded in great detail via copies of the statements that had been made to the Home Office in the asylum applications. A similar number were sketched out. Social workers knew from another third of the group that they had not witnessed traumatic events or been personally subject to torture. For one in four of the young people, the trigger events were unknown, because they had not disclosed them to the social workers, or because the workers had not asked. The social workers described four ways in which they talked about departure, when they did talk about it.

- First, there were the ones who knew what was happening to them, and spoke about it openly. They had been part of the process of planning the escape and were clearly attempting to get away from persecution and were not afraid to talk.
- Secondly, there were ones who knew, but did not say, and for these the workers struggled to identify the boundaries between privacy and secrecy.
- Thirdly, there were ones who had little idea of what was happening to them, and had explained their bewilderment openly. Sometimes they were too little to understand, and had come with older siblings who 'held' the story. Others simply did not know which country they had landed in.
- Fourthly, there were those that the social workers thought knew little about why they had been chosen as the ones to go, and now were stuck in a confused silence, being unable to give reasons to themselves or others for their departure. One young person confessed to having 'lost the steering wheel of my life', without knowing how this had happened, or why those in charge of his life prior to departure had made the decisions that had so radically affected him.

These stories were about sudden and catastrophic events that had led to exodus, or a prolonged period of attrition, within which safety and belonging were eroded over months or years. The noose became tighter, freedom became restricted, the family was threatened, family members were killed, and arrangements were made with agents for flight, and put into effect in dramatic fashion. The workers knew the horrors that a minority of them had faced, including being raped, beaten, trapped, frightened and confused. They relayed these stories with a degree of sympathy and captured the stoicism with which the young people faced up to their loss and escape. In the example in Box 2, the social worker had a copy of the statement to the Home Office, and was able to narrate a young woman's story during the research interview.

Mementos and keepsakes

Only one in five of the young people were known to have brought any memento from the past; four out of five had no photos of family members, no souvenirs, toys, tokens or belongings – only the clothes they wore. Typically, and in keeping with many aspects of an occluded past, they arrived carrying a little bag of additional clothing, but nothing else – at least, nothing that the social workers had seen. Generally these workers had not

---

Box 2   Hana's story: escaping from harm

Hana is an Eritrean young woman currently looked after in a rural part of England. Her parents had briefly migrated to Saudi Arabia, where she was born 16 years ago. The family consisted of mother, father, Hana and five siblings, an older sister aged 17, a brother aged 15, and two other younger sisters. Life was good in Saudi Arabia, and the family saved enough money to move to Ethiopia and set up a business in one of the cities. But as war between Eritrea and Ethiopia flared, and the family's life began to close down around them. Neighbours started to threaten family members. Hana was suspended from school. Their daily movements were restricted. They were afraid to speak in their own tongue, and they felt visibly different in appearance as Eritrean.

Hana made a statement to the Home Office at the point of entry, containing these elements:

One night the father was arrested by the police. After one month the mother disappeared and the children fled to the care of a family friend in Saudi Arabia. They stayed with her for six months, trying to locate the exact whereabouts of each parent, without success. On hearing that the children were being

▐▌▌▌➡

asked them any questions about the absence of artefacts from their previous lives, and appeared to have little understanding of the importance of transitional objects to children moving from one context to another. Sometimes, even the clothes that they brought evoked memories that were hard to carry, and attempts were made to bury the pain of recollection, with the help of day-to-day carers:

> **SW**: *She has a coat that she came to England with that the courier man gave her. The foster carer bought her another coat because the coat was like a summer coat. I think they either threw her original coat away or they put it some-where that she would not be able to see it because she found that it was such a painful experience having it around, but it was not ideal for this weather. So she got another one, but*

---

sought by the authorities, the friend sold the family's posses-sions, and converted the cash into gold. She found the chil-dren's passports and arranged for the three older siblings to be sent to Sudan. The youngest two were left with another friend to be cared for while the older children flew to the UK with the family friend. On arrival at the airport, she made sure they cleared customs, and then disappeared.

The children's statement noted:

We did not know where we were. We waited for a very long time but she did not come. A lady asked us for our papers. We said we were waiting for our friend, but she had not come. We were taken to immigration. We all cried a lot. We did not know what would happen. We waited for about six or seven hours and then someone came who could speak Arabic. We claimed political asylum. We were eventually collected by the social services and we are now safe.

Hana knew nothing about her parent's situation now – whether they were dead or alive, or where they were, and had lost contact with her other siblings.

> *that coat it was so traumatic for her to put it down and now that it is down, she doesn't want to see it. I'm not actually sure, I think maybe the foster carer might have destroyed it or put it somewhere she couldn't trip over it.*

In contrast to this process of shedding and burying the past, the young people who had brought something kept their mementos in a pristine condition – a prayer mat, a photo, a ring given by a parent as a birthday present, a necklace, and on a single occasion, a birth certificate. The unusual presence of these objects stood as a marked contrast to the majority. In instances where they knew that extended family members could be contacted to supply an artefact, they made great efforts to pursue the possibility of getting hold of something, no matter how small (see Box 3).

Arriving in the UK

When they landed on UK soil, asylum was, for some, tied closely to a simple idea of safety. The social workers noted that for those who had faced catastrophic events prior to departure, the memories of persecution had clearly followed them. They arrived at the port of entry frightened about being beaten and abused. One worker described an African child whom she met for the first time at the airport:

> *She knew she wanted to be safe. When she was on her knees saying, are they going to come and beat me? Are they going to come and take me away? And I was saying to her, you're safe. Nothing is going to hurt you here. You're safe. And that's all she wanted to be was safe. It is the same for a lot of young people. Some do know they are coming to England, some have never even heard of England.*

Six of the thirty-four minors came to the UK as part of a sibling group. All the others arrived alone, the majority with the aid of an agent. In many instances, particularly when the young people had been in the UK for some time before the Social Services' involvement, or in instances where the port authorities

---

Box 3   Simon's story: the empty photo frame

Simon is a 16-year-old Ethiopian boy. He was born and brought up in Addis Ababa, the son of a wealthy property developer. His father was politically active in opposition to the Ethiopian government. One day, government soldiers attacked Simon's house. The father was shot and killed. His mother committed suicide on the same day. Simon escaped, and the house was ransacked. An aunt helped to get him out of the country. He arrived in the UK and was referred to Social Services by Immigration. For a while he lived in a children's home, and made a strong attachment to the female manager. This relationship broke down around the first anniversary of his parents' death. He was diagnosed as suffering from post traumatic stress disorder, for which he received effective help from the local Child and Adolescent Mental Health Services. He moved on to independent living. The social worker described him as gregarious, liking company, a humorous and friendly young man, who still suffers from the trauma of his pre-flight experiences. She visited him in his new flat. On the mantelpiece in the front room she noticed an empty photo frame. She asked why it was there. Simon said that one day he hoped to get a photograph of his mother and father. Then the frame would be filled with their picture. The social worker noted,

> *Even though there's a loss around he has an aunt who can probably help him better than anyone else in the whole world. She could give him his identity back. Quite significantly he's got nothing in this photo frame on the mantelpiece in his flat. And what he was saying to me was 'I'm waiting for a picture of my parents, waiting to get a picture from my aunt'. An empty photo frame in his room. That's how the whole thing started about getting these pictures. And I could feel the urgency.*

---

had not been the main referring agencies, information about how they came to Britain and to the locality where they were found was hidden from the social workers. But in assembling the fragments that the workers could see, the main emergent impression was that an adult came with them, took them through the port of entry, and abandoned them shortly afterwards. The ones either travelling through mainland Europe, or from Europe, were smuggled into the country in lorries. The authorities noticed them, either wandering around the port of entry, or at major terminals, by the side of the road. Sometimes their direction of further travel was arbitrarily assigned by the immigration officer determining their initial claim, as shown by the story in Box 4. The impact of such events led to unexpected consequences.

Searching for resettlement

The young people had come to the notice of Social Services in a number of ways (see Table 5.2), depending in part on the choice of port of entry. If an airport was used, then port authorities with established protocols with Social Services would act as the main referrer to the duty social worker – in this sample eight of the young people came to the attention of the local Social Services in this way. Twenty six of them however, were referred after entry to mainland Britain. Transport police or local police officers refereed five of them, after they had been 'abandoned' by the agent or carrier on the road, in supermarket car parks, and at railway stations. Sometimes, they were picked up by strangers, who, like good Samaritans, took care of them temporarily, before alerting Social Services. Four of them were brought to the duty

Table 5.2 Referral source

	Frequency	Per cent
Self	11	32.4
Immigration authority	8	23.5
Police	5	14.7
Friend or friendly stranger	4	11.8
Community organisation	4	11.8
Other sources	2	5.8
Total	**34**	**100.0**

Box 4   Albert and Erijon's story: turf wars

Albert and Erijon from Kosovo travelled to the UK together and made an asylum application at a seaport. They were given separate interviews and each was told by immigration officers to head for a different part of the same UK city. They protested, saying that they wanted to remain together. Their request to be sent to the same destination was refused on the grounds that they were not related to each other. On arrival in the city, Albert referred himself to Social Services as an unaccompanied minor, and his story was accepted at face value. He was placed with foster parents. Erijon referred himself to a neighbouring borough, and was housed in a hostel for single adult asylum seekers. Albert's social worker wanted to reunite them by transferring Albert to the care of the neighbouring Social Services with the promise of financial backing for his care. But the neighbouring borough refused this offer. Albert said he could not understand what this dispute was about because his friend lived on the other side of a local park from him, just a few minutes walk away. The park had become a major demarcation line between the two authorities, and workers – for a time at least – had become caught up with guarding boundaries, supplemented by cross-border sniping in a sad, albeit less dangerous, re-enactment of conflicts left behind.

> *And for about a year, there was a lot of boundary wars between other local authorities and there was a lot of 'he's yours, he's mine, he's yours' and not a lot of acceptance. And I think the more overworked we became, the more we became obsessed about location. 'Where in the park did you say exactly, is it their side or our side?' And it became a focus about not listening to the story at all, but listening to exactly which part of the park they had slept in? It was very depersonalising, very much about 'We've got enough work, go on somebody else's patch' basically.*

Albert and Erijon did not live together. Albert continued to live with foster parents, and carried a degree of confusion and unhappiness at the bureaucratised demarcation. The foster placement broke down. He now shares a small flatlet with another looked after Kosovan boy, who is a stranger to him.

desk by these 'friends' or 'friendly strangers' whom they had 'bumped into' on the streets; these people took no part in the initial assessment of need, and left no traces of their encounter with the child apart from the stories told to the duty worker at the point of assessment. Four of them were referred by community-based organisations, which had become aware of their need for care through extensive informal networks of communication. The line between 'friendly strangers' and community contacts was not always clear to the social workers, as illustrated below. Particularly in the inner city teams, a standard narrative would involve a chance encounter, leading to temporary shelter, leading to the duty desk in search of care. The last domino to fall in this set of relationships would usually be the (emergency) duty social worker, asked by an adult to admit the child into care, on the basis that they could not afford or offer the longer-term care that the child needed.

However, the majority of 'in country' applications to the Social Services departments were by the young people themselves (eleven of the thirty-four), finding their own way to the duty desk, and asking for accommodation. In a process parallel to the friendly-stranger encounter, they sprang up like mushrooms in the locality, sometimes puzzling workers with their familiarity with social care provision, as discussed in the next chapter. Despite this many of the workers were clear that at the time of entry into Social Services, the young people were frightened, disorientated, bewildered, and clearly 'in need' of protection and care. Their comments reflected those of social workers who had been summoned by immigration authorities to the initial points of entry at airport and seaports. One worker, who had been the social worker for a group of siblings from Eritrea for a number of years, conveyed the following memory of the first encounter at a foster parents' house.

> *I'll never forget because I entered that room, it was a dark room and I don't think the carers were in the room at the time. The three of them were sitting huddled together on a little sofa in this dark room watching television and you could just see if they hadn't had each other, they would be lost. I'll never forget that moment, you know. They looked so sad the three of them, all sort of huddled together . . . Like little kittens.*

Some of the young people did not know the country they were in, particularly those abandoned at ports of entry. Some had never seen white people, knew little of the language or customs and did not know Britain was an island. The aim of securing sanctuary was noted by the social workers as a predominant feature for the new arrivals. They were seen as tough, resilient, resourceful and single-minded in their wishes to remain in Britain, as in the case of this 14-year-old who had spent three months in a bed and breakfast hotel before being able to prove he was a minor in need of care. His social worker noted that,

> *He comes across as an incredible survivor. He's very self-contained, he's very quiet, he doesn't say much, but when he says something it's meant, it's thought through. And we had to place him in a residential home because he was so sure, so focused on where he wanted to be and he wouldn't budge. I don't know whether he's stubborn or whether he's strong, but this child would not budge. And he's very clear about what he wanted in his life in this country. He wanted to live in a residential unit, go to school and play football. That's all he wanted in this country, and he's got all three.*

Initial experiences of care

Unlike the varied circumstances of unaccompanied minors being supported under section 17 and placed in Bed and Breakfast establishments or hostels without support and supervision, as reported by Stone (2000), Stanley (2001) and Dennis (2002), these young people appeared to receive an attuned service in relation to their needs. Their social workers told stories that had a particular rhythm and pattern, partially recognisable in the placement patterns of indigenous children. For example, for all of them, akin to the patterns of placement-finding for indigenous children, first placements were a matter of chance, driven by what was available on the day they came to the attention of Social Services (Packman and Hall, 1998).

Typically, once the formal admission to care had been administered in accordance with section 20 of the Children Act 1989, each young person was placed on a short-term basis, using any

Table 5.3 Length of time looked after by SSD by number of placements

		Number of placements			Total
		2 or less	3 to 4	4+	
Length of time looked after by Social Services departments	0–2 years	19	5	1	25
	3–4 years	3	2	1	6
	4+ years		2	1	3
		22	**9**	**3**	**34**

available emergency resource, whether a family or a residential unit. However, in most instances, the stay was no longer than a few days or weeks. Few of them (two out of thirty-four) had to wait for longer than a month for an allocated social worker. For the majority, the allocated social worker would begin the search for a longer-term, more durable placement. Children under the age of 16 were usually found foster families and those over 16 a children's home or supported lodgings in the locality. All sibling groups were placed together, unless they expressed a preference for living separately. As illustrated in Table 5.3, nineteen out of thirty- four had experienced two or fewer placements, particularly within the first two years of resettlement. Of the nineteen, seven had remained within these first placements. Altogether twenty-two of them had experienced relative stability up to four years after arrival. Twelve of the thirty-four had experienced numerous moves, for a number of reasons. Entering these new territories was reported to be as difficult for some of them as the shock of arrival had been on landing. The social workers said that the young people found the task of having to negotiate their ways through a fresh set of borders difficult and arduous. People kept asking questions. There were solicitors, social workers, police officers, Home Office officials, foster parents, residential workers, teachers, doctors, therapists, and new children at home and at school. There were forms to fill and information to record. All these people wanted to know things, and have answers in a language that was still being learnt by many of them. Sometimes the busy and demanding outside world that they processed was matched by an inner turmoil. For example, not all of them could bear re-entry into family care if there had been ruptures to their familial and kinship networks in the recent past. Some resisted and refused to be looked after in families, and made their social worker listen to them.

> *He had always said from the day I met him, 'Don't send me to foster care', don't send me to foster care, and he really had terrible anxiety about going to live with a family, real anxiety. I think it was very much about the loss of his family. He didn't want that sort of intimacy of a family to replace his. He wanted care at a distance.*

The resistance that they showed to the types of care that were possible had a genesis in other aspects of their past lives, not just those related to the flight to asylum. Muslim girls refused to mix with boys in residential homes, insisting on independent living or a same-sex hostel. Many of the young people expressed an initial preference for white English people because of perceived advantages of assimilating more easily into the UK. Several workers related their experiences of Eritrean children refusing Eritrean carers, even in circumstances where provision had been planned organisationally in a careful way. In one instance a project had been set up by the Social Services Group, and as one said,

> *It was felt that the project would meet their needs because it was run mainly by Eritrean workers who had actually been through the same circumstances as these kids. We felt that they would provide extra knowledge about the Horn of Africa experience and also the ways of coping with being a refugee, rather than the kids having to be with non-Eritrean, non-refugee people like ourselves. That, in my opinion, backfired because the kids didn't want to have a home from home. They came to this new society and they wanted to enjoy it to its full and therefore they felt they were being held back by whoever wanted them to stick to the old ways.*

Sometimes they 'got lucky' and accidentally landed in placements that appeared to accept them in a fluent and coherent way, not necessarily because the experiences and backgrounds of the carers matched those of the young people, but because the carers could 'hold' them in mind in a number of ways, and they tried hard, as key-workers or as foster parents, to make them feel at home. For example, they made trips to specialist shops, buying palm oil, cassava leaves, prayer mats, and 'industrial size' feta cheese blocks, aubergines, dual-language dictionaries and cook books, etc. They learnt rudimentary elements of the young person's birth language, or were sometimes sufficiently fluent in French and Italian to allow these languages to act as a bridge for communication. When faced with recurrent headaches, lack of sleep and nightmares, the carers contacted GPs for neurological and therapeutic referrals, or tried to find herbal remedies, massages, and relaxing bedtime routines for them to benefit by. Where the young person considered it desirable, the carers tried to extend their own networks of support to include people from the young person's country of origin. In this way mentors, befrienders and companions were cultivated for the young people, adding to the supply of contacts they established for themselves over time. Sometimes the carers' personal qualities won the young people over, as in the case of two sisters, both Sunni Muslims, who were offered and accepted a family placement.

> *The foster parents are devout Christian, but not evangelising, or anything. They're a very warm couple. Compassionate. I noticed they had a Liberal Democrat sticker on their door at the local elections, so they're not rabid Tories. So they're a liberal Christian family. I think their sons have got friends from China and Africa and they also think the girls are great, but not in a stifling, overpowering way. They just give the girls space and distance when they need it.*

But first placements were resting points for twenty-seven of them, not a final destination. Placements sometimes changed for a number of different reasons associated with their behaviour. Social workers related events that ranged from the 'normal teenage stuff' of stretching, bending and breaking household rules, to trauma-related anniversaries that triggered breakdown. One social worker offered a typical picture of the unsettlement of a troubled young Kosovan within an English family. Here, in the first of four placements within a 9-month period, the ordinary trials of adolescence and the extraordinary circumstances of asylum engineered a collision that neither party was able to avoid or repair.

> *There were communication problems between Ishmael and the host family, which was white UK. Ishmael went out of his way to annoy all the family and didn't communicate, broke the rules of the place, would not come in when he was supposed to, wouldn't eat with the family. When the family walked into a room that he was in, he would get up and walk out. If he went into a room that the family was sitting in, he would not enter the room, he would not talk to them.*
>
> *I think it was difficult for him because he wasn't able to put over his views about what he wanted because he had so limited language and he decided to distance himself from the family. We had set up interpreters who would go in on a regular basis so that they could communicate, but it was moan after moan after moan. Ishmael really wasn't prepared to give and take. The language barrier made the situation much worse at a time when he was finding it very difficult to deal with the sudden separation from his parents.*

The placement ended with mutual recrimination, and Ishmael moved to a flat shared with another young Kosovan man. Here he re-created, with a more culturally familiar person, another important aspect of the journey to resettlement – that of entering occupied territory, where someone else had already worked hard to establish their own territorial advantages. In these instances the new arrivals had to be careful to mind the pecking order to ensure that peace was preserved. The carefully accumulated possessions of the earlier arrivals, their shelf in the fridge, their food, their clothes, and their space all received a wide berth as the young people docked alongside them in the new homes.

The other important aspect, referred to in passing by the social worker above, was the issue of timing in relation to the crisis before the move from a placement. Several workers told stories of anniversaries of parental death, or separation from the family, leading to complicated confrontation with carers, particularly in instances where the carers had been invested with the power of the parents in the young people's eyes, and were seen to be depriving them in some way, or not giving them enough of something. Many of these conflicts would ebb and flow, and not all resulted in placement dissolution. Most were resolved within the family or home by the people involved or by a carefully authoritative intervention by the social worker. Calm – the sort of inner calm that the social workers hoped for in their young people over time – appeared to take years to establish for some, after periods of storming around: very much reflecting the extensive nature of the resettling over time, as noted by Silove and Ekblad (2002) earlier (see Chapter 1).

Resettlement on the outside: calling somewhere home

While it appeared to be difficult to replenish the feeling home they had left behind, the social workers said they saw an organic growth of relationships and possessions as the young people worked out the things they needed, to feel stable and settled in their new environments. In getting through a stage where life had fragmented, they were, in their current circumstances, holding different segments of their lives together in a cohesive way, but still waiting for a sense of wholeness and coherence to emerge.

As far as the social workers could see, there were some signs that those who had been well cared for after arrival, who were not personally wrecked by the departure or landing, and who had their wits and intelligence to guide them, could re-establish a fluid and coherent life, but for many of them, day-to-day life was still about crossing borders towards safe havens in their inner and outer worlds, and edging towards resettlement in both.

Very little is currently known about the type of care that works best for unaccompanied minors reaching industrialised nations (Zulfacar, 1987; Steinbock, 1996; Tolfree, 2004). In that sense the social workers in this study had very little to guide them in their search for the types of placements that would work best in relation to resettlement. However, 53% of the minors were in foster care, 23% in children's homes and hostels, and 12% living independently, reflecting the national percentage figures. The rest were living in a variety of arrangements provided, administered or purchased by the local authorities, including private and

Table 5.4 Types of placement

	Frequency	Per cent	Compared with national % figures in 2003 (DfES and NS, 2003a)
Foster care	18	53	68%
Children's home/ hostels	8	23	20%
Independent living	4	12	10%
Other resources	4	12	2%
Placed for adoption	0	0	0%
Total	**34**	**100**	**100**

voluntary-sector housing with adult supervision. A few of the young people had moved on to independent accommodation after arrival, on leaving their first placements, again reflecting the national average. Social workers' stories of their circumstances at the time of the research interviews indicated that 65% of the young people had told them they felt a substantial degree of satisfaction with the current care arrangements. In part, this was a reflection of moving to placements that the two parties had chosen together, that the young people had hoped for, and obtained through a solid determination to get what they thought was the best place for them to be.

Calling someone family and finding companions

A key aspect of finding a sense of home, said the social workers, lay in being able to call someone 'family', and in establishing a network of friends, relatives, companions and sponsors. The growth of networks was a complicated task. Some of them simply found indigenous people puzzling, not knowing their habits, rules and customs, and taking time to work these out. Others, in a rush to safety, would latch on to the first good, reliable and affectionate person they experienced, and a process of imprinting would happen as they dutifully followed this person out of the immigration holding area like little ducklings racing towards safety. Social workers knew that some of them had links already in the UK that were probably hidden away from the authorities. These hidden ethereal people were like extended family members, or like the traffickers who had funded the transition into the UK and were waiting for their investments to come to them after crossing the border. Some members of the networks were momentarily visible, like the 'friendly stranger' that they had found – or had found them – on the streets. Several of the young people had kept in touch with them after accidental encounters, and visited them at home, or met them at church and in wider community gatherings. Some longed to reconnect to the adults who had brought them in to the UK and then disappeared. As discussed in the next chapter, social workers dealt with these ghostly figures in ways that tried to keep the long-term interests of the young people in mind, for their protection, care, and independent resettlement.

For those young people who came without knowing anyone in the UK, and were circumspect about who they trusted from their own communities of origin, it was teachers, social workers, indigenous carers, Refugee Council Panel of Advisors members, therapists, and independent visitors who were the adults with whom they were most likely to connect over an extended period. Their friendship networks grew slowly, seldom consisting of more than a handful of trusted people. However, within the first year, the majority had established connections for themselves that the social workers considered useful to them in living their day-to-day lives. In each instance, utility was measured in relation to the perceived dependability of the carers or friends, and their capacity to offer practical help to the young person. These were the people who, according to the social workers, were most likely to pilot the young people towards a safer future, and stay around to repair the fabric of ordinary living (see Table 5.5 and Box 5).

Siblings

As previously noted, six of the young people were part of a sibling group, so had family representation; five of these individ-

Table 5.5 Social workers' view of the young people's most important relationship in the UK

	Frequency	Per cent
Carer(s)	17	50.0
Friend(s)	7	20.6
Sibling(s)*	6	17.6
Social worker	4	11.8
Total	34	100.0

Note All cases in this group of young people.

Box 5 The flower: a representation of networks

A social worker, who had just ended an 'eco mapping' exercise with a young man, brought the product of her session to the research interview. The drawing took the form of a flower with many broad petals, like a fat gerbera. The petals contained a name, or list of names and places. They were laid out in a radially symmetrical fashion around a broad central stigma, carrying the young man's own name. All the petals were crowded towards the centre – school friends, carers, home community members, the mosque, favourite schoolteachers, the social worker, the public library, and three houses, each one referred to as 'home', because people lived there who made him feel at home, he said. Many of the people from his own community were nominated familial roles 'like a sister', 'like brothers', with affirmative arrows joining them to the centre. The young man had lost all members of his immediate family, killed just before his departure, and had struggled in putting his thoughts to the drawing. The social worker had waited 8 months before beginning the process of drawing things with him. She was concerned that the first anniversary of the family members' death was approaching and that this young man would find that anniversary difficult to manage. She also felt that he had established a safe and protective network that was likely to help him in managing.

uals were younger siblings in their groups. All the sibling clusters, according to their social workers, regarded their brothers and sisters as their main support in the process of resettlement, their history carriers, and their greatest asset and hope for the future. Without the older sister or brother to hold them in place, noted the social workers, many of the younger children would have been sadder and less able to manage day-to-day living. Brothers and sisters looked out for each other, and helped each other to move on if one of them became stuck in worry about the past, present or future. For a few, an insular self-management replaced the need to find and establish fresh friendships or dependencies on other people.

Within foster families, the social workers said that the sibling groups could sometimes exist as self-sealed units, guarding their secrets. The younger ones would be told to be quiet by the older ones if they cried or missed home too much, and the older ones took on the main responsibility for being the go-betweens in the process of resettlement. At times, however, the burden of responsibility appeared to be hard for the older ones to bear, with much falling out between the siblings and conflicting demands for independence needing to be managed alongside a broad, parent-like responsibility towards younger members of the family. As much as life was made more manageable for the younger siblings by the presence of older ones, for the older siblings, life was more complicated than some were prepared to cope with. They sometimes wanted to leave and strike out on their own, and delicate balances were negotiated between independence and inter-dependence, in order to aid resettlement. For example, one social worker talked about an older sister wanting to leave for university to study nursing, but raising this idea tentatively at a review after having established that the foster carers would continue to care for her younger brother while she was away, and with the promise that the local authority would place the brother in her care after she had graduated. As one social worker said, in the case of a family of children from Eritrea who had been in the UK for a number of years,

They pull for each other and that's what makes them survive. Even though when they were in a foster place, they fought like cat and dog, but just like any brother and sister really. And the older

sister has now taken over that motherly role. I can go to the older sister and say, 'Come on, help me talk to your brother, because I can't get through to him.' So they have each other for support. They can talk to each other. They can share secrets, whereas if you are on your own it's more difficult to know who you can trust.

The main carers

The trust that the young people did find, after a time of being in their settled placements, appeared to be usually in their main carer. Half of them, according to the social workers, would have nominated their day-to-day carer as their most important relationship in their current circumstances, typically because these relationships were warm, reliable and affectionate. While few of the young men in this cohort were seen to give and receive hugs – in fact many of the boys struggled to express affection in simple ways – the young women were more openly expressive with women carers.

> *She absolutely enjoys being with the foster mother. The foster mum is very warm, and the kid herself is a very affectionate person, and things like in the evenings, just sitting down on the settee cuddling with the foster mother, watching television, that's important to her. The foster carer has said it time and time again, 'She's one of the family.' She calls the foster carer 'Mum'.*

The social workers noted that apart from being seen as representational parents themselves, many of the day-to-day carers of these young people were used to being seen as parents too, and none appeared to buckle under the weight of expectation this placed on them. Rather, some saw it as an honourable title and a gift from the young people as long as there was a clear understanding of their role and tasks. There was only one instance of a carer having mooted the idea of adoption in relation to an unaccompanied child amongst these cases, and the workers could not recall any other instances of adoption being discussed or planned for any of the others on their caseloads.

Several carers were said to have established clarity by means of stating rules and establishing routines that they expected the young people to attend to in relation to household chores. They maintained boundaries that demonstrated a form of remote control, with an emphasis on cleanliness and order. These households were stricter than those that offered an amalgamated hurly-burly of care, and appeared to have their own value for young people who the social workers said were trying really hard to introduce order into their own lives. As long as the rules were followed, then the young person could get by quietly.

> *He's really, really short-sighted and has to hold everything really close to his face. His foster carer just won't let him anywhere in the kitchen for hygiene reasons in the sense that he can't actually see to wash up properly, and it's just a little obsession that the foster carer's got, in my opinion, at the moment. She's very clean. It's her home, it's her palace. So even if he wanted to, the foster carer won't let him loose in the kitchen.*

But in a minority of cases – about one in every five – rules were reported as broken and this resulted in continued unsettlement. The story in Box 6 shows a young woman, accustomed in her former life to being a full member of a vibrant family, now living as a satellite in a stranger's household in a distant land.

Homeland food and personal belongings

One of the striking measures of success used by one of the social workers when asked about how he knew his young person was managing his life was to refer back to a recent home visit he had done, and say:

> *He showed me that he had aubergines in his fridge. Now I think that for a 15-year-old to manage to cook an aubergine is good. They're not the easiest vegetables in the world to cook. I was surprised to see aubergines because you don't see them in my fridge.*

For all the young people, having access to homeland cooking was said to be a significant aspect of resettlement. Food appeared to represent safety for many of them, even if they led

---

Box 6   The broken bowl: a representation of troubled resettlement

Nasira, aged 16, from Ethiopia, was placed with a house-proud foster mother. This was her first and only placement within the UK. The first few months were relatively quiet, and Nasira established a routine for herself that fell into the rhythm of family life within the foster family. Unlike her own family, that had done everything together, members of the foster family cooked and ate separately. There were no mealtimes. Nasira was told that there was food for her in the fridge. But she was confused about whether to ask for permission to open the fridge door, and ate very little at home, relying on school meals. When she did open the fridge she found some bacon and sausages near the food reserved for her. She became distressed and rushed out of the room, knocking over a glass bowl that shattered to pieces. The foster mother shouted at Nasira, insisting that she pay for another bowl through her allowance. Nasira was frightened. She locked herself in her room and refused to go back into the kitchen for weeks. The story emerged at a review meeting a few weeks later. Nasira said that she wanted to move because she was frightened of breaking any more things. She was told she could not move as no other placements were available. The review chair asked the foster mother not to cook pork while Nasira remained in the household.

---

a carbohydrate- and calorie-rich life in the first few months after their arrival. In comparison with the few who were dealing with the shock of displacement by not eating, as illustrated below, many of the young people had healthy and vigorous appetites. Pizza and burgers and chips were consumed as interesting additions to their repertoire of taste, before they faded into a repetitive blandness in comparison with their homeland foods. With help, and the purchase of utensils, ingredients, cookbooks, outings to homeland restaurants, and community contacts, their palates found their food bearings over time. As one social worker said,

> *They've all had to learn since they came to England. They were used to their mothers doing the cooking and now they do it and there's always lots of lovely smells. He talks about that quite a lot because he's learnt to cook. That's good independent living skills.*

But before this state of independent grace there had been struggles for some of them. Two of the young people were too bewildered to eat, shocking themselves into a withdrawn silence. They were the unusually troubled ones in the group, and caused great concern to their carers, and required detailed and extensive attention in order to feel that they had moved to a place of safety. In the case below, the social worker, a team of residential staff, and the other residents in a children's home were working together to take care of a new arrival who was forgetting to eat.

> *My fear a few weeks ago was the fact that he wasn't eating and I was beginning to get really fearful about that. He wasn't refusing to eat, but he just wasn't eating. There were days when I was going to see him and I said, if you don't eat you'll die. He said he feels so sad and people don't want to eat when they feel that bad. To have an appetite you need to feel reasonably OK, don't you, and there was nothing. So it wasn't like 'I'm not going to eat', it was just 'I don't need to eat and I don't feel like eating'. You could tell there was no motivation to eat, so when he had a good day we had to give him a lot to eat. I've been keeping him closely monitored actually.*

The social workers also told stories of food being hoarded in family placements. There were stories of anger at the absence or the withholding of food within residential establishments, told with affection, not malice:

> *When he's upset with the children's home he'll lose his temper about the food. Nothing else. Always the food. Any time he has any level of anxiety, it's always about food and he was shouting, shouting to my team leader who was in the review. Shouting about how they didn't feed him. And in the meantime he's holding his arm flexing this big huge bicep that he has, obviously a healthy young man.*

The urgent need to feed and hoard was also present in the relationship the young people were said to have with things that they owned or could own. Hanging on to possessions was important for them, if a little sad in some instances for the observant social worker. As stated in Simon's story (Box 3), if a picture frame was empty, or Christmas cards were still carefully displayed on a shelf in the heat of summer 6 months after the event, or a medallion with the Albanian eagle was held for comfort in review meetings, the workers quietly estimated the importance of having something that provided them with a certain sort of gravitational weight, to stop them floating away (see Table 5.6).

The social workers said that the young people gathered possessions about them by carefully saving up their allowances and spending them on things they valued. They liked having things that they could call their own, adding bits and pieces to their lives as they bedded down. The social workers felt that these material possessions often reflected their attempts to order their own lives, and this extended to fastidiousness about personal appearance and keeping their rooms tidy. They described the young people as spick and span and fashion-conscious, trying very hard to be like any other teenager with designer label clothes, who had 'big, built up, wedgie trainers and Reebok stuff'. One social worker offered a characteristic glimpse of a young man's journey towards a self-contained flat she had found with him, recounted in Box 7.

Table 5.6 Young people's care of self and possessions, as appraised by the social workers

	Frequency	Per cent
Excellent	15	44.1
Good	13	38.2
Poor	6	17.6
Total	**34**	**100.0**

> ### Box 7 Moving on with belongings
>
> After he'd arrived in the UK, he had one bag. When I picked him up from his first placement and took him to the next he had three bags and when I took him from the last foster carers I could hardly get his stuff into my little Ford car. He had so much stuff he'd accumulated, he had about five bags. And he wanted to take his little wardrobe with him. When he's in his placement he puts his things like his toiletries out and he's got his school work in a folder and keeps it all nicely in a folder inside, and he just has his things, hangs them up, puts them in the wardrobe and spends time putting things away. He looks after them. He is tidy, he's organised and he's very proud of what he's got. I have to say, all the young people I've seen, their rooms seem to be quite immaculate. But I think it's very much about, you had nothing, you've got here and then you've been given these things and you're going to look after them because you don't know what you're going to get next or you haven't had anything before, so it's probably part of that as well. Hanging on to your things, they're your own things.

Resettlement on the inside: health, education and behaviour

But it was not just belongings that the young people held on to; the social workers said that they had also brought with them a capacity to be engaging, combined with a broad determination to keep their heads down and succeed in their new environments. They coped with adversity with a level of energy and commitment that the social workers admired. The general pattern that was described by the social workers was one of them being physically healthy and rarely needing more than the requisite level of childhood immunisations to establish the beginnings of a proper medical profile in the UK. The first medical after admission to care often confirmed good health. Immune systems being compromised through HIV and Aids, extensive illnesses or continuous treatments were rare occurrences across the whole group of young people. Good health and energy were the prerequisites for engaging fully within their new worlds.

Many were reported to be strong willed. While tantrums, shouting, and a bullish attitude towards getting things for themselves were apparent in them, the majority of young people were regularly described as well mannered and personable, easy to be around, bright and 'sparky', shy and stubborn, causing no trouble to anyone; or as being a concern in relation to bad, sad or dangerous behaviour.

None of them had broken any laws in the UK. They were also experienced as creative, resilient, intelligent and charming, proud, smiley, sociable, accommodating, philosophical, self-contained, sometimes being able to 'sulk for his country and win gold medals', and interested in other people and curious about new things. These clusters of fond attributes – the social workers rarely resorted to simple descriptions of traumatised victims or chancers and charlatans – are exemplified in the comments by this social worker, taking a whole person into account in reference to age, circumstances, and disposition.

> *In a way I think of him like any young teenager who caused you a lot of hassle, – he can be extremely demanding. I think because he's got a very strong personality, he's very determined and he knows what he wants, but he also needs boundaries. At the same time he's amusing, he's got a lovely personality. He really has compassion for others and that comes over, and he's able to reflect on his behaviour as well, so when he has done something that hasn't been right, he will come back and say, 'Look, I'm very sad I did this'. It's a real asset to him, actually, his personality . . .*

The social workers were also aware of instances when politeness was a heavy burden for the young people, particularly when they appeared disengaged. The external world and its events appeared to glide off them, as if they had glass skins. These young people appeared to stand in contrast to the ones who were visibly sad, or passionate or engaging – they were said to carry themselves as if they had a deep sense of calm, that the social workers thought was a way of fending off distress. They were super-organised, very controlled, and cautious, and managed their day-to-day lives without drawing attention to themselves, for good or bad. These were the ones for whom the social workers waited, hoping to see the young person become less guarded over time, and for the external glaze to be replaced by a more permeable and liveable skin.

An extended pattern of sadness did not always warrant clinical interventions. The young people were reported as rarely needing psychiatric interventions. For example, only two of the workers told stories of referring their young person for assessments in relation to post-traumatic stress disorder. However, there were indications that all the young people experienced times of being psychologically dishevelled. They often worried about things, and the social workers indicated that despite their capacities to endure loss and uncertainty, they would lose sleep and feel miserable and become fearful on a regular basis. Not even the most robust amongst them escaped demons that chased them from time to time. While there were no reported incidents of self-harm, even amongst the few who were more deeply distressed than their peers, headaches and recurrent nightmares were disabling for several (seven out of the thirty-four) of them – at least episodically – and required attention from doctors, carers, opticians, and therapists.

> *He's started to talk about bad headaches and some days not being able to move from his seat, just thinking about the past and his head is going round and round and round. So I think some time soon or in the future that's going to have a great impact on him.*

Their faith in medical services was skewed towards physicians rather than psychiatrists or therapists. Through somatising some of their distresses, they would seek medication rather than therapy. Analgesics were understood and valued, but therapy was not. The

Table 5.7 Formal therapy

	Frequency	Per cent
Not needed	17	50.0
Needed/used	5	14.7
Needed/refused	12	35.3
Total	**34**	**100.0**

social workers considered that the young people could have bene-fited by the use of therapeutic services in half the cases but when therapy was offered, it was likely to be refused (see Table 5.7), for a variety of reasons, to do with age, timing, lack of understanding what therapy was, or being too busy prioritising ordinary living. As one social worker said in reference to age and stage,

RK: *Does she get to see a therapist at all?*

SW: *No, she doesn't want it. It's a quite clear 'No' at this point. It'll be on the agenda all the time. But she needs that inde-pendence really, of being able to say no. And I would say that at her age it is particularly difficult to actually engage in that process. Much younger, much older – no problem – but in the middle of adolescence, no.*

The few who did take up the offer of therapy appeared to benefit most from a resource aimed particularly at victims of torture, where the need to tell someone about what had happened to them was pressing for the young person. A success-ful engagement with local CAMHS (Child and Adolescent Mental Health Service) services was rare across all contexts, with only one case coming to light of a CAMHS-employed therapist, who, on retirement, continued her association with the young person who had been referred to her, by becoming his inde-pendent visitor. Feeling at home on the inside took time, and was possible only when they had made a mark for themselves in the outside world. Across all teams, 'the present first, the future next, and the past last' was reasserted as the main pattern of resettle-ment by the social workers on behalf of their young people. In the domain of the present, one key element emerged as the focus for making a mark, and achieving success – education.

Education as a balm

The social workers said that education offered the young people a way of dealing with difficult feelings, as well as of keeping hope alive. It appeared to act as a balm, and to fill their minds with learning, pushing some of their preoccupations to the margins for a time. As one noted,

I know that education helps to keep these flashbacks away and helps young people to stay sane. They say to me 'When I'm at college I can't think. When I'm doing studying I can't think'. The activity dispels the feelings. So it's very, very important. I think if your life is getting into some sort of routine, you know what's happening from day to day. It keeps those memories away for a time and it just helps young people to cope.

Their social workers said that the majority of young people they worked with were keen to go to school, and worked hard (see Table 5.8). Teachers had reported that many of them tried to remain focused and ambitious and would concentrate in class, keeping away from individuals and networks that threatened to disrupt their learning, and that they valued an atmosphere of ordered calm. A few were known to their social workers to have come home seething at incidents where their indigenous peers had been collectively disruptive or disrespectful to teachers. But school also offered a chance to socialise and integrate into ordinary society, and none were known to talk to indigenous friends about their own past experiences, unless their friends themselves were seeking asylum.

Some were quite clear to their social workers that being known as an asylum seeker would get them into trouble, or push them to the margins of a friendship network, even though there was little evidence that they had been picked on for being refugees within the school context. Invisibility of this sort mattered to them, and social workers not coming to parents' evenings (the

Table 5.8 Education

	Frequency	Per cent
Full time, attendance and achievement good	26	76.5
Full time, attendance or achievement poor	5	14.7
Excluded from school	2	5.9
No school provision*	1	2.9
Total	**34**	**100.0**

* new arrival

key-worker or foster parent was acceptable) meant that records of attendance and achievement were relayed second-hand to the workers.

Having a timetable provided a structure to weekdays, and education was experienced as rhythmic, predictable and safe. Particularly for those that had waited for a place at a school or at college, there was much relief brought about by walking in through the gates of the establishment, and finding a niche, so long as the establishment wanted them, and had provisions that could meet their needs. Social workers referred to English-language classes, or individual teachers, and to previously settled pupils from refugee communities acting as connectors and networkers within the school systems.

> SW: *She's a very hard worker and clearly wants to achieve and make the most of the education. She welcomes going to school, she has used her year head very well and she is taking advantage of the English lessons that they've got at school. She is using the foster mum to help her with her homework.*

Education was clearly stated as a reason for them being here. Their families had sent them away for reasons of safety, but also for improvement. They wanted to make their families proud. Akin to the young people in Williamson's (1998) study, they wanted teachers who were strict but fair, and recognised that failing in education would be 'a disaster'. Social workers noted the very different engagement with education that these young people appeared to make in comparison with many indigenous looked after children they had worked with, having absorbed many reports and experiences of children in care performing poorly educationally; these successes were reported with a degree of pride by the social workers.

> SW: *I think she worked exceptionally hard. She's done very, very well at school and she goes to the library most evenings. I just think she's a bright and intelligent young person and she knows she's been sent here, and if she's here, she knows she has to work hard to get on. I think that's a big focus for her and I imagine that comes from her family. I imagine that's something within the family that has been fed to her*

> *before she's come here. The idea is that she's come to England and she should take this opportunity to receive an education. And I think her foster carers encouraged her a lot. They've said it's important that you work hard if you want to get on.*

The young people were said to make concerted efforts to get to school on time, and five of them had elected to remain in their first school in the UK, even though placements had changed and their journeys had become extensive and complicated. They got themselves ready in the mornings, travelled across town, reliably returning at the end of a day. Many of the young people learned English quickly and the social workers believed that they were intellectually capable, adaptable, and could use their own mental faculties to organise their learning in an effective way. They kept their schoolwork organised, and seldom missed deadlines. They enlisted the help of others, and pushed aside other interests and commitments in order to maintain the focus on school.

> *He's done brilliantly. He started on a computer course and English course when he arrived in the UK at FE college and did very, very well. He's very good at sciences. And then he started doing a BTEC course in computer studies and now he's starting the Higher Diploma soon. And he passes all his exams with excellent results. The records show how well he's done and he rings me up every time he gets a good grade. He's very proud of his grades.*

In order to attend school they could forgo going to the mosque, or pressing appointments with doctors and therapists, or community gatherings and outings with friends. But on occasions too many things needed to be managed simultaneously, and the burden of needing to succeed academically, practically, with immigration, and emotionally, could be punishing, despite their best efforts.

> *Her Head of Year says she's very bright. I myself have looked at her books, I've actually done homework with her as well, and all I see are ticks, ticks, ticks. She had an exam and two weeks ago she had a therapy appointment at the therapy centre on a Thursday. She got home quite late that evening. She had a French exam on*

Friday. She didn't do so well. Now I spoke to her tutor last week who said that she wasn't very happy with her results. But 'I said to him, I can understand that, she had a really gruelling experience at the therapy centre and then to have to go home and prepare for a French exam.' But she was actually very angry and very upset that she didn't do very well, so she's got very high standards with regards to her work.

The drive to success was exhausting in this way, and also for those who were not academically minded, but felt the imperative to succeed none the less. The level of energy needed to plug the gap between expectations and results for these young people, who wanted to but could not manage to grasp academic prizes, left them feeling disorientated. Achievements and attendance became noteworthy for the wrong reasons. Low self-esteem, and a diffused 'can't do, won't do' atmosphere grew around them over time, causing some concern to their carers and social workers.

I'm not being nasty – but he's not able to get from A to B very easily in terms of answering a question. I'm not saying he's 'thick' but he's not a bright spark. I don't think he's ever going to be a brain surgeon, and neither am I, so it's clearly not a criticism, but I just think he could have done better. When he left school he went to FE College. But he dropped out after about five months, just prior to them kicking him off for non-attendance, not having particularly good excuses about why the work wasn't being handed in.

The loss of structure, rhythm and momentum that school provided was also reflected in the stories of the four most unsettled young people, who had confronted teachers and other pupils aggressively at times. Their attendance, in direct contrast to the majority of their peers, was poor. These were the same people who were known to lose their temper unexpectedly, to lack concentration, to be agitated and restless day and night, and to have threadbare connections with others, and a vision of their future that was cloudy.

The story (Box 8) about the destruction of travel documents for a refugee was told without irony by this social worker. In fact,

---

Box 8   The travel card and school exclusion: Bahri's story

Bahri is 15 years old, from Kosovo. He was given a travel card by his social worker to go between his foster placement and the school. The home and school were some distance apart, and his usual journey involved using a train and two buses. After his first placement had broken down, Bahri was offered a chance to attend a school near his new foster placement, but declined. The school agreed to this arrangement, even though there was some concern that Bahri was unsettled, and not always a calming influence on his peers. One day Bahri had a fight with an indigenous child. The other child tore up Bahri's travel card. This meant he had to get home by foot, a journey that took him 3 hours. The next day he took a skewer to school, and used it to threaten the boy who had destroyed his card. He was immediately suspended from school. The social worker met with him the following day:

> He accepts that he was wrong in pulling a skewer on the boy that he got into a fight with, but feels that he's been hard done by because the other boy started the fight and tried to rip up his travel card. He says 'He is the one that has the worse blame because he committed a terrible act on me.' But you pulled a skewer, you threatened to kill him,' I said. And he said, 'Yes, but I was defending myself.' And I said, 'Which is the more serious of the two?' He goes, 'My travel card being ripped up'.

---

many of the workers took the young people's experiences of education at (sur)face value, not linking them in any way to the refugee experience itself. Instead they were understood within the broader frame of capable, likeable and ambitious people wanting to do well for themselves. For example, amongst those who had reached a stage of expressing career preferences, their aspirations were to become a social worker, a doctor, a nurse, a midwife, a builder, an electrician, several IT specialists, business men and women, a tourism and leisure guide, a scientist, a hairdresser, a footballer, and an air hostess – in many respects the nucleus of a functioning society, not least one where reconstruction and free travel were possibilities. One boy wanted to be the country's best bricklayer, and found the construction of perfect walls at his Further Education (FE) college acted as a balm:

> *He actually says it helps his mental health and he'll just build and build and build.*

Healing, protection, regeneration, making money and enjoying one's life were broadcast as coherent elements of career choices that the social workers hoped would aid the process of resettlement. But they also knew of substantial uncertainties that were obstacles to resettlement now and in the foreseeable future. As they moved forward, the height and width of these obstacles cast shadows over the young peoples' expressed hopes. The social workers, as go betweens between the past, present and future, commented on their lives, and on their journeys thus far, in the following way, illustrating a diversity of experiences:

1   *He got what he wanted, but he hadn't expected the consequences of getting it. He's lost what he had.*

2   *He doesn't have any sense of where he came from any more.*

3   *We often said 'This can either ruin your life for ever and ever or it's not going to, and it's in our hand here. Let's work forward.' And I think she's very much taken that on: 'It's not going to finish my life forever, I'm going to get on, I'm going to do well.'*

4   *They'll become an asset for this country. In fact, I see assets practically everywhere I look with the kids I work with. They're educated, motivated, make good citizens.*

5   *She was saying to me the other day that she quite liked living here now, 'I've got lots of nice clothes now and I've learnt a lot, I've learnt to speak a new language and I have learnt about how English people don't like it when you shout, do they,' and things like that. So she feels that she is settling and I hope she will.*

Resettlement as an ordinary life in the future: balancing 'outer' and 'inner' worlds

When talking about the future for the young people the responses by the social workers appeared very familiar in the context of the following observations made by Ressler et al. (1988), about Basque unaccompanied minors escaping the Spanish Civil War in 1936. Of these children, they say:

> Once the children had been separated from their families, there were many obstacles to return. First, the war continued longer than expected. . . . Some children lost contact with parents as a result of population movements, or death or imprisonment of parents during their absence. Some parents did not wish their children to return for other reasons, believing it better for them to remain in interim care. In some cases, children were so integrated into the foster family that neither the child nor the foster family wished to separate. Some children did not wish to return for other reasons, such as better educational opportunities in the host country, and some could not return because of logistical difficulties and political problems. . . . During these years children grew to young adulthood, sometimes married, took jobs, and became integrated into the host society. (Ressler et al., 1988: 16)

Sixty-five years later, the social workers in this study confirmed similar prospects for these unaccompanied minors. First, they said that if there was one word that the young people wanted to hear from the authorities, that word was 'yes' – to being allowed to remain in the UK, if not as a refugee, then on humanitarian grounds; being allowed to travel freely; being able to attend FE college and then university with financial support; and remaining in a locality of their choosing with friends and carers around them, and being allowed to reunite with their family or extended family members. Resettlement in the future meant being able to stop in a place of their own choosing, or at least to move at a pace that they themselves dictated, not others. A 'yes' from the authorities gave them a chance to reconstitute a home.

> *To help with resettlement he needs his immigration status sorted. Otherwise you don't know when or if you're going to be sent back*

home. The likelihood is he won't, but you just don't know. How can you start making roots in a place and start developing when you don't know whether you're going back? I think stability is what this particular child wants.

In the meantime they were said to be tense about the future. For the newer arrivals, not hearing any news from the Home Office in relation to their asylum claim was expected in the sense that the other asylum seekers they met, their solicitors, Refugee Council staff, their social workers, and community links all told them that extensive waiting was the norm, and that achieving refugee status was unlikely. They remained frightened of being deported in young adulthood. For those with Exceptional Leave to Remain (ELR), or other anchors based on humanitarian grounds, the medium-term future was a little more certain – the longer they had ELR, the less likely it became that they would be expelled, as their friends and advisors told them. After four years they would get Indefinite Leave to Remain. They waited in hope. Sometimes, as a counterpoint to waiting for others to decide their future the young people appeared, to the social workers, to declare a mastery of their destinies in bursts of optimism in their meetings together. They would work hard; they would make a success of their lives and earn a lot of money and have cars and houses. They would make their parents proud. One young man made the following list and gave it to his social worker, combining aspirations with worries:

Things that are important to me in the future

To become a good professional and earn money to live happily
To have peace and harmony
To be able to practise my religion
To have friends and professionals around me
To be able to cope [with] the situation
To be able to always remember my family
To look after other peoples and children who need care like me

Worries that may occur in my future

Bad dreams which I like to get rid of
Thinking negatively

Those who are closer to me may be lost in future
Having bad habits like smoking and so on

His social worker knew that he and others had made considerable efforts in helping him to resettle. He had a close bond with his carers, a friendship network that included English people, and an excellent record of academic achievement. But his parents' death could not be put aside, simply by putting down new roots, in the same way that he could not extract an answer from the Home Office about his future. Something on the inside also needed to fall into place over time, with help from the outside:

> *I think he's well settled on the outside. But I think inside he's really struggling. He says 'I'm happy when I'm at school because I don't have to think, but as soon as I come home I worry.' He's just worrying and feeling so sad and lonely, even though he's got a lot of people around him.*

So far as the practitioners could see, the young people could take a pragmatic hold of their future responsibilities when circumstances allowed. There were those who had a gritty, scavenger-like approach to surviving. One young man had been able to substantially furnish his flat by rooting around in skips finding sofas, music systems, and other artefacts, which were clearly valuable to him even if they had been discarded by other more affluent people. Another earned extra money as a DJ at a local club, while attending FE college in the day. Some bought and sold clothes, others became mentors for younger asylums seeking children in their schools, and interpreters for others. They welcomed work experience opportunities. Whilst the young people were known to avoid criminal activity, the social workers worried that those who were very distressed or disorganised through grief, or were part of a hidden trafficking network, could enter worlds where there were bad or dangerous people who would exploit them particularly if they could not protect themselves.

> *Inside herself she's very chaotic and a bit over-confident and she feels she's a lot older than she is, but she's all of 16. And I think she's also quite easily led. I'm worried because you should see her, she's so beautiful. She's got amazing long, long braided hair and*

I'm quite worried about her being drawn into prostitution. She wants excitement in her life. I think that's a risk. I'm worried about her settling in the UK. There's an expression in my country that would fit exactly but I don't know if there's an actual equivalent in English: 'She doesn't stand with her feet on the ground.' So I think she could be easily led into things that are not good for her.

Overall, a situation that was a limbo for some was purgatory for others, depending on their own capabilities, their history, and the continued support of companions. While many of the young people attempted to lead ordered lives while waiting, a few of them drifted along, sometimes in a sullen, reclusive and confused way.

And he always wants to work so that he can send money back to his family, but when you ask him what kind of job are you going to get, he doesn't know. And I say, 'But how are you going to get a job?' 'Oh, I'll get one somehow. Yeah, it'll be uninsured, no insurance, cash in hand, dishwashing or something in a restaurant. There's ain't much out there for you kid unless you realise that you've got to learn your English to enable you to survive in this country.'

There was no evidence that this bullish and frank exchange motivated these young people. The drifters carried on drifting, and the social workers carried on worrying about them. A bleak *cri de coeur* from the workers, as they envisaged support from Social Services ebbing away, was similar to this one:

There's no support. I just think what are we setting these kids up for? Are we unleashing an emotional time bomb on society that a year or two years down the line, all these kids are going to have loads of mental health problems, totally isolated, no money, totally disaffected?

One in four young people had had no discussion with their social worker about repatriation, partly because they were at an early stage of resettlement, and partly because the social worker had not thought about discussing this with them. Only two of them

Table 5.9 Repatriation, removal and dispersal

	Frequency	Per cent
Refuses to go back	23	67.6
Wants to go back	2	5.9
Not discussed	9	26.5
Total	**34**	**100.0**

wanted to go back to their countries of origin, and were reluctant sojourners in the UK. The rest were clear that enforced return was something they did not want, and that their lives and livelihoods would be in jeopardy if they returned (see Table 5.9). They maintained that their primary intention was to remain here, and that there was nothing to go back to in their homeland. Dispersal also worried them. The majority were frightened by the thought of being dispersed within the UK by the National Asylum Support Service (NASS), or forcibly removed from the country and sent to another country, mirroring their fears about repatriation. Some said that they would resist being forced to move, probably by disappearing into the shadows, as they had already done in their countries of origin prior to departure. One social worker told a story of a young man who had lived in the UK for three years before having his asylum claim turned down, with instructions for his deportation arriving hand in hand with the offer of a place at university.

> *He was such a lovely young man and he was about to go to university and it was all just snatched away from him. He ran away and disappeared completely. I used to get phone calls every year at Christmas to 'Mother', really heart-wrenching stuff. Then I heard from him and his mother was still saying, 'You can't come back, it's too dangerous' and that was the bit that made me angry because he clearly wasn't lying in his original claim. My last phone call was last Christmas and I didn't have one this Christmas, so I don't know where he is now.*

The reluctance to return to the homeland was qualified, however. As they became more confident about the Exceptional Leave to Remain being extended to Indefinite Leave, they talked to their social workers about voluntary return as British citizens, at a time in thew future when their own safety and well-being were less likely to be in jeopardy, and when their travel documents were in order. They hoped to return as bountiful visitors to a peaceful land, and as helpers, friends and extended family benefactors, regenerating for themselves the return journeys of migrants, not political escapees. Success in the UK needed to precede the return.

Contact with family of origin

Contact with the family left behind was seen as a risky endeavour, primarily because the young people worried about breaching the family's safety or anonymity in some way through trying to send messages to them or find out how they were. They also risked getting bad news that would puncture whatever stability they had managed to establish. As one social worker observed,

> *They don't want to know about family tracing because if it's bad news then they have no hope. And uncertainty is better than clarity. Because it allows hope to exist, even as a fantasy.*

For these reasons, nineteen had no contact, and a further three refused any attempts to have contact made on their behalf. Only

Table 5.10 Length of time looked after by SSD before contact with family of origin

		Contact with family of origin				Total
		Established	Sought	Refused	None	
Time in UK	0–2	6	4	1	14	25
(years)	3–4	2		2	2	6
	4+				3	3
Total		**8**	**4**	**3**	**19**	**34**

four of them had agreed to use the Red Cross Tracing Service to make tentative enquiries about family members (see Table 5.10). Extensive periods of time had passed for a few of them since any news had been exchanged between themselves and those left behind. A general pattern appeared to be that contact was established either within the first year or so after arrival, or not at all. Five of the young people had spent much of their adolescent years with no news from those left behind. While it was rare for immediate family members to be known to be alive, eight out of the thirty-four had been able to identify uncles, aunts, cousins and other extended family members with whom they had made intermittent contact. These people were themselves spread across the world, mostly in countries bordering the homeland. The contact was made by telephone, by letter, or by sending taped messages to them confirming their safety and well-being. On three occasions extended family members were known to be resident in the UK, all of them young adults, and social workers were testing the feasibility of these men taking care of their young person in the future.

Mobile phones and phone cards were used to connect with family, sometimes covertly – carers would only discover the contact after the receipt of a large telephone bill, with itemisation that was unexpected and, in some cases, unacceptably expensive. While the social workers deemed overt and covert contact acceptable so long as it brought a measure of peace to the young person, there were instances of contact generating more turbulence than the young person could manage. In these circumstances, the social workers had some sad tales to tell (for example, Amina's story, Box 9).

If they could not go back to their parents, they hoped that parents or close family members could join them. Yet reunification – even in a neutral country – was a dim prospect for those who wished it, in chief because their immigration status was temporary, with no promise of resettlement for themselves or others, and in part because their financial dependence on Social Services meant that money to travel to meet family members outside the UK was rarely going to be made available. In only two instances, where Exceptional Leave to Remain had been granted, were the young people funded by Social Services to travel to other parts of Europe to re-connect with family, with

> ### Box 9   Amina's story of displacement
>
> Amina is a quiet, self-contained 17-year-old, and had been separated from her family in an African country for six years. For the first two years there was some intermittent contact between her father and Social Services, and a return to her home country was planned. Amina wanted this to happen, but her father declined because the country was too destabilised. He said that Social Services could 'adopt her'. Contact with the father stopped. It had recently been re-established through community networks bringing news of him to Amina. She wrote to him. The social worker saw her after she had received a response from the father.
>
> *I said, 'If you'd like to share the letter with me, I'd like to see it.' 'I don't have it,' she said, and I thought she'd decided not to bring it. Then she said to me, 'No, I've burned it.' He wrote in the letter a bit about himself. He is now married and he has two children. One of the children is called Amina, after her. It's quite incredible the emotional impact something like that has on her and how she feels, separated from him. He has another Amina there now, and he said that he had not been able to make contact with her before.*
>
> *After all this she said to me, 'But I've written him a letter anyway, do you want to see it?' She showed me the letter and I was practically moved to tears. She said over and over in the letter 'I love you so much, there's not one day that goes by that I don't think about you, and you'll always be my dad, no matter what.' Every paragraph begins and ends like that; it's like a Koranic verse, the mention of Allah at the beginning and end, like poetry really. I think that was quite revealing about Amina, about feelings that don't come out in direct conversation with her.*

the hope that reunification could lead to the adult members assuming care for them. But in all other instances, they expected to grow up without being cared for again by the adults they had left behind, even though they carried them in their thoughts. So, looking towards a future that was so uncertain, the social workers commented on who the young people would belong to or with, either in a familial sense, or in the sense of being embedded in a community that was safe and sustaining for them. The answers were wide ranging:

> *He feels that he doesn't belong anywhere. He doesn't want to be in England. He says he has no identity.*

Identity meant the past and the future, the family and the British passport. Not being able to have access to either of these sustained a sense of rootlessness for the young people. Putting down fresh roots in the future brought a series of challenges that were met by using their own sense of resilience and experience of surviving adversity. In several instances this response was supplemented by a view that the young people themselves would need to regenerate whole families, having lost the family of origin. In order to get a family they would have to make a family.

> **RK:** *Who will he belong to when he gets older?*
> **SW:** *Nobody. It would be nice if he had his own family.*

While the social workers understood the strength of purpose that the young people needed in the future to succeed, they also identified key participants in the current networks who would help them in the future. Brothers and sisters were expected to carry on together – not necessarily living together, but part of a nucleus of history that was helpful for the future. Friends whom the young people had invested in, carers who had become family figures, and community members who were safe, were all nominated by the social workers as people who could help to pick up the threads to their lives again, and act as catalysts for regeneration. Only two of the stories told of young people who were so isolated that no helpers were visible, either currently or on the horizon. For the rest, a series of connections appeared to be possible, as illustrated by these responses from some of the workers.

> 1 *I think he'll belong to his friends. I think he'll make significant friends.*

2   *I think the foster carer will always be a very important person to him, but obviously depending on what happens with his asylum status.*

3   *I think she will always be very connected to her sister, although they have a complicated relationship. They've helped each other through a lot of things. The common background and the common memories and the knowledge about their country. But apart from her, I don't know who they would belong to. I've never thought.*

4   *I think her links with the Eritrean community here are quite strong. They are the main bridge. She'll keep quite a strong link with them.*

When the social workers themselves felt a bond with their young person, particularly when they knew their histories, and admired their attempts at resettlement, there was a strong wish to see a happy ending – not a fairy tale as such, but because so much pain had been endured in leaving and settling, they simply wished the young people a future that was easier than their lives had been so far.

I think probably when he does have a relationship or a longer-term relationship with somebody, it will be quite volatile knowing his nature, but also I think it will be very supportive, he will probably be very respectful. He's very compassionate because that is his nature generally. Whatever's happened to him, I think that's the way he is. We'll see how he develops over time. You never know, I might be there for the wedding.

Summary

The stories known to the social workers indicated that in their countries of origin, the young people appeared to have led unremarkable lives until a catastrophe overtook them, or their lives became untenable for reasons of hardship associated with the disintegration of civic structures. In exodus, they unplugged their connections, wrapped up the ties that bound them to their homelands, and were bundled onto ships and aeroplanes that took them far away. They knew that no matter what, there was no going back to the past even though some of them had not been able to leave it behind in their minds. Others had tried to bury the past and concentrate on making the best of the present and future. There were those who had had to hide their roots, for fear of being found out to be economic migrants or trafficked children. Whatever their genesis, they sprang up as blank, or nearly blank faces in front of social workers, either at ports of entry, or in reception areas of Social Services departments. They were often frightened.

As they settled in the UK, a whole coherent picture of their lives was rarely visible to the social workers. Silence hid facts as well as suffering. They were said to respond in a complex way to the prospect of connection to others in reference to race, culture, language and religion. There were faint traces of their ordinary lives before leaving. But their social workers thought that their feelings about the past were strongly present, carried forward into their everyday lives in the new country.

Many appeared to make firm attempts to resettle, guided by their own capabilities and needs, and helped by a series of companions, both adults and other young people, and of these networks, some were known and some hidden from the social workers. Placements were often stable, and social workers offered some evidence that the young people could make and sustain attachments to their carers, and live through the uncertainty that was part of their everyday life. In time, they regenerated a sense of home, through relationships, belongings, and in making the best of educational opportunities. A minority were said to be troubled, yet the use of therapeutic services was rare. The future in reference to their immigration status was unclear for the majority, and the fear, noticed by their social workers at the point of entry into the care system was now manifest as anxiety. In these circumstances, hope replaced a clear vision of what would become of them, who they would call 'family', and where they would be allowed to refer to as home. As one social worker observed,

> *I've got somewhere some photographs of him when he first came and I'll make sure he's got them before he moves on from here.*

There's nothing physical, no object, no photograph from his life when he was little, so there's nothing. It's like a record of his life started when he was 10, after he came here. He'll keep in touch with me I think.

Their UK life was the one that was best known to the workers, and the one that contained the beginnings of shared experiences and memories. These experiences and memories were the key reference points that the social workers used in describing their practice, as discussed in the next chapter.

6 Social work practice with unaccompanied asylum seekers

As discussed in Chapter 2, the term 'resettlement' describes a process and an outcome, the journey towards a new home, as well as the home itself. In this chapter, the fluidity of process and firmness of outcome are measured in relation to the ways the social workers described and understood their work. The analysis shows that on the whole these social workers liked the young people and enjoyed working with them, even though the work was demanding and strenuous. The stories that they had been told by the young people held their attention, and engaged them emotionally. In turn, by retelling the stories, the workers became actors in the stories that they knew, and tried to bring some order to the 'narrative threads' that the young people brought to them. In a sense, through taking part in the research interview, they became the loom through which the stories of the young people's lives were woven. A few of them acted as defeated sceptics, sometimes demonstrating a weary awareness of tales that they said they had heard many times before from young people. But the majority of them also showed, as a broad pattern, optimism about their practice, and an ethical commitment to providing and coordinating welfare for unaccompanied minors. While gloom, drudgery, high drama and heightened emotions were part of the worlds in which they worked, their stories also contained humour, civility and affection. Here, an attempt is made to describe this tapestry of experiences.

The chapter begins by conceptualising three 'domains' within which social work practice with unaccompanied minors can be framed, described here as:

1 **The domain of cohesion**, where resettlement meant bringing order to the 'outer world'.
2 **The domain of connection**, where resettlement of their internal worlds was sought and sometimes found.

3 **The domain of coherence**, where resettlement allowed
    whole histories to be carried forward safely into the new
    land and into a new future.

It then considers the importance of developing a trusting relationship in a context of silences, secrets and deep disturbances in
the young people's lives. The relationships between social worker
and young person that appeared to provide the best framework
for the work to be done were those where there was trust.
Without trust there appeared to be no permission to enter the
worlds that the young people lived in, or to travel across them.
Often, for reasons of safety, the young people became the border
guards of their own personal worlds, and the social workers knew
this, and many waited patiently for leave to enter and remain, and
worked productively towards resettlement for the young person.
The main part of this chapter, then, discusses and explains this
productive work, and shows the detailed ways in which the social
workers went backwards and forwards between the three different 'domains'. The chapter concludes by presenting a table
summarising these approaches to resettlement.

The domains of practice conceptualised

1 *The domain of cohesion – bringing order to the outside world*

When working within this domain the primary focus was on the
'here and now' and the practicalities of resettlement – providing
shelter, care, food, money, schooling, medical support, welfare
advice; making sure that the young person had good legal representation in relation to the asylum claim, and a safe network of
friends and community to hold them in place and in mind. In this
domain the social workers are referred to as 'the Humanitarians',
using models of practice that are familiar to many NGOs offering material assistance with refugee resettlement (Spake, 2001).
The social workers said they were perceived by the young people
themselves as people in authority who could both help and
hinder outer-world settlement. They were the resource holders,
who saw themselves as 'realists and pragmatists', getting the

young people the practical help they needed to get by on a day-to-day basis. As stated in the previous chapter, the young people's own reported concern was to deal with 'the present first, the future next and the past last', and within this sequence, all the social workers appeared to adhere to at least the first stage of this process when establishing working relationships with them. The young people looked to the social workers to act as advocates and mentors when they came to trust them. If they did not trust them, then the social workers continued to be viewed with suspicion and in silence. In turn, the social workers regarded at least some of the stories told by the young people as inauthentic, and some of their demands as unrealistic. Within this domain, the rough and tumble of practice ranged from scepticism and mutual suspicion, to purposeful interventions designed to avoid social exclusion by generating supportive and robust local networks of protection and care as citizens in the UK.

2   The domain of connection – resettlement of inner worlds

The second of these domains was that of connection, leading to resettlement in the 'inner' world. This domain was where social workers responded to the emotional life of these distressed young people, attempting to connect events, people and feelings in ways that helped them to experience containment. These workers are referred to here as 'the Witnesses' (Blackwell, 1997; Papadopoulos, 2002). As I have said, while few of the young people were seen as needing psychiatric or therapeutic services, many were said to be psychologically dishevelled as a consequence of dislocation and the shredding of roots. Some of the distress was apparent from the start of the relationship, but in most instances it remained hidden, only to emerge over time as a consequence of mutual trust and affection. Social workers, who saw this domain and entered it after a time, believed that the young people's experiences of abuse, disconnection and flight had a powerful bearing on their daily conduct and their capacities to manage their lives. The workers bore in mind that there were connections to be made between past and present, between inner and outer worlds, and that the free flow of emotional traffic between them would aid resettlement (Schofield, 1998). They were also conscious of significant absent people – those who were dead or missing, but who lived in the young people's memories and minds. As part of stepping in to this domain with palliative intent, they offered the young people a chance to tell their stories, not just of seeking asylum, but of loss. In time they became memory holders for the lives the young people.

3 The domain of coherence – resettlement as feeling reconstructed

This was the place where social workers framed the experiences of 'traumatised asylum seekers' within a broader view of ordinary children coping with extraordinarily adverse circumstances and trying to make the best use of their own strengths and capabilities. The workers within this domain are referred to as 'the Confederates'. These workers said they found the young people interesting, and elastic in their capacity to survive and do well at times of great vicissitude. They looked for and found resilience in the young people and their contexts. They expressed fondness and an attachment towards them, making the line between friendship and professional help less distinct than in the work of their colleagues working in other domains. Within a framework of friendship and loyalty, they acted as collaborators, getting the young people what they wanted or needed. They were protective, subversive and optimistic. They also helped the young people to deconstruct and reconstruct stories of asylum and trauma into complex stories of departure from families that they missed. These 'new' stories were broader and deeper – and more honest – than the linear and thin explanations given to the Home Office in the asylum application, and contained portions of ordinary, well loved lives, not just fragments of sudden departure. As the young people began to trust the workers, their reputations as safe, reliable and capable practitioners were broadcast amongst hidden networks and they acted like beacons for new arrivals. They tried to make the young people feel at home, and became companions for them, not just understanding, but becoming part of the young people's new lives.

The overlapping domains

The domains themselves did not exist as distinct entities. Their borders were diffuse and permeable. Also, in practice only a minority of the social workers stayed exclusively in one domain, as illustrated below. Figure 6.1 shows that many of them were on the move between domains and in moving from one to another and back again, they appeared to use the young person's needs and capabilities, as well as their own practice preferences, to guide them in negotiating the focus, range and depth of work.

The eight thoroughfares used by the workers are illustrated (arrowed), with the thoroughfares used most frequently appearing in bold type. Nineteen of them began their work within the domain of cohesion and five of them remained there and focused on work of a practical nature with the young people. Yet the rest

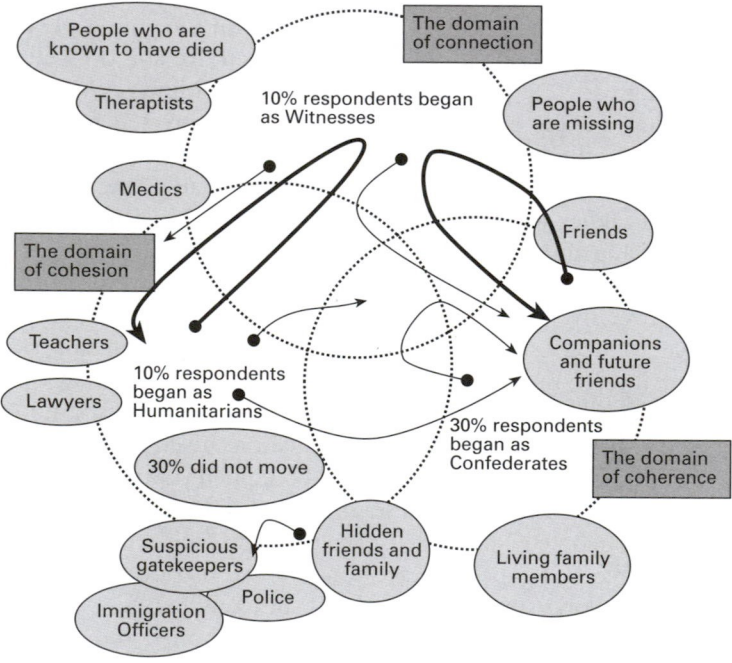

Figure 6.1 The overlapping domains of social work practice with unaccompanied minors

of the humanitarians appeared to have the greatest variety of directions and movements, ranging from becoming guards to Witnesses, and to Confederates and future friends. Three of the Witnesses and seven of the Confederates also began in their own domains. Those who began their stories as Witnesses, *all* appeared to move towards either humanitarianism or confederacy. None stayed as or came back to being Witnesses in their domain of origin. The Confederates, on the other hand, were the ones most likely to move from and return to their origins, and the ones who clearly articulated a hope of continued companionship with the young people. They started and finished within the domain of coherence.

An important feature to note about the domains is the existence of people from the young people's formal and natural networks of care, and their positions within the diagram. For example, people who were dead or missing were most likely to be held in mind by the Witnesses, working alongside therapists and medical practitioners, particularly psychiatrists. In the Humanitarians' work, a range of professionals were used for 'outer world' reconstruction, including GPs, teachers and lawyers. Also, immigration and police officers were part of this domain, particularly when suspicions arose about the young person and their circumstances, as discussed below. For the Confederates, the natural networks became accessible over time, including hidden family members, as they gradually came to know the young people more fully.

The majority of workers appeared to adapt their focus of work to the circumstances that would yield the best outcomes for their clients and themselves as they travelled across domains. In any case, what many of them emphasised in working within and across the domains was the need to be emotionally committed to the young person, to make the relationship work at its best.

The relationship between the social worker and the young person

Resettlement contained at its core an emotional commitment by the social workers towards the young people, based on a complex and robust relationship. Unless the worker was emotionally engaged by the young person's story, there was little prospect of it being re-told in the research interview with any degree of warmth, and indeed none of them spoke of young people that they disliked, even if the young people were reported to be graceless, demanding, not always truthful, and difficult to manage sometimes. For those workers who had worked with indigenous looked after children, the asylum seeking young people drew favourable comparisons, and they were seen – as noted in the previous chapter – as engaging and civil, and worth investing in. However, the expression of warmth did not simplify the complicated reality of dealing with a troubled adolescent. Nor did the absence of warmth in the social worker mean that s/he failed to engage at a practical level with the young person. At the time of the research interview the relationship between the social worker and the young person had been sufficiently well established in most instances to allow the workers to reflect on its nature and relative importance in the process of resettlement.

The issue of trust

The basic view put forward by the workers, partially in recognition of the complexity of the situations they were dealing with, within which secrets, silences and lies existed as common currency, was that the young people would not talk to them unless they took care to establish a trusting relationship. Trust in itself contained several sub-components and meant the social worker acting in particular ways towards the young person. For example, they said that being honest, clear, realistic and precise in receiving and transmitting information was of critical importance to the young person they worked with.

> *If I promise her I'll do something that she's asked me to do, I will do it. I'd never, never let her down. I've always been totally honest with her. If I don't know something I'll tell her I don't know and I'll get back to her and make sure I do. And I've always stated exactly what my position is and I will go back and say it again just in case because she's not familiar with our systems and won't always take everything in the first time.*

By doing this, the workers hoped to lay down the foundations of reciprocity, where over time the young people would also be honest, clear, realistic and precise with them, if not about their origins and reason for flight, then about their current circumstances and future intentions. The workers also wanted the young people to experience an authority figure as being helpful to them, not an interrogator as much as an enquirer into their well-being. They claimed they were alert to the sensitivities generated by persecution in this way – whether in the country of origin or since arrival in the UK. Workers speculated that sometimes these children and young people had been warned not to speak to anyone who might test and reject their claim for asylum, particularly those in authority, exactly mirroring Anderson's (2001) findings.

> *They're schooled before they come here to think you don't trust anybody in authority, you must never ever say your true identity or the truth because bad things will happen to you*
>   *I did a survey a few years back about when did you feel safe? Who did you feel safe with? And this young person put* **'I thought my social worker was a spy for immigration, but after six months she was just like my mother'**. [emphasis added]

This transition from being seen as a guard to becoming a guardian was welcomed by the social workers, and brought much relief to both parties over time. In these instances the workers speculated that the young people themselves had little notion of safe authority, or indeed what a social worker was or did. The frame within which an effective relationship was established referred in simple terms either to a hostile and remote authority figure, or to a missing parent. A key balancing act in practice became one where the social workers presented themselves as neither, while making attempts to see why these extreme care-and-control positions were manifest for the young people themselves. The workers also emphasised the need to be consistent, reliable and kind, and the need to develop a pattern and rhythm of warmth over time, so that the young person could (re)experience order and care as aspects of reorganising their lives. Praising the young people for their achievements, finding their interests interesting, acting on their behalf by permission, and having faith in their future, even when the young people were frightened about what was going to happen to them, all established threads of trust between the social worker and the young person, and provided the foundation in many instances of a coherent, flexible, and worthwhile relationship – worthwhile for both parties, as illustrated by the following comment made by a social worker:

> *He'll leave messages on my mobile phone and say, 'Hello, I'm ringing up because I need a car and I want you to buy me one.' And then he laughs and puts the phone down. And the next time I speak to him, I'll say 'What was that message?' He said 'I need a car and I want you to buy me one.' And I said, 'Well, you know what the answer is to that,' and he said, 'Oh I know, I'm just teasing.' He's got a really good sense of humour, although he's stopped asking me for silly things. He just rings me up sometimes to tell me how he's doing in his college course or if he wants money to go on a trip somewhere, and he'll just chat sometimes.*

The journey towards this trusting territory was often complex and long drawn out, yet several workers described it as having reached a point of mutual satisfaction, sometimes after years of hard work. Many of them saw trust as a way the young people invested in them or came to believe in them as good people who could come and go from the different worlds that they lived in and moved between in their search for resettlement.

> *I think our relationship is one of trust. She does trust me. In five years she's grown from a child to a young woman. I think she likes me as a person as I like her as a person. I think we've come to a stage where we can laugh and cry together. Yes, and I think we've sort of grown together really in a way.*

This growing together illustrates the powerful sense the workers sometimes conveyed of companionship-based journeys being undertaken in the resettlement efforts. Just as the young people dipped in and out of different worlds – some open and some hidden – the social workers also entered, worked within and moved between their own domains, given their own preferred orientations, and the young people's needs as perceived by them.

I now turn to a closer examination of social work within each of the domains. Examples from practice are used to illuminate important defining features of each domain.

The domain of cohesion: the Humanitarians in action

On the young people's behalf, the Humanitarians tried to rebuild the outer world and give it some order, particularly in relation to belonging to a country, a family, and a community. The alleviation of legal and procedural difficulties and the lifting of barriers to accessing resources were perceived by them as key elements of effective practice. Many of them wanted the young people to settle in the local community, and disappear into the folds of common citizenship as quickly as possible. As confirmed earlier, the young people themselves focused on this aspect of resettlement in the first year to eighteen months after arrival, and wanted 'real' help of a type that swept away uncertainty. At the heart of the humanitarian endeavour lay a capacity to see the young people as children in need of care and protection, and the majority of workers appeared to subscribe to the view that they were working with children first and foremost (Stone, 2000), not asylum seekers, whose claim needed to be evidenced before services were provided. But around the periphery of the Humanitarians' vision, there were suspicions about the authenticity of claims, and muddles about how to respond to secrets and lies. Both the centre and the edges of the Humanitarians' position are examined here.

Saying hello

The young people in some instances appeared to imbue the social workers with authority. They respected them, wanted to be directed by them, and to be provided by them with guidance in the absence of knowing any firm rules of engagement within their new worlds. The common explanation by the social workers for this unexpected level of positive attribution to them was to say that perhaps the young people experienced them as the equivalents of community elders, particularly on the part of those from contexts where there were no state systems of welfare provision. They also speculated that at least some of the young people had grown up in contexts within which children were compliant in the face of adult decision making (Mann, 2000). In these instances the Humanitarians offered some examples of what they understood their responsibilities to be when authority of this sort was deposited in their laps. They became mentors and introduced the young people to the territories within which they had grown up, but which the young people knew little of:

> *I took them to* [City X] *with a big multicultural population; I took them in a shop there for body creams and specific lotions and oils for their hair. They were pleased. We did a grand tour one day; saw all the sights in* [City X], *like tourists.*

This 'explaining the new world' from the perspective of a helpful British citizen became part of the repertoire of conversations that provided the initial hooks into the territories the young people entered. Health and welfare systems, legal definitions, school timetables, and a range of customs and practices were carefully and simply delineated in the hope of making encounters with others in the outside world less mysterious to the young people and more worthwhile than they otherwise would have been.

Attending to the young people's habits and customs

The Humanitarians also ensured that some important habits and customs could be carried over from the young peoples' countries of origin. For example, where direct and easy access to places of worship was not possible, social workers made concrete efforts to recognise and hold in mind the possibilities of devout expression. The practitioners maintained that the young people should be allowed to integrate their former religious observances into their new environments where possible, if they chose to do so. Money and time was spent in understanding the type and level of continuity the young people wanted, particularly in reference to religious practice.

RK: *You said he was quite a devout Muslim. How do you know?*

SW: *He talks a lot about his religion. Fridays are his favourite days because that's when they go to the mosque and everybody comes around and they cook a meal together before they go. When we talk about what support he has, he always brings up his religion and praying and that as being something which gives him comfort when he's anxious. And he also prays at home, he wanted a prayer mat for his room and things like that. So we bought him a prayer mat for £15 and a copy of the Koran.*

As stated in the previous chapter, the young people were sometimes taken to restaurants specialising in food from their countries of origin, or the social workers made sure that the carers understood the need to eat 'home food'. In one instance, a social worker had spent some time doing an internet search for a dual-language dictionary, and came across a recipe book by chance.

SW: *I actually found an Albanian–English/English–Albanian dictionary on the Internet, that we bought for him. And that was about £12. When I was looking for his dictionary, I managed to find an Albanian cook book in English as well. I told his children's home about that and they bought it and used it quite considerably, not just for him but the other kids who were there. The young people were incredibly delighted that they could eat Albanian food.*

Networking

The process of joining things together was apparent in other aspects of the 'outer world' work of the Humanitarians. For example, these social workers spent considerable thought and time in the construction of local safe networks for the young people, using a variety of service providers. They ensured that contracts between foster carers and the young person were translated into languages that both understood. Referrals were made to specialist educational services, interpreters and lawyers who had a good reputation for dealing quickly and efficiently with asylum cases. Social workers came to know and identify these 'good people' over time, and as their reputation spread within the locality, more and more young people were referred to them. The notion of finding someone who would be committed to the young people succeeding in getting Leave to Remain was part of a recurrent pattern of measuring good outcomes. A similar example was given, by another social worker, of a local voluntary-sector resource used to prepare the young people for entry into mainstream education.

> *The teacher has two groups, one in the morning and one in the afternoon, and it is literally to work with young people who come into the country, who basically know no or little English. And she does everything with them. She has very small groups and she'll do everything from numeracy, maths, to things about the country, where they come from, cultural issues, and most young people love it. They go there and think it's brilliant. It's the best thing for them, it's the structure.*

While key members of other professions helped to peg the young people down in this way, what many of the Humanitarians did not appear to do was extend the scope beyond the use of formal local networks. This had two consequences. First, expertise in refugee matters that was available in distant resources was not accessed. For example, specialist medical and therapeutic services or the Refugee Council were seldom used to understand or help with individual cases. Secondly, networks linked to communities of origin that could have been used to assist with resettlement remained untapped. As discussed in the previous chapter, these networks were sometimes regarded with scepticism or suspicion, especially when the social workers felt that they had been used by the young people to seek assistance, through the strategic emergence of 'friendly strangers' who brought the young people to the duty desk. In all, the Humanitarians were more comfortable with forms of assistance that they could deliver by themselves and via trusted – often professional – local sources.

Placement provision

When thinking about placements these workers appeared to understand and exercise their responsibilities fully when they adopted the humanitarian aid paradigm of 'the need for durable solutions'. They hoped that the choices they made on the young peoples' behalf would provide stability over an extensive period of time. As stated in the previous chapter, the majority of initial placements were determined by availability on the day the young person was accommodated. It was at the stage of making a planned move towards a second placement that these Humanitarians showed their capacity to strategically capture resources on behalf of the young people. For example, one worker found an Asian family for a group of Eritrean siblings. They had initially been placed with an African Caribbean foster mother whom they disliked intensely. Their original bid had been to move to a white UK family, but this had been refused by the social work manager, who wanted to challenge the assumption that resettlement would be more fluent on the basis of this sort of cross-cultural placement. In this instance the social worker was the first in line to meet these newly recruited foster parents, and had this story to convey:

> **SW:** *The key thing was they needed a long-term placement; they were unhappy and that was very obvious. I knew we wouldn't be able to get them an Eritrean family and also they were saying very clearly that they wanted a white family I remember, and they wanted to learn English and felt that only an English white family could teach them proper English. So that was one of their things. For me, a key thing was my knowledge about the plight of refugees, and if it couldn't be an Eritrean family, I knew we'd need something that would come very closely to meeting all their needs.*
>
> *I visited these Asian foster parents. When the foster mum started talking about the fact that her parents were refugees my gut feeling was that this family, especially the mum, would be able to meet those kids' needs. They were new foster carers, they had only just recently registered so I had to go through the processes as well, asking the Adoption*

and Fostering panel for them to be a long-term placement for these three because that would block them immediately for years. Which in fact it did.

This type of judgement by the social worker and her manager moved beyond simply linking the siblings to someone who appeared superficially similar, or appealed to the young people on the basis of the perceived advantages of difference (Kohli, 2003). Similarity of experience was seen and valued as an important determinant in the decision to place, rather than race, culture, language and religion. The ability to find this 'third way' resolution, which challenged practice beliefs around same-race placements, or beliefs held by the young people, became a major feature of humanitarian practice. In this instance the placement had lasted throughout the middle child's adolescence and departure into independent life.

Even if placements did not always last, a key feature of the humanitarian approach was to not give up on trying alternative placements, and advocating within the agency for continued financial commitment towards resettlement efforts. In part, a strong humanitarian imperative appeared to be in place – namely that the young people 'deserved' a fair deal after what they had been through, and that they were decent people in an inhospitable context and could succeed given the chance (Kidane, 2001). The position of seeing someone who deserved something often indicated a fondness for the young person, born out of sympathy for their circumstances and disposition. The social workers reported a number of key actors who responded in similar ways, investing in the young people's stability, even if that stability did not last long. One worker reported the following scenario when moving a young person from a placement that had failed.

When I took him from his foster mother to the residential unit, he didn't even say goodbye to her. This foster carer had really invested a lot in him, spending a lot of time with him, and I felt for her because I could see that she had tried so hard with him in every way, by letting him eat in his room, by cooking him African food, by taking him out on his own and letting him sit quietly and getting him the books he wanted. She just wanted to make it work.

So when he left she said to him, 'I'm only up the road, if you want to come up here for a meal at any time and have some African food with me, then tell your social worker and you can come up and see me. Or if you would like me to come and see you, I will do that'. But he was so pleased to be going, he didn't even look at her. I knew then that there wouldn't be any contact maintained there.

In this respect, being a humanitarian provider in the domain of cohesion was sometimes experienced as a thankless, unrewarding role, reflecting turbulence in the relationship between the worker and the young person. Several of the workers described being frustrated at the level of continual demand placed on them by the young people as well as their agencies, particularly if they were doing their best in difficult, often extremely busy circumstances. In these instances, the workers described their difficulty in balancing the behaviour of the young person with the limitations on resources available to them. In one instance, a worker noted the debilitating effect of being perceived as an ineffective provider.

I can come out of a meeting after two hours and just feel totally drained. I've gone through the wringer with him because it can be a real battle, and I say 'Sorry, you're going to have to do this,' and he say, 'No I'm not.' 'Yes you are. I've got legal responsibilities that I've got to carry out and you are going to have to go to school and you're going to have to stay here.'

I managed to persuade my boss to give him £200-worth of clothing, additional money for clothes; at the end of it he said it wasn't enough. I said 'I accept it wasn't enough, but you know it's better than anybody else has got and basically you are supposed to get it out of your own budget every week.' And he said 'I want more', and I said 'Sorry you can't get more.' I'm not expecting kids to be grateful for what I do . . . but I expect them at least to acknowledge the fact that I achieved it for them in a way. It just felt like a total slap in the face. To get that £200 out of my manager took weeks and he's saying it's not enough.

This 'honest broker', like many of the Humanitarians, used images of war and peace to frame the work, not necessarily consciously, but because these were imbedded within the experiences that the young people brought to the surface. The stories were often of gaining and losing territorial advantages, money, 'things', friends and family. War and its impact rippled across many of their day-to-day exchanges, yet the Humanitarians seldom ventured into other domains to look for explanations for the young people's anger.

Scepticism and suspicion

The impact on the social workers of being peacemakers could also be debilitating, and they described colleagues who they said had been defeated by demanding behaviour, and become sceptical or suspicious over time. Suspicions were reported as arising from three broad areas:

1 authenticity of age;
2 authenticity of the asylum story;
3 whether young people had access to networks of care and support that they kept hidden from Social Services, either in the UK or abroad.

For example, they reported instances of Social Services personnel becoming cynical about claims made by young Africans and Kosovans to be younger than they appeared, and worrying that, amongst the general concern about the large numbers of asylum seekers they were dealing with, their services were being exploited and their resources drained. Similarly, some of them worried that through becoming familiar with asylum stories that all sounded the same, some of their colleagues had became sceptical over time, and rudimentary in terms if helping beyond the immediate needs of the young person for shelter and food. In their view, anyone could become sceptical, whether they were veterans or novices, and there was no simple explanation of how some people kept themselves engaged with the young people, and others became guards, protecting their services and resources from use. However, none of these Humanitarians identified themselves as being part of the culture of cynicism. On the contrary, many offered a sympathetic 'I believe what they say' approach to the young people's claims, or an agnostic, neutralised engagement. One social worker, from a 'child and family' team in an agency containing a specialist service for adult asylum seekers and their families, had this to say in relation to one of her cases:

> SW: *Initially the social services asylum team thought that the Home Office documents had been tampered with. On those grounds they decided not to accept him, and put him in B&B instead. It was believed he was over a year older than he is now known to be, so when they then placed him in a B&B alone, they thought his age was older than 14.*
> RK: ***What made them think that?***
> SW: *Because the papers he was given by the Home Office gave a different birth date. He disputed this and they then had to go back to the Home Office to get clarity about his birth date. He stayed there on his own and was referred to our office here, a couple of months later. The reason why he was referred was because they found out his actual age and had proof from the Home Office saying he was 14. At that point they referred him here to be accommodated. Because of his age being clearly determined, he became a child in need.*

Another noted that one of the young women had been to a medical prior to the care admission. Following this a review meeting took place. The social worker said,

> *At the meeting the foster carer said that the dentist said it was quite strange because all of her four wisdom teeth had come out quite a while ago, so that normally doesn't happen until you're quite older. And she's supposedly 14.*

Neither the social worker nor the foster mother had done anything more than note this as an odd occurrence, and the young woman's life in care was based on the age she gave at the point of entry into care. This suspension of disbelief, and the capacity to accept the young person at face value, was an important feature of humanitarian practice, a 'what you see is what you get' acceptance of the circumstances and features as relayed to them by the young people themselves. In these circumstances, as noted in the previous chapter, workers took the age that was given by the young person, and accepted it, or they guessed an approximate age. The composite humanitarian perspective was one of wanting to care for those having come so far away from their homelands at such a critical time in their development.

But there were instances where disbelief and suspicion were stubbornly present, for example in relation to hidden networks. One worker described a sense of scepticism associated with this network of kind strangers with whom magical encounters acted as the precursors to the referral to Social Services.

> *I think they were aiming for here. The information is very vague. Of all places, I have no idea how they ended up in our area? The Eritrean community said they found them and they have the same excuses as we're having now, people saying, 'Oh well we find this young girl wandering along the High Road.' And we think 'How is that possible? And how do these people spot them? How do they know?'*

But these questions were rarely investigated further by them. Similarly, contact with family abroad was suspected in a few cases, but not investigated, as in this example.

RK: *No contact with members of the birth family?*

SW: *No. Well, I'm saying no in the sense that he says no. As far as we know he's saying no. I can't be certain on that, I guess only he really knows the answer to that.*

RK: *Have you any guesses?*

SW: *Well, there's these calls coming in on the answer machine and sometimes I think maybe he's spending his money on telephone calls, although he can use the phone at the foster carers. And he does nip off to the phone box and says 'I'm just going to the phone box,' so the foster mum wonders who he's phoning when it's not with her. So we don't really know. It's just suspicion really. It may be completely harmless and he may be phoning somebody at school. I don't really know. I've said to him if he wants to make an overseas call and it's your family, come into the office and we'll pay for it. I can't really be any clearer than that with him.*

There were therefore opportunities for the social workers to be border guards, but for the majority in any of the three domains, becoming a police or immigration officer was antithetical to the position they preferred to adopt, and their knowledge of the factual details of the young person's life was smudged and imprecise. Suspicion and scepticism did not translate into investigation and interrogation. So in some respects this imprecision appeared to serve a purpose both for the worker and for the young person – neither had to enlighten the Home Office of circumstances that did not fit the official asylum story. Instead, both could focus on the 'child in need' as the primary reason for social work intervention, and both could take part in a 'don't ask, don't say' compact, and keep up a functional opaqueness to the relationship. In a sense, this opaqueness preserved the humanitarian focus by allowing the social workers to continue with their care functions while distancing themselves from the discomfort of too much disclosure, which could lead to control from immigration needing to be exerted. It also appeared to hide the young people's whole stories from view, generating a sketchy understanding of their circumstances.

Kind but vague bureaucracy

The Humanitarians were also sometimes vague about a number of important facts. For example, there was a record of the extended family of origin in only eight of the thirty-four cases, and of the nuclear family in seven others. In over half the cases, there was no information about any family, mostly because the young people had refused to give this information on being admitted to care. In five cases the social workers had failed to ask for this information. Apart from the 'don't ask, don't say' approach to information, sometimes the social workers appeared to regard the young people as particularly fragile, as if pursuing the sort of basic facts that they would automatically obtain from indigenous children before admitting them to the care of the local authority was dangerous to the health and well-being of these young asylum seekers. In their attempts not to bewilder, confuse or hurt them further by questioning, social workers sometimes did not ask, and therefore did not know, as in this example:

RK: *Ever done a family tree with S.?*

SW: *She has no brothers and sisters, and that's as far as we've got really.*

RK: *You know who the parents are, do you?*

SW: *Not by name. It's something I haven't pushed, you know. I haven't done a family tree. How embarrassing! I know she's got no siblings and that's as far as it's gone. If you ask her questions about family, it's 'yes, no' answers. So I'm reluctant at this stage to push it any further.*

RK: *What do you think that reluctance on your part might be about?*

SW: *Mm . . . I think just knowing that up until now she hasn't wanted to speak about anything from home and she's happy to talk at great length about things that have happened to her daily here in the last couple of weeks. Talk about what she wants to do in the future, and it's not that she's shy, it's not that she doesn't want to chat about things with me, so I think it's just respecting that she does find it difficult for whatever reason.*

This kind yet vague approach to facts was also evident in other records they kept about the young people. For example, while it remained much easier for the practitioners to relay information about the flight and the grounds for seeking asylum if they had a copy of the young person's statement to the Home Office, the majority of social workers (60%) said that they did not have the statement on file, so the stories of departure were gathered from conversations with the young people themselves. Also, many social workers had found their attempts to get copies frustrated by the young people or their legal representatives. An inconsistent picture emerged, with some workers, particularly in specialist teams for unaccompanied children, having well established protocols for gaining permission to make the statements part of their formal records, and others struggling to understand, in the absence of the statements, the exact nature of the flight. The research interview with the workers appeared to be the first opportunity to reflect on this missing part of the jigsaw.

RK: *Have you got a copy of his statement that went to the Home Office?*

SW: *No. I presume his solicitor has. I'm not sure. The only thing I know that enabled his application is that he was unaccompanied and the fact his country is one of a list of countries that you're certain it's not a bogus claim. So as far as I'm aware, it's for those two reasons.*

RK: **Is there any reason you haven't got a copy of the statement?**

SW: *Ahh. . . . To be honest, I didn't know I could get a copy.*

The journeys out of the country of origin, like the leave-taking stories, also remained puzzling in many instances. While many social workers believed that the young people had been in the care of their parents right up to the point of departure, or had been cared for briefly by extended-family members, or friends, this was simply what they had been told by the young people. No clear information existed about how the flight had been financed, where it had begun or the time the journey had taken. In many instances, the young people were said to be confused about these details, not in a deliberately obstructive manner, but because in their youthful way, they did not keep an accurate account of the process of leaving the homeland. Many workers said that they had no indication of their young person having experienced or witnessed violent or traumatising events prior to flight. Sometimes they attributed this to departure having taken place as the dangers of explosion, rather than the explosions themselves, became apparent to the families. Some saw the flight as a culmination of detailed planning by the young person's family, away from poverty as well as persecution, as suggested within the study by Robinson and Segrott (2002). Others were vague:

RK: **What happened to make her leave?**

SW: *This is an area I'm not sure how much to push for information or not. As far as I can understand there was the fear of persecution, but I don't know why that would result in her leaving alone rather than with her parents.*

RK: **Has she talked to you about seeking asylum, or what it was like coming here?**

SW: *I've just tried to look for the initial assessment and I can't find it in the file. But I know from little things she said that she was very scared obviously, and I know this man took care of her and he was paid by the family, so she felt some level of security because he was with her. That was a big comfort for her.*

RK: **Do you know when she last saw her family?**

SW: *No, but I think it was pretty close to when she left. She's hesitant about the contact with her family because I get the impression maybe the police* [in the country of origin] *are looking out for her family, I don't know. But I really don't know specific details about any of this, no.*

Forgetting

Unless the young people had arrived at a port of entry and were referred straight away to Social Services, how and when they got into the country were not often known in any detail to the social workers, because of the 'don't ask, don't say' approach. Occasionally, however, the social workers remained vague because they had forgotten the stories the young people had told. For example,

RK: **How did he get to the UK?**

SW: *I'm never quite sure where he arrived and that's not clear, but he arrived at a port and I don't know really what happened after that. There's a bit of confusion. I think he went to one port and was transferred to another port. He never knew where these ports were really. I don't know the exact details of how that happened.*

RK: **Have you any idea of the journey itself? How long it took, where it was from?**

SW: *The first journey I'm not sure. He got on a boat in Africa, but then I think he got on second boat which I think was a Belgian crew . . . I just can't remember, I have heard him but can't remember exactly.*

This lapse of memory was, in a way that would have been familiar to the young people themselves, a balm for the Humanitarians. This type of response did not always mean that the social workers were disengaged from the young person, or lacked commitment. As shown in the previous chapter, they struggled hard to stick to the practicalities of care, and the young people were said to value this practical orientation. Nevertheless, the Humanitarians often allowed themselves to believe that forgetting was better than remembering; closed doors were seen as functional, and a narrow perspective on the 'here and now' provided a sharper focus and more precise illumination of the young person's practical and material needs, capabilities and circumstances. There was the possibility of being released from the burdens of the past by burying it. As one worker noted,

> *There's an Irish expression – if you keep looking backwards you'll get a crick in the neck. I've adopted that approach in my work. It's the here and now and then you've got to move forward.*

For these reasons, there were some who sat very firmly in their own domains, and did not see it as their job to go elsewhere.

> *There's no focus here on counselling, we're not counsellors. What I do is very, very practically based social work . . . I don't know a lot about her childhood or anything like that, but that hasn't been the primary focus and I haven't aimed for it to be.*

This rationale for remaining in the outer world dovetailed well with the young people's silence. The social workers said they saw some merit in the position that they should not pursue the past insensitively, with poor timing, while ignoring 'primary' needs. They also appeared to accept that the young people had someone to talk to – from siblings, to therapists, to foster carers and key-workers, or community members – and that their role as a figure of some power and authority mitigated against open disclosure. But a few of the social workers appeared to be daunted by the prospect of witnessing distress. For example, in one case when asked if the young person had brought any memento to the UK, the social worker responded by referring to his own personal management of feelings;

> SW: *Not one of my children has produced a photo saying, 'Here, that's my parents.'*
> RK: *How do they remember them then? How do they hold them in mind?*

> SW: *I've never asked them that because I find that painful. I've had bereavements close to me. My father and my grandmother died in the same week and the type of person I am I have to clear it all. I don't want memories and mementos, it's gone now.*

So on the borders of the Humanitarians' work towards resettlement, vagueness and forgetting, scepticism and suspicion, and action and inaction existed as part of the responses they made to the young people, even if they liked them. In its centre, big efforts appeared to be made to provide material and practical help. Some of the workers knew that they needed to move from the outer world towards the inner world to make a contribution towards resettlement of a different kind, where the past and the present connected, particularly when associated with expressions of distress for the young people. These practitioners then made attempts to move from the domain of cohesion to the domain of connection, as described below.

The domain of connection: the Witnesses at work

For some of the young people, said the workers, the past could not be easily hidden, and when, sooner or later, it caught up with them, many of the social workers took responsibility for moving beyond the surface into deeper territory. Unlike those working in and on the outer world, these 'Witness' social workers appeared to draw on some important phrases from the language of therapy, as well as the more fluent and familiar languages of practical social work. They did not describe themselves as therapists, and rarely claimed formal training as therapists. However, they adopted a broadly therapeutic approach as part of their casework, listening to stories of great suffering. In order to contextualise this approach, we need to reconsider the work of Blackwell (1997) and Papadopoulos (2002), who together give a clear exposition of the term 'witnessing' that gives a particular sort of meaning to the notions of working with the inner and outer worlds of refugees.

Papadopoulos (2002) proposes that we need to think of refugees as people who have lost their home, and, as was stated in Chapter 3, recommends therapeutic care for them rather than formal therapy as a way of promoting psychosocial well-being. He asserts that 'loss of home is the only condition that refugees share, not trauma' (Papadopoulos, (2002: 9). This is a complex assertion because home is not just a physical entity, or a geographical location, it is a *sense* of home as a psychological, deeply felt foundation of well-being. Home is a place that connects inner and outer worlds, where habits of the heart are practised and understood by the people who form the home community. It is a *flexible and protective membrane* (Papadopoulos, 2002: 16), which offers containment for good, bad and ugly experiences and feelings. It is the loss of this every-day foundation through forced migration that leaves people temporarily disorientated, as if they were frozen – a type of *psychological hypothermia* (Papadopoulos, 2002) – and they need to thaw out, in order to proceed with ordinary living again. The frozenness itself is seen to have protective functions, not psychopathological ones, allowing them time and space to renew and reassess their lives. This process allows the sense of agency referred to by Blackwell and Melzak (2000), referred to earlier, to be present from the outset. It also offers helpers room for an optimistic shift away from diagnostically based interventions. In elaborating the meaning of *right conditions and circumstances*, welfare workers are invited to resist the temptation to impulsively 'rescue' people from their experiences because it makes *them* feel better and less frightened, to do so. Instead, they are asked to engage with the process of 'therapeutic witnessing', which Blackwell (1997) describes, in reference to psychoanalytic ideas, as having three elements – *holding, containing* and *bearing witness*. In essence, workers are asked not to become action-orientated helpers in the face of 'muck and bullets', but to stay still enough to bear the pain of listening to stories of great loss as they emerge at a pace manageable for the refugee. Containing pain is hard, and some of the muck sticks in an uncomfortable fashion. One way of mis-handling this discomfort is to respond by becoming split into sentimentality or suspicion of refugees' experiences, thereby losing a chance of hearing the complex, real and heartfelt stories that people can bring. The position of being a witness – that is, being still, unafraid, honest, kind and emotionally robust – is harder than rescuing, but ultimately more productive because it lets people name and exorcise their demons and ghosts in the process of self-recovery. Standing still enough to absorb the emotional impact of refugees' experiences is something that allows the movement hidden beneath the frozen state of psychological hypothermia to emerge in a tolerable way at the right time. The social workers who were 'Witnesses' in this respect, either in a phase of their work, or because of a preferred orientation, appeared to understand the need to be still, as well as the notion of movement, as a literal response to a catastrophe or natural disaster, as well as understanding the ways in which these events perturbed the young people emotionally and psychologically. In other words, they took account of what the events meant to the young people, and the ways in which these meanings affected their adjustment to their circumstances.

The young people that these social workers found themselves most drawn to were the ones who were clearly suffering from events associated with the horror of war, and stories of escape. They also appeared to understand that any of the young people could be frightened by dislocation, and needed reassurance and warmth, no matter what their reason was for being in the UK.

Waiting

In many instances the social workers needed to wait before history and its impact became clear to them from the young people's own accounts of what happened to make them leave. A commonly expressed view amongst the witnesses was that the young people were 'totally lost and abandoned and frightened' by the flight and entry into the UK and used silence productively, as suggested by Papadopoulous (2002), watching and listening to others and processing the impact of their own presence on others in the new context. In these circumstances, as one social worker noted, the young person needed to 'rest his feet' before talking.

> *I've tried to discuss his feelings in leaving the family home under such strenuous circumstances and my opinion is that he is not ready to address that emotionally and psychologically. He has been sent over here by his family, he's been given instructions on what*

*he should do with his life and he's just trying to get on with it.
He's in no position to start, I think at the moment, to even dwell
on it. I hope that once he's found some form of stability in the UK,
some sense of stability in himself, then we can start worrying with
him about why he's here and what it's like being in exile. But
I think to address that, whilst he's not even able to rest his feet
properly, would be torture.*

These social workers waited, and some said that they had
waited for a long time, to hear the young person talk about why
and how he or she had come to leave home. Silence was frustrating for the workers sometimes, as were monosyllabic answers
to standard questions about family history in completing the
Action and Assessment records. But the protective functions of
silence for the young person were understood by the Witnesses.
They hypothesised that *not* talking had a link to the management
of distress that they needed to understand rather than try and
puncture it in any premature way before the young person was
prepared to do the talking. Having said this, there were three
types of situations that could trigger the social worker gaining an
understanding of the young people's distress.

- First, if they were brand new arrivals, they sometimes
  tended to talk more openly than they did after a few
  months of settlement. Some workers observed a pattern
  of relatively open discussion at the point of entry into
  care, followed by long periods, perhaps years, of silence,
  followed by more openness in early adulthood.

- Secondly, conflict in the home country sparked upsets for
  some of the young people, and kept them focused on
  political and personal recollections. They would then be
  sensitised by reports in the media, continually picking at
  details of conflicts as they unfolded, and compare them to
  their own experiences, or worry about those that they
  knew lived in the countries they had left, who continued
  to be exposed to war.

- Thirdly, some came with the need to talk, clearly
  distressed beyond their own capacities to contain their
  feelings or deal silently with their experiences.

At these points where the young people were opening up, there were two options available to the social workers. The first was to respond directly in some way to the distress themselves, and the second was to find suitable resources that the young people could use.

Witnessing distress

The social workers who were Witnesses appeared to be able to listen to waves of pain coming from the young people, and resisted becoming busy in practicalities when they cried. Unlike some of their Humanitarian counterparts, or themselves in a 'humanitarian' phase of their work, they could bear to look back. They described deep sadness being expressed in different ways by the young people. For a few there was a fearful watchfulness that would slowly blend into loss of appetite, headaches, lack of sleep, recurrent nightmares, and tears. There was anger in some others that would be launched if little things did not go according to plan, or if they were denied in some way. Some just cried. The stories they told about their own suffering and survival, as discussed in the previous chapter, drew out a range of responses from the Witnesses, that they hoped would stem the hurt that they saw in the young people's faces.

Within the telling of the story of John (Box 10), the social worker identified key components in the witness's repertoire – first, not just the capacity to look back, but the willingness to enter the story by permission, depending on the young person's own willingness to talk at a pace that was manageable for him. Secondly, she described a general trend in her practice of not enquiring about their history during the first phase of the relationship, but being prepared to wait. However, she knew that, for some of the young people, it emerged immediately, and that it ebbed and flowed, depending on their own day-to-day preoccupations. Thirdly, with John, the social worker showed some understanding of the difference between relationship and role in terms of John's experiences of his sister as a mother, and in the research interview she was able to speculate that other people taking on the role of the main carer for John might need to understand that he would compare them with his sister when

Box 10   Witnessing John's story

John came from Sierra Leone, from an impoverished rural background. His parents had died when he was a baby, and he was
raised by his older sister. They owned a small farm, and lived
there until he was 15 years old. One day he went to collect
cassava some miles away. When he returned, he found his village
had been raided by soldiers. His sister had been killed by them. He
was not allowed to see her body. The soldiers captured him, and
he was sent to Liberia, and from there (probably) recruited by traffickers, who smuggled him into the UK. He was told he had been
sent to America, and when the social worker met him two days
after his arrival, he was very frightened and thought he was in
America. He was 16 at the time of entry into local authority care.
The social worker said,

> I never ask young people when I first meet them why they're
> here and what happened to them, but he straight away just
> came out and told me about being on the farm and everything
> that had happened. It was very spontaneous. So since that time
> we've sat down and we've talked about what happened to him.
> But then another time I'll go and see him and he doesn't want
> to talk about anything. So it's very spontaneous. It depends
> what's going round in his head. In his statement to the Home
> Office he talks about coming back to find his sister dead, and
> the men wouldn't let him in the house to say goodbye to her.
> He's mentioned her name a lot. She was his maternal figure
> because of the age difference and because she cared for him.
> He now says he won't and can't stay with a family and I think
> it's because he misses her so much, he can't bear to be close to
> anything that reminds him of being looked after by her.

they offered him care as a parent figure, and that this could
require a complex negotiation.

In this instance, she moved John at his request from being
cared for by an African foster parent to a residential unit, where
two white staff who became his key-workers were described as
'very nurturing, very caring', helping John to eat, to sleep, and

to be uninterrupted for long periods of silence as he recovered. In understanding the history in this way, the practicalities of John's care arrangements were tailored to fit his capacity to resettle. Within this description of her efforts, the social worker held the absent sister in mind and her importance in John's inner world, and made sure that the sister was not usurped by providing a 'proxy' sister/parent in the African foster mother. This capacity to allow and encourage the young people to bear in mind those people who were no longer accessible in the real world became a feature of practice for many of the Witnesses, and they acted as mediums in the sense of having a keen intuitive understanding of the meaning of loss and the importance of communion with people who were dead or missing. Remembering and mourning the dead and missing, at a time ,and at a pace that the young people could tolerate, became components of a collaborative stay in the domain of inner world resettlement, reflecting Summerfield's (1995:496) suggestion that the dead and disappeared should be remembered as part of the process of healing. He says,

> This is not an exercise in simple humanitarianism. . . . It helps those left behind to generate a meaning for events and to provide a social context for mourning. The dead are lost, but they may be redeemed to the extent that their names and fates have a place on the public stage.

Responding to deep sadness

On occasions, the Witnesses took direct responsibility for structuring time with the young people to allow the them to rely on social workers as people who could bear the weight of their burdens. In one instance a worker discussed a series of meetings that she had culled from a busy and demanding schedule, because the young person had asked for her to be with him at a time when he felt frightened and unable to go to a therapist. The purpose of the sessions was to open up a space for ease of reflection, and to act as a contrast to the bureaucracy of reviews and administration or the intensity of a tightly focused encounter with a therapist.

We've set up six sessions, because I've talked to him about a specialist therapeutic resource we quite often refer young people to. He's terrified of going somewhere to somebody he doesn't know. He wanted to meet up with me and talk to me. But I think he's afraid of losing control. I think he's afraid that if he starts talking and if he starts letting the emotions come up, he's afraid he won't be able to stop. So he needs someone like me, who he knows and trusts.

This was the middle ground, within which the skills of attentive listening to a young person's story were sharpened by many of the Witnesses over time. They said they intended it to be a demystified process – many encounters acted like pockets of investment for the young people that they could fill with whatever they wanted. Many of them did, over time, fill them with such an intense sadness that it left the workers themselves shocked. As one social worker said in reference to a young woman who had been raped by a number of men prior to leaving her country of origin,

It just all came flooding out again and again. And sometimes I thought, what am I doing really? Every time I see her she talks about it and I leave her in tears. She used to worry me to death. The first time I heard the story was when I was taking her to her placement. I dropped her off and then from the placement to my home is quite a long way and I can honestly say that I was just so choked up. I just could not believe what I just heard, it was just awful. That one human being has done this to another human being.

I cried, but not in front of her. I hate to cry with the young person because what does that mean to them? You assist them by making sure that nothing is showing, if you're holding it all in because sometimes I think you just have to. It's about saying, My God, that's awful.' And it's about hearing their story and being a witness to their story, I think. And you are, you're a witness to their story and it's just so important.   [emphasis added]

In these circumstances, the workers stressed a number of important aspects of intense encounters. First, that their act of helping involved them being still enough to absorb the strength of feeling coming from the young person. Many said that they found it distressing, frightening, and confusing. It made them feel angry and isolated, and helpless, mirroring the young people's own feelings of dispossession and harm. They said they felt as if they had become the lightning rods through whom powerful feelings were conducted. Secondly, the witnesses said that the only way to earth themselves was to look to their peers for support and comfort, rather than towards the piecemeal training and consultation offered by the agency. Thirdly, they noted that no matter how well they managed proximity and distance helpfully for themselves and the young person as an aspect of witnessing, there would always be occasions when other helpers needed to step in, in order to assist the young person.

Referring: using specialist others

These social workers noted that what they witnessed also needed to be visible to others, and that their own skills were limited in the face of overwhelming experiences. They turned to therapists for help with the young people. Sometimes, nothing that they did themselves or provided felt good enough to be of any benefit in light of the amount of loss that the young people were experiencing. As one worker said,

> *I think if this was an indigenous child, who saw his whole family killed, you would put in all sorts of resources wouldn't you. And because so many of our asylum seeking young people have been in that situation, we try and help them as best we can. But it's not a patch on what you would do if it happened to an indigenous child in the child care team. I sometimes wonder if we're doing enough with all the loss and traumas that they've been through.*

In saying this, the worker encapsulated a frequent concern about the gaps between services and needs, and the differential criteria by which asylum seeking people were sometimes treated. Despite their own good efforts, many of the social workers absorbed a sense of not doing well enough in light of the young people's perceived therapeutic needs. This also appeared to apply to other local resources. Even though there was a view that the young people could benefit from the help offered by specialist therapists working with refugee communities, there were reports of hurdles that needed to be crossed. In some instances the young people's own reluctance to accept therapy coincided with local CAMHS services being seen as 'a complete and utter disaster'. There were long delays in offering initial appointments, no facilities for non-English-speaking young people, no interpreting service, and sometimes the therapists, the social workers said, had managed to 'spook' the young people by not adjusting the pace of entry into their inner worlds, given the relationships they had with silence and secrets. Young people were described as going for an initial consultation, finding the process odd, intrusive or frightening, and withdrawing quickly into the networks of people that they knew well. Given these local disengagements, the witness social workers tended to persist with referrals to specialist therapeutic resources that had a national reputation for working with victims of torture. Here, the chances of young people finding a balanced and attentive therapist were reported as being much higher in comparison with the local context. But even then the practicalities of travel interfered with accessing these therapists on a regular and frequent basis.

> *I did refer her to a specialist therapeutic resource in another city because I just felt I wasn't doing a good enough job, or maybe I wasn't doing enough. And she would just start crying, feeling very depressed, having nightmares, having flashbacks. But it was a long journey, and we tried to arrange it so she could go there in the morning, and her key-worker would meet her in the afternoon, and meet her from the train, but it just didn't work. Doing long journeys, coming home, going to school, she just could not keep it up.*

In these circumstances these workers said that they could do little more to help the young people even though they worried about those they thought needed help, but who had steadfastly refused. They hypothesised that so long as psychiatric intervention was not necessary – and none of the cases discussed by the social workers indicated this – then the process of resettlement in their inner worlds appeared to require the establishment of supportive, affectionate and reliable relationships within their own networks of care. Social workers recognised that their task lay in helping to reconstitute or replace networks, rather than provide referrals that the young people could not bear, or could not reach. One social worker told this story of a young woman, part of a sibling group, who had been sexually assaulted after arrival in the UK:

> *She said 'No I don't want counselling, I don't want to talk about this any further. I've talked enough and I can talk to my sister about it.' So she will find avenues where she can take it within her own family and friends, rather than professional helpers. We offered for her to see a therapist, but she chooses not to because she has, for herself, found a better way of dealing with it.*

In many instances the choice remained with the young person in relation to using 'opening up' or 'closing down' as a way of managing feelings, and deciding whom they turned to for help, and when they accessed a resource if needed. Overall, the workers said that the young people often expressed a wish to disappear into the folds of common citizenship and find a 'talking cure' in the anonymity provided by their own networks of care and support.

The Witness social workers were particularly careful to explain in the research interview that as time passed, they too could become part of the web of comfort and support that the young people considered to be part of their 'natural' network. They noted that they and the young people had a history to share, and could look back together. These social workers themselves became memory holders, in contrast to their forgetful or vague Humanitarian colleagues, and could remember the past, and tell stories about individual childhoods as they had been lived out within the UK.

> *He was only eight when he came to England; he was very unhappy and he cried. My memories of him as a child were that he cried constantly to go home. The impression we got was that he knew very little about his family because his elder siblings chose not to tell him because they probably felt that he was too young. And he's still quite quiet, and I think he's completely different to the child he would have been if he'd stayed at home and been brought up in normal family life.*

What these workers recounted, in part, was that the young people – whatever their emotional temperature over time – were looking to root; that is they were searching for ways in which ordinary human contact could be established with other people whom they had come to trust, in the absence of family members, and that this contact would be extensive and durable, modulating over time as their needs and capabilities changed.

Part of the resettlement process, and therefore part of the young people's hopes in relation to the outcome, was that the social workers would provide friendship as part of their established relationships with them over time. However, many of the Witnesses themselves were hesitant about the creation of a diffuse boundary between friendship and professional assistance. For them, smudged boundaries of this sort were difficult to sanction or maintain, and whilst they appeared to understand why the young people sought friendship, they continually reminded them of their professional roles and responsibilities within the context of a relationship that was likely to end as soon as the transition from the care of Social Services had taken place. As a complement to their depth of focus, particularly in reference to past suffering, was a clear delineation of the limits of their involvement as part of a friendship network in the young people's future. In contrast to this position, the parameters of friendship and professional assistance appeared to be much more permeable in the work of the confederates within the domain of coherence, as discussed below, as were some of the consequences for the young people's move towards resettlement.

The domain of coherence: the Confederates as companions

This third domain lay close at hand to the worlds of the Humanitarians and Witnesses. In this domain there were social workers who are recognisable in Parton and O'Byrne's (2000: 2) term 'constructive social work'. Firmly based on ideas derived from narrative therapy (White and Epston, 1990), itself embedded within a wider social-constructionist frame (Burr, 1995), Parton and O'Byrne's (2000) approach suggests that the way people use and tell 'thick' stories about themselves can help in reconstructing their lives, particularly when they have become trapped in their own thin narratives of victimhood. In that sense, their emphasis on social workers understanding, uncovering, and using stories of survival, capability and resilience to work along-side clients, fits very well with the narrative-based approaches in the literature. As Melzak (1995b: 112) says when writing about her work with refugee children,

> My central aim in assessing and listening to children is to enable them to integrate their experiences, to tell their own story in all its complexity – its political, social cultural, emotional, relational and physical aspects. To tell the story of memories connected with shame, guilt and extreme emotions such as fear and rage, and memories connected with feelings of pleasure, and deep feelings of well-being connected with home and community.

This 'whole' approach, where the value of a thicker story is emphasised, characterises important aspects of constructive social work, and those elements within it that reinforce the idea of the social worker and the client companionably being involved in the co-management of a process. These social workers appeared to offer this type of companionship for the young people. But there are several distinctive aspects of their practice that are discussed here that meant that they moved beyond the terms of construc-tivism, into what I have referred to as the notion of confederacy. Here, these practitioners became, as I will now explain, ethical subversives, making up information about the young people in an attempt to protect their interests, and friends, as they looked to accompany the young people into the future.

Holding complexity and ambiguity

These social workers, about one in four of those interviewed, appeared from the outset to be interested in the young people not just as refugees (or credible asylum claimants), but as adoles-cents flung far from danger and familiarity and retrospectively having to reclaim and reinvent their lives in deeply uncertain circumstances. They recognised that a complex set of reasons had led to departure from the homeland – for some, clearly associated with civil unrest and persecution, for others with economic fragmentation in the country of origin, and for a minority, with being trafficked children. In any case, they saw that wanting to get away from poverty, and get an education or make money, could co-exist with asylum stories and be legitimate reasons for departure. Like most of the Humanitarians and the Witnesses, these social workers resisted being drawn into positions of being border guards, either at ports of entry, or at in-country access points to local services. Instead they maintained a position of gatekeepers who would open the gates where possible, and keep them open to 'children in need', no matter what the push factors had been that had exiled the children from their countries of origin.

> *Obviously the Albanian boys are fleeing for economic reasons on the whole; there's a few exceptions to that I think, a few genuine exceptions. So I can understand that their focus here would be economic, they're not political refugees, they are economic refugees. And the government doesn't recognise that. I actually find it difficult because I think there's a fine line between the two. Obviously, there's different degrees of political refugees as well as economic refugees but I think at the bottom end of one and the top end of the other, there's a very, very fine line. I've always said that it's not an issue for me.*

A basic shared proposition amongst the Confederates, exactly paralleling the description of 'thin' stories in the literature, appeared to be that some people lied about their reasons for coming to the UK because only lies would fit the narrow channel that was generated by the current legal definition of asylum. They said that the young people had to tell simple, linear, asylum-based stories to enter. In not being able to be honest about the whole of their contexts of departure, some of them were trapped inside these stories. In contrast to a few of the Humanitarians, the Confederates did not themselves appear to view lying as problematic, only the burden that the lies created for the young people, who could not talk of other reasons that had led them to come to the UK without fear of being summarily ejected. In this respect, the Confederates came to reframe 'the problems *of* asylum seekers' as 'problems *for* these young people'.

Their own broad position was presented within the research interviews as one of sympathetic understanding, rather than the narrower pursuit of acceptability of the asylum story. As one social worker typically noted,

> *You're doing it for* their *best interests not because you're colluding with the authorities to find stuff out.*

As such, 'the authorities' became a type of shorthand for the police and immigration services for the Confederates, even when they had referred to the young people seeing social workers as authority figures, at least at the initial point of contact. This somewhat ambiguous positioning of themselves in relation to the continuum between friend/collaborator and judge/prosecutor illustrated both the advantages and the dangers of a labile role adopted by the Confederates, and many of them could have been lost in a collusive huddle with the young people, had it not been for a capacity to show that they could challenge not just the provision of services, but also the young people themselves, when it came to the maintenance of boundaries, and the assertion of order in a confusing and complicated world, as illustrated below.

Looking past the given story and reaching out to the young people

Given that the Confederates' clearly articulated position was that at some point economic and political reasons coincided and jointly pushed the young people out of their habitats of origin, to separate the 'deserving' political refugee from the 'undeserving' economic migrant was not something that they were prepared to do. They were, however, able to move away from simple dichotomies towards a more complex world. For example, a particular feature of the Confederates' work was a capacity to look beyond the given story that they had heard many times before and see a storyteller who was frightened at telling the story for themselves for the first time to a social worker. Particularly in the specialist teams, where the main clusters of Confederates appeared to occur, the following pattern was described in relation to how they had learnt to deal with the young people's stories. Initially, as new entrants into a team dealing with young asylum seekers, they said they had been simply struck by the awfulness of some of the descriptions, and wanted to rescue the children involved from any further harm. However, as they came across more and more stories that were similar in content, they experienced themselves becoming cynical and feeling that the young people were looking to manipulate their sympathies, or treating them as if they were naive. Sometimes they found the repeated stories 'a bit droll', and particularly in a team culture of disbelief, these stories would be caricatured by team members. At times of heavy demand for services, the caricatures would lead to depersonalised encounters, and the sort of turf wars described in the previous chapter. But this distancing and 'remote control' approach to practice could dissipate over time, an effect triggered by a number of factors including a growing affection for the young people, or by perceiving the vulnerability of the young person in front of them in the duty interview room. Some of the confederates hypothesised that once they had decided to 'really listen' to a story – to take into account the stage, the play, the actors, and the dialogue, so to speak – there would be a Damascene moment that would convert them from scepticism to faith. Some had previously struggled because they had found some of the young people's accounts frightening, just as the Witnesses had, or had noted the young people's fear of them as social workers. They wanted to broaden the constricted channels that fear could generate in a way that made their exchanges with the young people 'real'. Opening these channels required them to be brave, they said, as much as it did the young people themselves.

To get to this reality, the Confederates said that they had had to make a choice about their practice, by not dismissing the young peoples' stories as tired fiction, but by looking underneath them to see the world through the eyes of a frightened teenager looking to them for care.

> *I look back and can see now that they're told to say that [asylum] story. That's what they have to say. If I were in their place, I'd say the same thing, and even if I'd heard it a thousand times, they don't know that I've heard it a thousand times. Often I tell them I've heard that story several times and it's OK to tell me that*

story. I'm more inclined to be doing the assessments along the lines that they're young people in need, and I'm just going to assess them regardless of what the given story is.

They made the young people feel welcome. In this respect a key element of confederate practice appeared to be a willingness to reach out to the young people, rather than react to their practical demands once they had approached the duty desk. This was allied to an invitation to the young people to say what was tolerable at any particular time, with the hope of the thin asylum story being transformed into a less rehearsed and more honest account of their motivations, circumstances and past lives, within which multiple explanations could co-exist. In contrast to those who pursued the truth of the asylum story, these social workers appeared to draw a distinction between truth and honesty. They did not appear to pursue fact or look for independently verifiable evidence of an asylum claim's authenticity. Instead they appeared to generate opportunities for the young people to be as honest as possible in the circumstances about their current and past experiences. Authenticity of process rather than validity of outcome appeared to be valued by them, and they were prepared to wait to hear the whole story:

I've seen young people who are trying to remember what they've been told to say and they're just wailing because they can't remember the story they're meant to be telling you and it's just not right. It's caused such awful distress and you're just adding to their fear and the pressure if you carry on asking them. So it's best just to back off and wait.

In these circumstances the Confederates appeared to offer care without the precondition that a 'truthful' story was offered in return.

I've been caring with or without a story as it were. I haven't pushed for the story because if that needs to come out it will come out. And I think staying with it is a very, very important part. They will tell you in time. People 'come out' at different stages and you just have to accept that and respect that, you know.

As trust developed within the relationship and the young people could see that they had a choice about the speed, direction and scope for talking about their lives, stories of suffering were uncovered in optimistic ways to reveal other stories of capability in the face of distress. Within these the young people were protagonists, and had an elasticity which allowed them to bend but not break with the pressures exerted on them. Thus, the stories that the Confederates heard were not just related to asylum or trauma – although they were given due consideration by these social workers – but also of ordinary lives before leaving, of growing up in families and communities where 'habits of the heart' were practised in familiar ways that the young people had now lost and needed to recover, before feeling settled in the UK. For example, the young people were reported as missing their families, and the sights, sounds, smells, and texture of living in their childhood environments. They were said to be angry at their parents for making decisions that had led them so far away; they were grateful for having got away; they felt guilty and worried about those left behind, particularly other siblings; and they wanted to succeed, knowing the material and psychological investment that had been made in them by the family left behind.

The Confederates said that they picked up a strong and urgent sense from the young people of wanting to be ordinary again, unconfined by the label of 'asylum seeker' or 'refugee', and tracked this feeling back to a time when the young person in their charge had been an unnoticed citizen in their country of origin. As one social worker noted:

> *It's very difficult to live an identity which is just about asylum seeking. He's just an ordinary kid in some ways.*

Promoting resilience and optimism

The way back to this ordinariness was described by the Confederates as being based on a confirmation of survival and adaptability, and a reassertion of resilience. Evidence for the type of toughness that the social workers thought the young people needed came from several directions, the first being a set of personal characteristics that the Confederates admired.

RK: *You've referred often to this young woman in terms of her own resilience. What makes her resilient? What keeps her going?*

SW: *I think she wants to succeed; she wants to do well here, which ties up with education, wanting to succeed, wanting to obviously have a good job. And I think it's as if she's thinking, 'My mum and dad would have been proud of me if they could see me now.' Because I was saying to her, 'I'm very proud of you and I know your mum and dad would be so proud of you.'*

As noted in the previous chapter, these social workers said that the young people were tough, resilient, resourceful and single minded, having a sort of stubbornness that could be both exasperating and helpful. Just a few of the known stories indicated the pre-existence of a broad, deep and loving attachment to their families and networks in the past, and where some of the young people had been able to regenerate protective networks in the present, the social workers had put current circumstances together with past experiences to conclude that some key elements of resilient strategies were at play that allowed the young people to conduct themselves in a composed and effective way in a variety of contexts, at home and at work or in education. Their memories, their intelligence and a will to succeed were combined regularly with a social grace that the Confederates clearly valued as offering a more cheerful and coherent future. As one social worker noted,

She wants to become an air hostess. She will be OK. When she was younger, she would get so depressed and say she was ugly and needed her teeth fixed because she would never become this air hostess, you know. But it's not like that any more, she just knows what she'd like to be and she doesn't talk about not being pretty enough any more.

Resistance: saying no and responding to racism

Having said this, several of the Confederates were at pains not to construct a scene of sentimental whimsy in terms of their direct work; they confirmed that their own relationships with the young people could be confrontational and tense, especially at moments when they denied access to someone or something that the young person said they urgently needed. They reported many examples of having to say no, or of setting limits to behaviour and resources. What made their approach unusual was that they could often re-interpret confrontation as being helpful to the young people, as in this example of a social worker who was asked whether he knew of anyone whom the young person would consider to be supportive, affectionate and reliable:

> *Well, I don't think he'd nominate me. I don't think he views me as a support mechanism. I think he views me as a source of money and a source of saying no to him. I know that I've found his strong will and stubbornness incredibly frustrating, but I think in a way that's been something he's been able to hold on to and to own for himself and there's an element of survival isn't there, in that if he wasn't stubborn in that way, then he might not have survived.*

This capacity to see beyond the given, as in other aspects of their work, and to re-interpret behaviours that allowed the young people to be seen in the best possible light, had led many of the Confederates to relationships with them that were experienced by both parties as robust, in that the rough and tumble of day-to-day existence did not destabilise a growing and strong bond. In some ways, a 'warts and all' young person was seen as an authentic and graspable character in contrast to the smooth-edged, silent and remote individuals who had first come into view at the duty desk. These social workers were also able to express understanding towards those young people who exhibited racism by responding to it in a way that did not obliterate the young person. As noted in the previous chapter, racism was apparent in many of them particularly when faced with the prospect of being cared for by people who were not the ones they had hoped for in terms of race and culture. Confederate social workers appeared to locate its appearance through understanding its genesis, and gently resisting rather than resenting the consequence. For example, they could see that many of the European and Asian young people were simply not used to diversity, and that some of the children from the Horn of Africa had come with explicit expectations of being cared for only by white people. They could see that integration into the host community alongside disintegration from the community of origin were complex processes to manage, and attributed expressions of racism at least in part to the ways that the young people dealt with uncertainty by falling back on simple stereotypes of good and bad. They also appeared to recognise that as much as the young people rejected some carers on the basis of race and culture, many of them were also frightened of being cared for by people from their own national and ethnic backgrounds. Similarity and difference brought opportunities and threats, and the Confederate social workers appeared to take these into account in practice. In other words, workers showed a capacity to think beyond simple and schematic formulations of anti-racism. The young people, on being told that they had little choice about the race of the carer and that they might be reacting to negative artefacts rather than responding to the complexity of life, were said to accept the choices made on their behalf, sometimes with positive consequences. African-Caribbean carers cooked Albanian food and English carers learnt rudimentary language skills. Where workers held on to the notion of the richness of difference, rather than following the rules of preference used initially by the young people, resettlement in their new circumstances became easier, and the workers reported a sense of attachment emerging within the newly founded networks of care.

In itself, the sense of attachment that the Confederates expressed in their own relationships with the young people was not substantially different from the ways the Humanitarians expressed a degree of warmth towards their charges, nor from the ways in which the Witnesses talked about making an emotional commitment to those who were distressed. But in this instance it could lead to some surprising strategies to aid resettlement.

Being ethical subversives

In their determination to maximise the possibilities of the young people remaining within the UK, the Confederates were sometimes prepared to be subversive. At a simple, practical level, subversion could take the form of inventing parts of the young people's lives. As noted in the previous chapter, the issue of not knowing the exact age of the young person troubled many of the workers, but was primarily resolved by accepting that they were the age they said, unless there was a *prima facie* case for suspicion based on appearance. But a few of the Confederates went a small step further. In one case a worker described the process of making up dates of birth for a group of siblings from Eritrea in her care. She was hesitant about disclosing this aspect of her practice, perhaps mirroring the processes that the young people themselves engaged with in gaining validity and acceptability from the authorities. She saw her inventive intervention as being necessary, and subversive.

> **SW**: *It was very obvious that if you didn't have a date of birth in this country, you're not going to get anything. So we played a little game with regards to what kind of dates they would like. They had the approximate timing, the years, but they had no idea of the months or the day of the month they were born. So we were sitting together and I was basically asking what date of birth they would like for themselves, and I remember the youngest one saying 'September', and here we were in October. So I said to him, why not have it in October and then you're in for your birthday present, if not you'll have to wait a whole year. So that's how we agreed his birth date.*

The worker, like her Confederate colleagues, was keen in the research interview to point out that this strategy, whilst rare, had been developed as an ethical response to the situation. Without her intervention, the children in this family could not have been anchored in bureaucratised systems that required them to have a precise birth date. She said that she was not prepared for questions about their 'true' age to continue to confront them as they lived their lives in care, and that an invention that approximately fitted their appearance had settled at least that part of their lives, even if other major uncertainties remained.

Another aspect of subversion was the capacity that some workers showed to act like lighthouses for young people who were drawn to them by their reputations for care, inclusivity and attention. Whilst they recognised that their organisations did not want, could not afford, and would not condone a mass presence of asylum seeking people within the locality, they felt proud of having a reputation as beacons. In these instances, the pattern that appeared across teams was that one or two social workers would gather a reputation for themselves as people who were receptive and attractive in the sense of providing the young people with a confidential and safe welcome, as in the following example of a social worker referring to the work that she and a colleague had undertaken with some young men from Kosovo:

> *The boys see me as having a high profile in the department. So they know what position I hold within social services and it means that I'm always a beacon for them to come to and they know I'm here, they know where to find me. And the other beacon beside me is my colleague Ian, and they know that Ian and I work together and that we're honest with each other and that we can be discreet about the sort of information we share and with whom.*

During the research interviews, these confederates confirmed the circumstances that had led to this individualised beacon status. They were proud, but not loud, in the sense of promoting their reputations within their work contexts. Their stories were displayed in a way that quietly exemplified hard work, focused commitment, and a capacity to peel back layers of untruths that the young people had told in order to protect themselves from harm, as in the example in Box 11.

These struggles of depending on the young person's expressed story, knowing that it cast light and shadows in complex ways on who they were, how old they were, and where they were from, meant that the route to authenticity was difficult for both parties. For the Confederate social worker, building a trusting relationship, and using that relationship to safely pilot the young person towards authenticity, appeared as a fundamental element of effective practice. Similar struggles were apparent across different teams in different settings, dealing with young people from Africa. In the African context, some young people claiming to be from war-torn parts of Africa had disclosed their Nigerian origins, sometimes because they were unable to hold secrets, or by revealing them by accident or through persuasion. In these instances too, the workers referred to a sense of reclamation experienced by the young person in their charge. But being honest about national origin, amongst other aspects of the claim, both jeopardised the young person's ability to remain within the UK as an asylum seeker, and offered a chance for a sense of authenticity to emerge. Fragmentation and coherence co-existed in these instances.

The Confederates, on the whole, appeared reluctant to use this information to tell the Home Office the whole story as they had come to know it, and this choice did not appear to trouble them a great deal. Having drawn the boundary very firmly between themselves and the immigration authorities, they stayed on course towards helping the young people manage the process of re-creating coherence for themselves in ways that allowed them to find and establish new connections as well as connections with people from their past. Ethical subversion, from their point of view, was purposeful, in that it helped the young people to embed themselves in their new lives after having uprooted themselves from their past and allowed a sense of coherence to trump feelings of fragmentation.

Companionship

The majority of the confederates showed a tendency to doggedly stick by the young people that they had chosen to talk about in the research interview. Their relationships were extensive and enduring. They saw themselves as people in whom faith had been placed, and to whom the young people turned in times of uncertainty and trouble. Those who upheld their beacon qualities also reported instances of being the first point of contact for the young person, often when picking them up at the port of entry. They reported a sense of 'imprinting', where the first kind, trustworthy face in the UK had led the young person to sustain an emotional bond that had led to the social workers being regarded as powerful parent-like figures. The warmth exhibited by the young people in these circumstances appeared to take some of the practitioners by surprise, before settling into a welcome part of the relationship.

> **Box 11   Revealing and re-telling: Bekim's story**
>
> Bekim came from Albania, and had claimed to be Kosovan in his asylum application. His allocated social worker knew through the interpreter that he had lied, because his accent was Albanian rather than Kosovan, and there was some other circumstantial evidence that had come to light during the six months she had known him. She also knew that he had contacts in the locality, including an uncle who he claimed was a friend. One day Bekim said that he wanted to stay with this 'friend' over the Christmas holidays, and the worker offered to do a home visit to make sure that she was satisfied that the 'friend' could care for him. During the home visit, neither the uncle nor Bekim admitted to their relationship.
>
> *I knew from history and from my own experience of working with these young people that there is no way that this is a stranger who he met and he's befriended in London. It isn't that, it can't be. And I just couldn't believe that. This guy's been there from day one. There was a lot of innuendo in my conversation about their relationship and I gave them a lot of 'outs', a lot of ways of jumping in there if they wanted to. But neither of them bought it. And I was surprised I think, and a bit disappointed in some ways that Bekim was not quite at that point where he could trust me. But I could feel this sense of shame that he had to lie to me. He couldn't look at me when I left, he couldn't look at me at all.*
>
> ⟶

I feel that many of the young asylum seekers I've met, they can surprise me. When I first started this job I noticed how they are very tactile. They'll see you and give you a hug and normally in child protection work you don't get any of that business. With these kids you have to change your way of working because you have adjust. This is a very different way of working, that's nice; it's informal, as long as you're quite clear about your boundaries and everything.

Despite this the home visit led to continued contact with the friend/uncle, and the relationship between Bekim and the social worker developed into an affectionate and reliable one. During this time, the worker visited Kosovo with some Kosovan friends, and they made their way there through Albania. By chance, she had stayed in the city in which Bekim was born. In one of their regular meetings, she said,

> I was talking to him about my trip to Albania because at first he didn't believe that I went. All he heard really was that I had been to Kosovo; it didn't really sink in that I had been to Albania.
>
> So I started talking about Albania and so he started talking about Albania, and then he started talking about wanting to go home to Albania. And then the conversation just had a momentum of its own. And Bekim started talking about his home and his mum and dad, and how he wants to go back to see them, but he's got reasons why he wants to be here. And he talked about his uncle who's kept an eye on him all of this time, and said, 'This guy who you met at Christmas is my uncle'. And I said 'I know,' and he said 'I know you know. But I hadn't been able to say anything.'
>
> So it was really quite an emotional and good exchange. He felt I was ready to hear this information and I felt he was ready to tell it, so it was good. I know that Bekim's level of respect for me is high. It's made things a little bit easier for him because he doesn't have to pretend in front of the person he really respects and that's good for him.

In part, an awareness of boundaries for the Confederates meant that they made sure that the young people understood that they were not their parents, even though they were prepared to act *in loco parentis*.

> *It's almost, as with quite a few of them, you're the only person they've got, so it can be quite intensive – it can be parent-like.*

The Confederates generally appeared to like this level of emotional

Table 6.1   Social work within the domains of resettlement

Domains	Cohesion	Connection	Coherence
Trust	Trust needs to exist across all domains. It is based on a demonstration of reliability, regularity, consistency, affection and kindness, honesty, precision, clarity, praise for achievements, acting by permission, faith in the absence of certainty about the future.		

Orientation	The Humanitarian	The Witness	The Confederate
Representation of the social worker	Someone in authority who is a realist and pragmatist; a resource holder who will get them what they need in order to get by, and act as an advocate, protector and mentor.	Someone who represents the missing parent, acts like a medium and is a memory carrier and searcher for meaning, can understand silence, can witness distress.	Someone who is an optimistic collaborator and has become the parent *in situ* – a rediscovered parent – and acts as a confederate to ensure the best desired outcome.
The story that is heard by the social worker	The asylum story and its practical and legal consequences including authenticity of claim. Little knowledge about past life is sought from the young person or records.	The asylum story plus the clinical history of events and responses are understood within a therapeutic frame. Young people are represented as sufferers and victims with some aspects of resilience.	All stories, including the 'capability' stories of early experiences, are used as a foundation for durable resolutions. Young people are experienced as survivors and agents of change.
Key aspects of social work practice	The emergence of order. Focus on the 'real world' issues and offer practical help. Make sure they obtain the right to remain in the UK indefinitely, have a home,	The quest for peace. Understand expressions of dislocation and distress in the context of trauma. Work with those whose distress is leaking, but wait for those who are silent. Focus on the	The offer of companionability. Talk about ordinariness in the past. Find evidence of love or capability in those stories and work these into their stories of survival. Survey capabilities and

	friends, education, a doctor, contact with extended family or use of Red Cross Tracing Service.	meaning of events and people. Continue to offer time to talk. Refer to therapist if needed.	resilience of the young person for (re)constructive work and help them find a sense of agency.
Networks	Use of local map of contacts, resources and helpers. Cohesion of resources that fit together to make a safe place for the young person. Suspicion of hidden networks.	Mapping the world of experience and meaning. Memories and ghosts are connected to the present. Connection between then and now, the lost and found.	Coherent links between people, resources, memories, personal capabilities; tolerance of hidden networks and implicit support for manufactured 'truth'. A 'living' map.
Boundaries	The worker acts as a citizen maker, against social exclusion, especially for credible claimants.	The worker acts as a go-between linking inner and outer worlds, past and present.	The worker is an 'ethical subversive' deconstructing boundaries, a companion.
Lies	The worker judges the truth of the asylum story. Knows that the young people lie sometimes. Is troubled by this.	The worker understands that lies can help *and* contort resettlement.	The worker accepts that lies may be functional in providing the best chance of a successful asylum claim.
Secrets	The worker believes that secrets can hide lies. Silence may be a cover for secrets. Should this be investigated further or disclosed to the relevant authorities.	Secrets and silence can sometimes be protective, especially in managing deep distress, but in the longer term are harmful.	Secrets can be functional because they are part of surviving. The worker accepts some element of assisting resettlement through keeping the minor's secrets.
Remembering, forgetting, and revising	Workers say 'Forget and move on, the past is gone, we can only change now and the future.'	Workers say 'Remember what is forgotten and by remembering, make peace, lay ghosts, move on.'	Workers say 'Rebuild or deconstruct stories of victimhood into stories of resilience – see past strengths as offering future potential.'

investment that the young people were prepared to make in them, and responded warmly to the invitation. As noted above, instances of being proud of them were liberally used by the Confederates to confirm a sense of a responsibly managed attachment that sustained an organic growth in companionship over time – going to parents' evenings at school, helping to review art work that they were exhibiting locally, and standing in the crowd in a nightclub as they took their first steps as performance artists and DJs, were some examples that illustrated a permeable boundary of extended involvement in the ordinary aspects of resettlement. Some of the Confederates, in continuing their responsibilities as ethical subversives, made sure that nothing destabilised the relationship even if there were times when they had to respond to organisational pressures to close or transfer a case.

> *I mean, I'm not really supposed to be his social worker, I was always told to transfer it ages ago and I just haven't. Well I have thought about it, but I'm still waiting for a letter from the Home Office and I can't do anything until I get that, can I?*

Yet even the Confederates shared a pattern of involvement with the young people that meant that an intensive early phase of the relationship had moved on to less frequent contact by the time the story was told in the research interview. This was regarded by all the workers as a necessary part of both managing demand, as well as the young people establishing an effective network of support for themselves. Re-settlement as a co-evolutionary process and re-settlement as an outcome were described by one of the Confederates in this way:

> *I hope and believe I will go to her wedding and I'll be around when she has her children. She will belong to someone one day but I think I'll be around, most definitely. I said, 'Don't you dare get married without me.' I've been to a few weddings. . . .*

Summary

In summary, it can be seen that there were similarities and differences in living and working in the three domains. In each, the social worker could be effective. Across all of them, effectiveness was tied to developing a trusting relationship with the young person. In each of the ways of working, different aspects of resettlement based activity were displayed. These are summarised in Table 6.1 (on pp. 204–5).

7 Conclusions

In this book, one image that has been used in describing social work practice with unaccompanied minors is that of weaving together threads which have been scattered. As indicated in the introduction, the threads themselves are not new, in that they have existed for some time across a variety of disciplines and lines of enquiry. Neither is the idea of the 'loss of narrative threads' (Summerfield, 1998) new, because researchers within social work and researchers within refugee studies have been looking for many years at stories of loss and continuity for vulnerable children who cross different borders in search of safety. What is new, in the ways in which it has been applied in this study, is the generation of fresh perspectives for stories of social work in the context of forced migration. While the nature of this enquiry and the methods used do not lend themselves directly to the production of recommendations for practice, they do reveal important details about the lives of asylum seeking young people and their social workers. These can be used in two ways. First, to understand in some depth aspects of the lives of young asylum seekers which show them as people coping with the rough and tumble of resettlement as best they can. Secondly, to think broadly about social work as more than an impoverished response to their care needs, so that social workers can reclaim some optimism about their practice.

In this book, I have proposed that new pictures are constantly being created by acts of integration and evolution following forced migration, and that different types of loss *and* gain are visible as the details within them. In developing this proposition, I have attempted to offer some understanding of resettlement for refugees and its various meanings, from a theoretical point of view, from research studies, as well as from the stories told by social workers about their practice with young asylum seekers. Within the ebb and flow of refugee movement, I have suggested that resettlement is not simply an 'outer world' outcome, but also a process, and that it has political, social and psychological aspects that are complex and fluid, that occur together, and need to be co-managed by refugees and their helpers as they move between different 'domains' of resettlement.

Locating social work with unaccompanied minors in context

Within the UK, being a social worker and being an unaccompanied minor are both difficult positions to hold. In a sense, they both belong to the margins of respectability and their movements towards a more central and reputable space within public perception are hesitant and uneasy. In all, social work services and practices have been, and continue to be, viewed within this arena in a dystopian frame (Ferguson, 2003). So finding the 'good enough' in the lives of unaccompanied minors and in the practices of their social workers became, over time, one of the major areas of enquiry for the study. In delineating the findings, I have suggested that many of the social work practitioners appeared to work in contexts that were fraught with practical, procedural and political obstacles that impeded progression towards an ordinary life for the minors. Typically, these obstacles appeared in the forms visible in many of the UK studies discussed in Chapter 3. For example, organisational ambivalence towards unaccompanied minors, to some extent mirroring and reinforcing the need to 'keep them out', was outlined by a number of those interviewed, confirming the findings by the Audit Commission (2000) and Stanley (2001) of poorer standards of care and protection being offered in circumstances of perhaps greater immediate need in comparison with vulnerable indigenous children. The contexts appeared hostile, 'a lottery' in terms of the ways these children and young people came to be assessed, understood and provided with services. In this study the social workers confirmed that an accident and emergency response rather than a preventative service was likely to be the default position unless they themselves struggled to maintain a sense of anticipating and dealing with the range and types of threats of marginalisation that the minors faced on a daily basis. The sense of 'unbelonging' and vulnerability appeared as a consequence of the young people facing 'internal border guards' at the interface of a number of services related to health, education and care. It also exerted a particular gravitational pull away from ordinary life towards marginal living in relation to immigration, where the constant prospect of repatriation halted any movement towards citizenship. In many respects, the practitioners themselves felt 'on the edge' as social workers, with their role and tasks being represented negatively within media reports and within the UK-based research literature. Not being impervious to bad representation, like the young people themselves, the social workers felt a sense of marginalisation at times. This sense of not being good enough appeared to make them hesitant about claiming effectiveness. So, in some important respects, they appeared to feel less ownership of the process of rescuing ordinariness on behalf of the young people they were working with than they could have done, given the stories they told.

The unaccompanied minors and their lives

In all, the study's findings are sometimes at odds with and sometimes confirm and add to other established findings about refugee children within the wider refugee literature. In confirming some of the information visible through previous research, the study shows that the young people whom the social workers described appear to have come from diverse backgrounds, for a number of reasons. These ranged from what the social workers thought were relatively affluent young people moving for political reasons, to those who came from relatively poor backgrounds, moving for reasons which were less easy to fit within the conventional legal definition of 'refugee', but resonated well with the SCEP definition of 'separated' children. Particularly in the context of refugees needing to underplay any economic motives for their flight, and in presenting their political reasons for seeking sanctuary in credible and digestible forms to the authorities (Bertrand, 2000; Jacobson and Landau, 2003), the social workers uncovered stories that contained both political and economic reasons that were arranged in such a way that political triggers for flight were on display, and economic ambitions were hidden. In any case, however the pulse of movement was generated, it was known to their social workers that they needed 'sponsors' to buy their passage to industrialised nations far away from their homelands, whether these were parents who found the money, or others. They needed agents to get them through international borders. These elements are presented in the studies by Ayotte (2000) and Robinson and Segrott (2002), and confirmed through the informed guesses made by the social workers within this study.

Yet very little detail appears about the young people's pre-departure lives either in the existing literature or through the stories known to the social workers here. In line with the sketches contained in the literature, as discussed in Chapter 2, the impressions of history offered by the social workers were largely the ones given by the young people themselves as they approached Social Services. They carried no identifying information or mementoes. History was therefore smudged, and this resulted in many uncertainties about, for example, where they came from and the sort of families they have left behind, and their age – but few independently verifiable facts. The social workers in this study confirmed the existence of silence and 'thin' stories, and linked them in many respects to explanations given in a diverse range of studies within the literature. Here, the social workers said, were young people who could not or would not talk about where they came from with any degree of comfort or breadth, but would present the thin stories that they thought would give them the best chance initially of being accepted as refugees. For some of the young people, thin stories were all they could recall, because for one reason or another, these stories had displaced a sense of an ordinary 'thick' life through the deep fragmentation generated by war. For others they appeared to work like an entry key into systems of care and protection.

In some important respects, in offering a range of hypotheses about how the thin stories came into existence, many of the social workers gave, as Geertz (1973) observes, 'thick', multi-layered explanations for their existence, by asking 'What is going on here?' and not being content with one-dimensional answers. Even the more suspicious of those interviewed in this study said that they could see why the young people maintained silence or thin stories. Yet no matter how useful these appeared to be in the short term, the social workers also appeared to pick up on the need for the young people to discard thinness in favour of thicker lives during the evolution of resettlement, so that the cost of carrying thin stories did not rub out the thicker past, or impede the development of the need to refurbish their lives with people they could belong with, and memories they could live with.

The portrayal of the young people in this study also offers a chance to see them as a complex and 'alive' group. For example, an abiding impression that the social workers gave of them was that many of them wanted to be ordinary again, and not just defined by the labels 'asylum seeker' and 'refugee'. They did not want their movements of belonging to be arrested by these labels. Instead, they wanted back some of what they had lost – a sense of an elastic and individual identity that they could shape in the ways that they themselves wanted to over time. After all, said the social workers, they were in many respects like any other adolescents growing up in adverse circumstances and trying to make sense of them. In all, the stories that the social workers told about them suggested that, unlike the commentaries within much of the literature, they did not experience the young people in simple ways, for example as a cohort of injured or psychologically dishevelled people, or innocents or charlatans, although there were elements of these impressions in many of the portrayals. As much as some of the young people were seen as battlers, demanding, silent, and distressed, they were also seen to be friendly, likeable, ambitious and hopeful. The young people were said to be able to make and sustain attachments with carers, their peers and the social workers themselves. The stories therefore contained elements of integration and disintegration, for good and bad, that were similar to the ones described in some of the literature, with the young people exhibiting broad capabilities and some quite specific war-related emotional disturbances. In this study, the young people were described by the social workers as wanting to be active in the reconstruction of their lives – at least in relation to the majority seeking out friendship networks, making sure they got themselves to school, and settling into routine lives. There appeared to be – so far as many of these social workers were concerned – resilience and persistent optimism about the way the young people resettled on the whole, despite the complexity and uncertainty with which they lived. These latter attributes appeared to provide both the social workers and the young people something to hold on to energetically as a counterpoint to the many vicissitudes they faced together, and enabled both to distance themselves from representations of refugees and social workers in simple, negative forms.

The social workers and their practice

In relation to the main focus of this study, resettlement practice by social workers seems also to be far more complex than the largely simple and negative constructions given to it within the UK-based research studies. For example, none of the agencies' informants, and very few of the practitioners who were interviewed, gave any view of asylum seeking young people that strayed far from the principle of 'children first and foremost' contained within the European and national guidance documents. The exceptions to this rule could have occurred in the agencies within which the generalist teams A and B were located. Here, at the time of the fieldwork, the policy to accommodate only those young people who were known to be sixteen years of age or younger appeared to contradict the view that all asylum seeking young people were treated as children in need, on a par with indigenous children. It also appeared to contrast with the more inclusive approach taken by both the specialist unaccompanied minors teams (C and D), which accommodated most of the young people at the point of application for assistance under section 20 of the Children Act 1989. Given the design of this study, it is not possible to say how those 16–18-year-olds who remained outside care provision under section 20 fared in comparison with their section 20 counterparts. What it does confirm, however, is that there appeared to be relatively few important differences across agencies in the ways in which the young people were treated by their allocated social workers once they were accepted for section 20 care.

For example, the details of ordinary day-to-day practice show that on the whole, the majority of social workers appeared to provide, where possible, a steady and dependable service to the young people, even if they knew very little about their origins. They appeared to understand that it was difficult for many of the young people to bear to look back or dare to look forward, and that at least for the initial part of the resettlement journey in the UK, they needed to focus on *the present first, the future next and the past last*. In fact, some of these practitioners, largely working within the Humanitarians' domain of cohesion, appeared to be much more confident with working in the present than with the future or past, and between them the young people and these practitioners kept a focus on the 'here and now', perhaps because it was more tangible, and because putting the 'outer world' building block in place offered the best chance of a stable structure from which the past and the future could be viewed with a degree of balance at a later time.

The practitioners appeared to sense the importance of trust for the young people, and that they needed to act as guardians, not guards. In the minority of instances when they did guard the trafficked young people, they said they explained the rationale for their actions clearly, simply, and with authority. In all there was some evidence that they thought about what safety meant for the young people in their varied circumstances, and worked towards ensuring that it became part of the ordinary rhythm of life.

They attempted where possible to find durable solutions in terms of placements with families, specialist residential establishments, and in semi-independent and independent units. This may in part be the reason for the majority of the young people appearing to be satisfied with their care arrangements. Siblings were never separated, unless they themselves requested this, and older siblings who carried the responsibility of care appeared to be supported practically and emotionally by the social workers.

Many of the practitioners, particularly in the specialist teams, were aware of the need for good lawyers and speedy resolutions to the asylum applications, as well as the ways in which educational and medical services could assist resettlement. Using formal local networks effectively appeared to be part of their overall practice orientation as they advocated on behalf of the young people to access resources. Unlike the social workers referred to by Ayotte and Williamson (2001: 26) who 'approached foreign embassies to request information about a child's family, or passed information to the Home Office without consultation', these practitioners preferred, on the whole to be careful in ensuring that the young people knew what was being done on their behalf, who was being contacted, and why this was being done. Consent and information sharing formed one of the threads of a trusting relationship over time, reflecting the importance to these young people, like their indigenous counterparts, of the social worker acting as a 'single champion and companion through the changing scenes and vicissitudes of a local authority childhood' (Utting, 2003: i). In that respect, many of those interviewed gave an account of themselves as the types of 'champions and companions' hoped for by Utting (2003). But they were not saints, in the same way that they were not inept, as described in some of the literature. They could be forgetful and vague about a number of important matters – basic biographical information, the details of the asylum claim, absence of planning regarding independent living or return to the country of origin – and this meant that the criticisms levelled at social workers within the UK research studies had at least some basis in fact. More importantly, no matter how or why their vagueness matched the young people's need to be amorphous themselves, a context was created within which a dynamic of 'don't ask, don't say' had displaced precision in some of their thoughts and action. Particularly as Humanitarians within their domain, they described their frustrations at the young people being demanding of money and resources. They struggled not to be sceptical of some versions of the 'truth' that the young people presented, even though they could understand why they lied, or only showed part of their stories. They worked hard to maintain order and civility.

However, even when working in this domain was about bringing order to the outside world, they did not create order by representing complex reality in simple terms. Instead they appeared to deal robustly with a multiplicity of meanings. For example in relation to race, language, culture and religion, they appeared to recognise complexity in practice and said that it partly reflected the young people's own complex relationship with similarity and difference. The 'prejudicial attitudes among social services staff', as reported by Ayotte and Williamson (2001), or the racism reported in the study by Stanley (2001), were not apparent in the stories told within this study. Nor was the notion supported that the young people are always best served by being placed within their communities of origin, because these could sometimes be dangerous. Instead, the social workers gave some rich accounts of practice within which similarity and difference were delicately negotiated when providing the young people with placements they wanted as well as in challenging them when they exhibited racism in reference to who looked after them on a day-to-day basis.

Within the domain of connection, those who could be Witnesses and remain quietly attentive when distress overwhelmed the young people, created opportunities to move from the surface into deeper territories of meaning and feelings. They appeared to understand, as described by Blackwell (1997) and Papadopoulos (2002), the role of stillness in the movement towards resettlement, where the grief that some of the young people displayed required them to wait and listen. This process of witnessing is probably not what Howe (1995) had in mind when referring to psychotherapy as an essential component of safely connecting inner and outer worlds. None of the social workers who worked within this domain would have described themselves as therapists. Yet they appeared to provide 'therapeutic care' (Papadopoulos, 2002), in ways that helped to settle disorientation and turbulence, and allowed the young people to find *a sense of home*, within which a feeling of being cared for could re-emerge. They waited to hear the young people's stories, and adjusted the rhythm and pace of their engagements, either offering themselves as attentive listeners, or by referring the young people who were deeply distressed to mental health professionals. In any case, the social workers who acted as witnesses – again, rarely present in the UK refugee literature in comparison with the list of shortcomings related to social work – stepped forward within this study to define both their domain and their work within it. As they remembered the young peoples' stories within the research interviews, their own were revealed as ones where the virtues of working with intense feelings, of holding and containment, of becoming the conduits through which the young people could discharge their distress, were still very much part of contemporary practice, rather than nostalgic artefacts. When Bilton (2003: 2) expresses some concern that in understanding child-care social work, 'what is needed is not so much the development of new knowledge as the recapturing of something which risks being lost', these social workers appeared to show that they could hold on to the traditional importance of a helping relationship that could make a bridge between inner and outer worlds, and with the past and present. Yet there was some evidence to suggest that being a witness was an emotional challenge. One way that the social workers dealt with the intensity of feelings generated by working within the domain of connection was to themselves move to humanitarian or Confederate positions.

Finding a third type of practice – Confederacy – was unexpected, given that the refugee-related 'humanitarian' literature and the literature related to psychosocial practice with children rarely discusses the notion of the type of protective confederacy that this study describes. The Confederates' roots lay much more recognisably in narrative family therapy and social constructionism, approaches that are rarely used in writing about social-work practice (Hall, 1997; Parton and O'Byrne, 2000; Hall et al., 2003). Yet the Confederates emerged as important contributors to resettlement, with a helping role based more on a sense of companionability and friendship than that of either the Humanitarians or the Witnesses, who maintained a distinct helper/helped boundary. They appeared to form the foundation for the young people to 're-member' their lives, through the reclamation of thick stories, as well as the establishment of networks of protection and care that would be steady and lasting (Meyerhoff, 1982). To them, multiple motives and explanations – economic and political – were permissible, within which the young people could rediscover themselves as protagonists as they reached a point in their resettlement when they could safely shed their thin stories. But it was this willingness to see multiplicity that could have generated a dilemma in practice, concerning how much of what they knew about the more economically motivated young people should be shared within their agencies and more widely with the immigration authorities. They appeared to deal with this dilemma by taking the young people's side in most instances, and becoming what I have referred to here as 'ethical subversives' – their preferred 'greater good' was to safeguard the needs and interests of the young people, rather than the interests of what they termed 'the authorities'. This smudged the issue, in many instances, of how they themselves were 'the authorities' and what they saw as their primary mandate within the care/control continuum of social-work practice, even if this was a helpful smudging so far as the young people continuing their lives in the UK was concerned. Certainly within the UK-based research studies, as well as in the broader refugee literature, there is no mention of social workers practising with unaccompanied minors in this way. For practitioners thinking about their various obligations to their clients as well as to their agencies and wider communities, there is no particular way out of the argument that confederacy carries elements of collusion. For these Confederates, the balance was struck by seeing the young people as children in need, and resisting any impulse or expectation to disclose their 'whole' stories to the immigration authorities.

As noted, the Confederates could exert control when necessary, particularly in challenging the young people's demanding behaviour, but like their Humanitarian and Witness counterparts, they said they did it to be helpful, and to allow the young person to experience the maintenance of boundaries in a safe manner. In the longer term, the boundaries themselves became permeable as the workers began to talk about the affectional bonds that held the relationship between themselves and the young people in place. Their 'reputation' as lighthouses spread amongst the young people and beyond, and being referred to in parent-like ways appeared to be something that they liked. They wanted the relationships to continue to evolve, and in some instances they hoped they would last a long time. As with the issue of ethical subversion, this element of confederacy, in which the social workers hoped for continuity of contact, is little reported in the refugee literature. Using the details in this study however, tentative hypotheses can be put forward as to why this might be. First, they liked the young people. Particularly in the specialist teams, some of them had been drawn to this area of work, favourably contrasting the circumstances and behaviour of these young people with those of indigenous children in care. They found them rewarding to work with, despite the complexity, or in some instances because of the complexity inherent in the cases. Something about the stories that some of the young people told – particularly in relation to the depth of suffering they had encountered – affected these social workers and made them feel committed to seeing them through from extensive uncertainty to a durable resettlement. They admired their resilience, and saw them as deserving of support. Sometimes, simply because the young people themselves did not have a construct of 'social worker' within their cultural frames, but did have 'family', friend, companion, and mentor, these latter roles became the salient ones through which the relationship came to be understood over time.

In terms of their contexts, these social workers appeared to depend on localised learning rather than generalisable knowledge to find their way around the work. The majority did not appear to use theory, research, policies, or government guidance in practice. They would have been hard pushed to articulate the different facets of resettlement presented in this study, or to describe the domains of resettlement or indeed their differing roles within those domains. Akin to having learnt a language, they would have found it difficult to give a technical explanation of the structure and syntax of their work, no matter how eloquently they expressed themselves. Moreover, they largely confirmed the findings by Stone (2000) and Ayotte and Williamson (2001) that training in working with unaccompanied children was piecemeal and poorly accessed. Given the design of the study, no conclusions can be drawn about whether further training of the type asked for by the social workers would have resulted in a better service. Yet there was little evidence to suggest that the absence of training created conditions within which the social workers stopped seeing the world from the point of view of the young people in the sense advocated within the SCEP guidance (Ayotte, 1999). Local learning in this sense meant using personal experiences and the culture of their teams to guide practice. The specialist teams contained experts who appeared to be more familiar with the details of the difficulties faced by the young people than their counterparts in the more generalist teams. In seeing such details, workers were able to give examples of how the presence *and* absence of people and resources affected these unaccompanied minors, clearly exemplified in a number of individual stories of loss, mourning, and rediscovery. But there was evidence across all teams that as workers became more committed to their work with young asylum seekers, they could see what was visible, as well as what was absent, what was shown and what was hidden. In time they could generate hypotheses about why individual young people might be presenting in the ways they were, tied to a deep understanding generated through shared experiences.

In each of the domains, the work was 'messy', and the workers' own explanations of practice did 'speak of experience, trial and error, intuition and muddling through' in exactly the way anticipated by Schön (1995). Each domain carried its advantages for the young people, and contained a range of building blocks necessary for resettlement. As they worked and travelled within the domains the social workers gave an account of practice that appeared to be multi-faceted and a more optimistic endeavour than presented in the UK studies on the lives of refugee children. Despite the high drama associated with some of the circumstances through which they had made their way to the UK, once the young people entered systems of care and protection under section 20 of the Children Act 1989, the social workers in this study turned out after all to care for them well.

References

Aciman, A. (ed.) (199), *Letters of Transit: Reflections on Exile, Identity, Language and Loss* (New York: The New Press).

Ahern, F., Loughry, M. and Ager, A. (1998), 'The Experiences of Refugee Children', in A. Ager (ed.), *Refugee Perspectives on the Experience of Forced Migration* (New York: Pinter).

Ahern F. L. (ed.) (2000), *Psychosocial Wellness of Refugees: Issues of Qualitative and Quantitative Research* (New York: Berghahn Books).

Anderson, P. (2001), ' "You Don't Belong Here in Germany . . . ". On the Social Situation of Children in Germany'. *Journal of Refugee Studies*, 14 (2): 187–99).

Apfel, R. J. and Simon, B. (1996), 'Psychosocial Interventions for Children of War: the Value of a Model of Resiliency', *Medicine and Global Survival*. www.ippnw.org/MGS/V3Apfel.html

Armstrong, A. (1988), 'Aspects of Refugee Well-being in Settlement Schemes: An Examination of the Tanzanian Case', *Journal of Refugee Studies*, 1 (1): 57–73).

Audit Commission (2000), *Another Country: Implementing Dispersal under the Immigration and Asylum Act 1999* (Audit Commission for Local Authorities, and the National Health Service in England and Wales).

Ayotte, W. (1999), *The Separated Children in Europe Programme. Statement of Good Practice,* 1st edn (Geneva: Save the Children, United Nations High Commissioner for Refugees).

Ayotte, W. (2000), *Separated Children Coming to Western Europe: Why They Travel and How They Arrive* (London: Save the Children).

Ayotte, W. and Williamson, L. (2001), *Separated Children in the UK: An Overview of the Current Situation* (London: Save the Children).

Barudy, J. (1990), 'The Therapeutic Value of Solidarity and Hope', in H. Jockenhövel-Schiecke (ed.), *Unaccompanied Refugee Children in Europe: Experience with Protection, Placement and Education* (Frankfurt: International Social Service, German Branch).

Beek, M. and Schofield, G. (2004), *Providing a Secure Base in Long-term Foster Care* (London: BAAF).

Bell, A. (1996), *Only for Three Months: The Basque Children in Exile* (Norwich: Mousehold Press).

Berry, J. W. (1991), 'Refugee Adaptation in Settlement Countries: An Overview with an Emphasis on Primary Prevention', in F. L. Ahern and J. L. Athey (eds), *Refugee Children: Theory, Research and Services* (London: Johns Hopkins University Press).

Berry, J. W. (1997), 'Immigration, Acculturation and Adaptation', *Applied Psychology: An International Review*, 46: 5–68.

Bertrand, D. (2000), 'The Autobiographical Method of Investigating the Psychosocial Wellness of Refugees', in F. L. Ahern (ed.), *Psychosocial Wellness of Refugees: Issues of Qualitative and Quantitative Research* (New York: Berghahn Books).

Bihi, A. (1999), 'Cultural Identity: Adaptation and Well-Being of Somali Refugees in New Zealand' (Victoria University, Wellington), cited in A. Gray and S. Elliott (2001), *Refugee Resettlement Research Project: 'Refugee Voices'* (New Zealand Immigration Service).

Bilton, K. (2003), *Be My Social Worker: The Role of the Child's Social Worker* (Birmingham: British Association of Social Workers/Venture Press).

Blackwell, D. (1997), 'Holding, Containing and Bearing Witness: The Problem of Helpfulness in Encounters with Torture Survivors', *Journal of Social Work Practice*, 11 (2): 81–9.

Blackwell, D. and Melzak, S. (2000), *Far from the Battle but Still at War: Troubled Refugee Children in School* (London: The Child Psychotherapy Trust).

Bloch, A. and Schuster, L. (2002), 'Asylum and Welfare: Contemporary Debates', *Critical Social Policy*, 22: 393–414.

Blomqvist, U. (1996), 'Social Work in Refugee Emergencies. Capacity Building and Social Mobilisation: the Rwanda Experience', in M. McCallin, M. (ed.), *The Psychological Well-Being of Refugee Children. Research, Practice and Policy Issues* (Geneva: International Catholic Child Bureau).

Böcker, A. and Havinga, T. (1998), *Asylum Migration to the European Union: Patterns of Origin and Destination* (Luxembourg: Office for Official Publications of the European Communities).

Bracken, P. J. (1998), 'Hidden Agendas: Deconstructing Post Traumatic Stress Disorder', in P. J. Bracken and C. Petty, *Rethinking the Trauma of War* (London: Save the Children).

Bracken, P. J. and Petty, C. (1998), *Rethinking the Trauma of War* (London: Save the Children).

British Association for Adoption and Fostering (BAAF) and Refugee Council (2001), *Where are the children? A Mapping Exercise on the Numbers of Unaccompanied Asylum Seeking Children in the UK: September 2000 – March 2001* (London: BAAF and the Refugee Council).

British Medical Association (2002), *Asylum Seekers: Meeting their Healthcare Needs* (London: BMA Board of Science and Education).

Burnett, A. (2002), *Guide to Health Workers Providing Care for Asylum*

Seekers and Refugees (London: Medical Foundation for the Care of Victims of Torture).

Burr, V. (1995), *An Introduction to Social Constructionism* (London: Routledge).

Cairns, K. (2002), *Attachment, Trauma and Resilience* (London: British Association for Adoption and Fostering).

Canadian Council for Refugees (1998), *Best Settlement Practices: Settlement Services for Refugees and Immigrants in Canada* (Canadian Council for Refugees).

Carey-Wood, J., Duke, K., Karn, V. and Marshall, T. (1995), *The Settlement of Refugees in Britain*, Home Office Research Study 141 (London: HMSO).

Centre for Inner City Studies (1992), *Refugees in the Inner City: A Study of Refugees and Service Provision in the London Borough of Lewisham* (London: Goldsmiths' College, University of London).

Chapman, R. and Clader, A. (2003), *Starting Over: Young Refugees Talk about Life in Britain* (The Prince's Trust). www.princes-trust.org.uk/main%20site%20v2/downloads/refugee08.pdf

Cheetham, J., Fuller, R., McIvor, G. and Petch, A. (1992), *Evaluating Social Work Effectiveness* (Buckingham: Open University Press).

Christiansen, L. K. and Foighel, N. (1990), 'Trauma Treatment for Unaccompanied Minor Refugees: Experience from the Work in OASIS in Copenhagen', in H. Jockenhövel-Schiecke (ed.), *Unaccompanied Refugee Children in Europe: Experience with Protection, Placement and Education* (Frankfurt: International Social Service, German Branch).

Coate, J. and Kamasa, K. (1997), *Refugees and Asylum Seekers in Haringey* (London: Haringey Council).

Craven, N. (2003), 'This devoted Christian couple took in what they were told were two 16–year-old orphans from Kosovo. In fact they were Albanian crooks . . . ', *Daily Mail*, 2 August 2003.

Daniel, B., Wassell, S. and Gilligan, R. (1999), ' "It's just common sense isn't it?" Exploring Ways of Putting the Theory of Resilience into Action', *Adoption and Fostering*, 23 (3): 6–15.

Davidson, S. and King, S. (2005), *Public Knowledge of and Attitudes Towards Social Work in Scotland*, Scottish Executive Education Department Research Programme, Research Findings no. 10, September 2005.

Davies, M. (1994), *The Essential Social Worker*, 3rd edn (Aldershot: Ashgate).

Davis, H. (1999), 'The Psychiatrization of Post-Traumatic Distress: Issues for Social Workers', *British Journal of Social Work*, 29: 755–77.

Dennis, J. (2002), *A Case for Change: How Refugee Children in*

England are Missing Out (London: The Children's Society, Refugee Council and Save the Children).

Department for Education and Skills (2003), *Every Child Matters*, CM5860 (London: The Stationery Office).

Department for Education and Skills (2004), *Analysis of Responses to the Green Paper 'Every Child Matters'* (London: DfES), accessed 3 June 2004.

Department for Education and Skills, and National Statistics (2003a), *Statistics of Education: Children Looked After in England, 2002–2003* (London: DfES, Issue No. 06/03).

Department for Education and Skills and National Statistics (2003b), *Statistics of Education: Children Looked After by Local Authorities, Year Ending 31 March 2003*, Vol. 1: *Commentary and National Tables* (London: DfES).

Department for Education and Skills and National Statistics (2004), *Children in Need in England: Results of a Survey of Activity and Expenditure as Reported by Local Authority Social Services Children and Families Teams for a Survey Week in February 2003* (London: DfES, Issue no. vweb01–2004).

Department of Health (1990), *The Care of Children: Principles and Practice in Regulations and Guidance* (London: HMSO).

Department of Health (1995a), *Unaccompanied Asylum Seeking Children: A Practice Guide* (London: Social Services Inspectorate).

Department of Health (1995b), *Unaccompanied Asylum Seeking Children: Training Pack* (London: Social Services Inspectorate).

Department of Health (2003a), *Children Looked After by Local Authorities, Year Ending 31 March 2002, England,* vol. 1: *Commentary and National Tables* (London: Department of Health).

Department of Health (2003b), *Guidance on Accommodating Children in Need and their Families,* LAC (2003), 13, 2 June 2003, Children's Services (London: Department of Health).

Department of Health and National Statistics (2002), *Children in Need in England: Preliminary Results of a Survey of Activity and Expenditure as Reported by Local Authority Social Services' Children and Families Teams for a Survey Week in September/October 2001* (London: Department of Health).

Department of Health, Department for Education and Employment, Home Office (2000), *Framework for the Assessment of Children in Need and their Families* (London: The Stationery Office).

Eisenbruch, M. (1992), 'Towards a Culturally Sensitive DSM: Cultural Bereavement in Cambodian Refugees and the Traditional Healer as Taxonomist', *Journal of Nervous and Mental Disease*, 180: 8–10.

European Council on Refugees and Exiles (2002), *Position on*

Integration of Refugees in Europe, December 2002 (London: ECRE). www.ecre.org/positions/integ02.pdf

Fadiman, A. (1997), *The Spirit Catches You and You Fall Down: A Hmong Child, Her American Doctors, and the Collision of Two Cultures* (New York: Farrar, Straus and Giroux).

Fazel, M. and Stein, A. (2003), 'Mental Health of Refugee Children: Comparative Study', *British Medical Journal*, 327: 134.

Ferguson, H. (2003), 'Outline of a Critical Best Practice Perspective on Social Work and Social Care', *British Journal of Social Work*, 33: 1005–24.

Finlay, R. and Reynolds, J. (1987), *Social Work and Refugees: A Handbook on Working with People in Exile in the UK* (Cambridge: National Extension College and Refugee Action).

Fisher, M., Marsh, P., Phillips, D. with Sainsbury, E. (1986), *In and Out of Care: The Experiences of Children, Parents and Social Workers* (London: B. T. Batsford).

Fraser, M., Richman, J. and Galinsky, M. (1999), 'Risk, Protection and Resilience: Towards a Conceptual Framework for Social Work Practice', *Social Work Practice*, 23 (3): 131–43.

Garbarino, J. and Kostelney, K. (1996), 'Developmental Consequences of Living in Dangerous and Unstable Environments: the Situation of Refugee Children', in M. McCallin (ed.), *The Psychological Well-Being of Refugee Children: Research, Practice and Policy Issues* (Geneva: International Catholic Child Bureau).

Geertz, C. (1973), *The Interpretation of Cultures* (London: Fontana).

Gilligan, R. (1999), 'Enhancing the Resilience of Children and Young People in Public Care by Mentoring their Talents and Interests', *Child and Family Social Work*, 4: 187–96.

Gilligan, R. (2001), *Promoting Resilience: A Resource Guide on Working with Children in the Care System* (London: BAAF).

Gilligan, R. (2004), 'Promoting Resilience in Child and Family Social Work: Issues for Social Work Practice, Education and Policy', *Social Work Education*, 23 (1): 93–104.

GLA Policy Support Unit (2004), *Offering More than they Borrow: Refugee Children in London* (London: Greater London Authority).

Goldstein, H. (1992), 'If Social Work Hasn't Made Progress as a Science, Might it be an Art?' *Families in Society*, 73 (1): 48–55.

Gosling, R. (2000), *The Needs of Young Refugees in Lambeth, Southwark and Lewisham* (London: Community Health South London NHS Trust). http://www.lho.org.uk/view/Resource.aspx?id=8757

Gray, A. and Elliott, S. (2001), *Refugee Resettlement Research Project 'Refugee Voices': Literature Review* (Immigration Research Programme, New Zealand Immigration Service, Department of Labour).

Green, E. (2000), *Unaccompanied Children in the Danish Asylum Process* (Copenhagen: Danish Refugee Council).

Hall, C. (1997), *Social Work as Narrative: Storytelling and Persuasion in Professional Texts* (Aldershot: Ashgate).

Hall, C., Juhila, K., Parton, N. and Pösö, T. (eds) (2003), *Constructing Clienthood in Social Work and Human Services: Interactions, Identities and Practices* (London: Jessica Kingsley).

Hamilton, C., Daly, C. and Fiddy, A. (2003), *Mapping the Provision of Education and Social Services for Refugee and Asylum Seeking Children: Lessons from the Eastern Region* (London: Children's Legal Centre).

Harding, J. (2000), *The Uninvited: Refugees at a Rich Man's Gate* (London: Profile Books).

Harris, M. J. and Openheimer, D. (2001), *Into the Arms of Strangers: Stories of the Kindertransport* (London: Bloomsbury).

Harris, T. (1993), 'Surviving Childhood Adversity: What Can We Learn from Naturalistic Studies?' in H. Ferguson, R. Gilligan and R. Torode, *Surviving Childhood Adversity – Issues for Policy and Practice* (Dublin: Social Studies Press).

Hodes, M. (2004), 'Refugee Children in the UK', in M. Malek and C. Joughin (eds), *Mental Health Services for Minority Ethnic Children and Adolescents* (London: Jessica Kingsley).

Hoffmann, E. (1989), *Lost in Translation: A Life in a New Language* (London: Heinemann).

Hollway, W. and Jefferson, T. (2000), *Doing Qualitative Research Differently: Free Association, Narrative and the Interview Method* (London: Sage).

Home Office (1998–2004), *Asylum Statistics United Kingdom, 1997–2003*. Statistics for each year from 1998 are available via www.homeoffice.gov.uk/rds/immigratiom1.html

Howe, D. (1995), *Attachment Theory for Social Work Practice* (Basingstoke: Macmillan).

Howe, D. (1996), 'Surface and Depth in Social Work Practice', in N. Parton (ed.), *Social Theory, Social Change, and Social Work* (London: Routledge).

Howe, D., Brandon, M., Hinings, D. and Schofield, G. (1999), *Attachment Theory, Child Maltreatment and Family Support: A Practice and Assessment Model* (Basingstoke: Macmillan).

Hulewat, P. (1996), 'Resettlement: a Cultural and Psychological Crisis', *Social Work*, 41 (2): 129–35.

Humphries, B. (2004), 'An Unacceptable Role for Social Work: Implementing Immigration Policy', *British Journal of Social Work*, 34 (1): 93–107.

Jacobson, K. and Landau, L. (2003), *Researching Refugees: Some*

Methodological and Ethical Considerations in Social Science and Forced Migration (Geneva: UNHCR Evaluation and Policy Unit). www.unhcr.org

Joly, D. (1996), *Haven or Hell? Asylum Policies and Refugees in Europe* (Basingstoke: Macmillan).

Jones, D. P. H. (2003), *Communicating with Vulnerable Children: A Guide for Practitioners* (London: Gaskell).

Jordan, B. (2000), *Social Work and the Third Way: Tough Love as Social Policy* (London: Sage).

Karpf, A. (1997), *The War After: Living with the Holocaust* (London: Mandarin books).

Kidane, S. (2001), *Food, Shelter and Half a Chance: Assessing the Needs of Unaccompanied Asylum Seeking and Refugee Children* (London: BAAF).

Kohli, R. (2001), 'Social work with Unaccompanied Asylum Seeking Young People', *Forced Migration Review*, 12 (1): 31–3.

Kohli, R. (2003), 'Editorial *Child and Family Social Work* 8 (3): 161'.

Kohli, R. and Mather, R. (2003), 'Promoting Psychosocial Well-being in Unaccompanied Asylum Seeking People in the United Kingdom', *Child and Family Social Work*, 8 (3): 201–12.

Koser, K. and Pinkerton, C. (2002), *The Social Networks of Asylum Seekers and the Dissemination of Information about Countries of Asylum*, Finding 165 (London: Research, Development and Statistics (RDS) Directorate, Home Office).

Kushner, T. and Knox, K. (1999), '*Refugees in an Age of Genocide: Global, National and Local Perspectives in the Twentieth Century* (London: Frank Cass).

Kvale, S. (1996), *Interviews: An Introduction to Qualitative Research Interviewing* (London: Sage).

Laming, H. (2003), *The Victoria Climbié Inquiry: Report of an Inquiry by Lord Laming* (London: The Stationery Office).

Levenson, R. and Sharma, A. (1999), *The Health of Refugee Children: Guidelines for Paediatricians* (London: Royal College of Paediatrics and Child Health).

Loizos, P. (2002), 'Misconceiving Refugees?' in R. K. Papadopoulos (ed.), *Therapeutic Care for Refugees: No Place like Home* (London: Karnac).

Lonigan, C., Shannon, M., Finch, A., Daugherty, T. and Saylor, C. (1991), 'Children's Reactions to a Natural Disaster: Symptom Severity and Degree of Exposure', *Advances in Behavioural Research and Therapy*, 13: 135–254.

Loughry, M. and Eyber, C. (2003), *Psychosocial Concepts in Humanitarian Work with Children: A Review of the Concepts and Related Literature* (Washington, DC: The National Academies Press).

Macaskill, S. and Petrie, M. (2000), '*I didn't come here for fun* . . . ': *Listening to the Views of Children and Young People who are Refugees or Asylum-Seekers in Scotland* (Edinburgh: Save the Children in Scotland/Scottish Refugee Council).

MacFadyean, M. (2001), 'Destiny's Children', *Guardian*, 10 March 2001.

MacMullin, C. and Loughry, M. (2000), 'A Child-Centred Approach to Investigating Refugee Children's Experiences', in F. L. Ahern (ed.), *Psychosocial Wellness of Refugees: Issues of Qualitative and Quantitative Research* (New York: Berghahn Books).

Mann, G. (2001), *Networks of Support: A Literature Review of Care Issues for Separated Children* (Sweden: Save the Children).

McCallin, M. (ed.) (1996), *The Psychological Well-Being of Refugee Children: Research, Practice and Policy Issues* (Geneva: International Catholic Child Bureau).

Melzak, S. (1992), *Secrecy, Privacy, Survival, Repressive Regimes, and Growing Up* (London: Anna Freud Centre).

Melzak, S. (1995), 'Refugee Children in Exile in Europe', in J. Trowell and M. Bower (eds), *The Emotional Needs of Young Children and Their Families: Using Psychoanalytic Ideas in the Community* (London: Routledge).

Melzak, S. (1995b), 'What happens to children when their parents are not there? The challenge of holding a developmental and child focussed perspective within organisations that offer therapeutic work with survivors of torture and organised violence', Medical Foundation for the Care of Victims of Torture.

Meyerhoff, B. (1982), 'Life History among the Elderly: Performance, Visibility and Remembering', in J. Ruby (ed.), *A Crack in the Mirror: Reflexive Perspectives in Anthropology* (Philadelphia: University of Pennsylvania Press).

Milgram, R. and Milgram, N. (1976), 'The Effects of the Yom Kippur War on Anxiety Levels in Israeli Children', *Journal of Psychology*, 94: 107–13.

Minority Rights Group International (eds) (1998), *Forging New Identities: Young Refugee and Minority Students Tell their Stories* (London: Minority Rights Group).

Mitchell, F. (2003), 'The Social Services Response to Unaccompanied Children in England', *Child and Family Social Work*, 8 (3): 179–90.

Montgomery, E. (1998), 'Children Exposed to War, Torture and Other Organised Violence – Developmental Consequences', in G. Van Bueren (ed.), *Childhood Abused* (Aldershot: Ashgate).

Muecke, M. A. (1992), 'New Paradigms for Refugee Health Problems', *Social Science and Medicine*, 35 (4): 515–23.

Newland, K. (2002), *Refugee Resettlement in Transition* (Washington,

DC: Migration Policy Institute). www.migrationinformation.org/Feature/display.cfm?ID=52

Packman, J. and Hall, C. (1998), *From Care to Accommodation: Support, Protection and Control in Child Care Services* (London: The Stationery Office).

Papadopoulos, R. K. (ed.) (2002), *Therapeutic Care for Refugees: No Place Like Home* (London: Karnac).

Papadopoulos, R. K. and Hildebrand, J. (1997), 'Is Home Where the Heart Is? Narratives of Oppositional Discourses in Refugee Families', in R. K. Papadopoulos and J. Byng-Hall (eds), *Multiple Voices: Narratives in Systemic Family Psychotherapy* (London: Duckworth).

Parker, R., Ward, H., Jackson, S., Aldgate, J. and Wedge, P. (eds) (1991), *Looking After Children: Assessing Outcomes in Childcare. The Report of an Independent Working Party Established by the Department of Health* (London: HMSO).

Parton, N. and O'Byrne, P. (2000), *Constructive Social Work: Towards a New Practice* (Basingstoke: Macmillan).

Petty, C. and Jareg, E. (1998), 'Conflict, Poverty and Family Separation: the Problem of Institutional Care', in P. J. Bracken and C. Petty (eds), *Rethinking the Trauma of War* (London: Save the Children).

Punamäki, R. L. (2000), 'Measuring Suffering: Conflicts and Solutions in Refugee Studies', in F. L. Ahern (ed.), '*Psychosocial Wellness of Refugees: Issues of Qualitative and Quantitative Research* (New York: Berghahn Books).

Pynoos, R., Steinberg, A. and Wraith R, (1995), 'A Developmental Model of Childhood Traumatic Stress', in D. Ciccheti and D. Cohen (eds), *Developmental Psychopathology*, vol.II: *Risk, Disorder and Adaptation* (New York. John Wiley).

Ressler, E. M., Boothby, N. and Steinbock, D. (1988), *Unaccompanied Children: Care and Protection in Wars, Natural Disasters, and Refugee Movements* (Oxford: Oxford University Press).

Richman, N. (1998a), *In the Midst of the Whirlwind: A Manual for Helping Refugee Children* (London: Save the Children).

Richman, N. (1998b), 'Looking Before and After: Refugees and Asylum Seekers in the West', in P. J. Bracken and C. Petty (eds), *Rethinking the Trauma of War* (London: Save the Children).

Riley, J. and Wood, B. (eds) (1996), *Leave to Stay: Stories of Exile and Belonging* (London: Virago Press).

Robinson, V. and Segrott, J. (2002), *Understanding the Decision Making of Asylum Seekers*, Finding 172 (London: Research, Development and Statistics Directorate, Home Office).

Rousseau, C., Said, T., Gagné, M. J. and Bibeau, G. (1998) 'Resilience in Unaccompanied Minors from the North of Somalia', *Psychoanalytic Review*, 85: 615–37.

Russell, S. (1999), *Most Vulnerable of All: The Treatment of Unaccompanied Refugee Children in the UK* (London: Amnesty International).

Rutter, J. (2003), *Working with Refugee Children* (York: Joseph Rowntree Foundation).

Rutter, J. and Jones, C. (eds) (1998), *Refugee Education: Mapping the Field* (Stoke-on-Trent: Trentham Books).

SCEP (2000), *Separated Children in Europe Programme: Statement of Good Practice*, 2nd edn (Geneva: Save the Children, UNHCR). http://www.separated-children-europe-programme.org/separated_children/good_practice/index.html

Schofield, G. (1998), 'Inner and Outer Worlds: a Psychosocial Framework for Child and Family Social Work', *Child and Family Social Work*, 3: 57–67.

Schofield, G., Beek, M. and Sargent, K. with Thoburn, J. (2000), *Growing Up in Foster Care* (London: BAAF).

Sen, A. (1993), 'Capability and Well Being', in M. C. Nussbaum and A. Sen (eds), *The Quality of Life* (Oxford: Clarendon Press).

Silove, D. and Ekblad, S. (2002), 'How Well do Refugees Adapt after Resettlement in Western Countries?' *Acta Psychiatrica Scandinavica*, 106 (96): 401–2.

Smith, D. (1987), 'The Limits of Positivism in Social Work Research', *British Journal of Social Work*, 17: 401–16.

Spack, T. (2001), 'Global Overview: Refugee Resettlement and Integration Models and Methods', Report to the International Conference on the Reception and Integration of Resettled Refugees, Sweden, April 2001 (unpublished).

Stanley, K. (2001), *Cold Comfort: Young Separated Refugees in England* (London: Save the Children).

Stein, B. (1986), 'The Experience of Being a Refugee: Insights from the Research Literature', in C. Williams and J. Westermeyer (eds), *Refugee Mental Health in Resettlement Countries* (New York: Hemisphere). http://www.msu.edu/course/pls/461/stein/MNREXP1.htm

Steinbock, D. J. (1996), 'Unaccompanied Refugee Children in Host Country Foster Families', *International Journal of Refugee Law*, 8 (1/2): 6–48.

Stone, R. (2000), *Children First and Foremost: Meeting the Needs of Unaccompanied Asylum Seeking Children* (London: Barnardo's).

Summerfield, D. (1995), 'Raising the Dead: War, Reparation, and the Politics of Memory', *British Medical Journal*, 311: 495–7.

Summerfield, D. (1998), 'The Social Experience of War and Some Issues for the Humanitarian Field', in P. J. Bracken and C. Petty (eds), *Rethinking the Trauma of War* (London: Save the Children).

Summerfield, D. (2000), 'Childhood, War, Refugeedom, and Trauma: Three Core Questions for Mental Health Professionals', *Transcultural Psychiatry*, 37 (3): 417–33.

Summerfield, H. (1993), 'Patterns of Adaptation: Somali and Bangladeshi Women in Britain', in G. Buijs (ed.), *Migrant Women: Crossing Boundaries and Changing Identities* (Oxford: Berg).

Taylor, A. (2004), 'Failed Unaccompanied Minors May Be Forcibly Removed', *Community Care*, 20 May 2004: 3.

Teoh, A. H., Lafer, J., Parton, N. and Turnbull, A. (2003), 'Trafficking in Meaning: Constructive Social Work in Child Protection Services', in C. Hall, K. Juhila, N. Parton and T. Pösö (eds), *Constructing Clienthood in Social Work and Human Services: Interactions, Identities and Practices* (London: Jessica Kingsley).

Thoburn, J., Norford, L. and Rashid, S. (2000), *Permanent Placement for Children of Ethnic Minority Origin* (London: Jessica Kingsley).

Thomas, S. and Byford, S. (2003), 'Research with Unaccompanied Children Seeking Asylum', *British Medical Journal*, 327 (13 December): 1400–2.

Thomas, T. and Lau, W. (2002), *Psychological Well Being of Child and Adolescent Refugees and Asylum Seekers: Overview of Major Research Findings of the Past Ten Years* (Australia: Human Rights and Equal Opportunity Commission). http://www.humanrights.gov.au/human_rights/children_detention/psy_review.html

Tolfree, D. (2004), *Whose Children? Separated Children's Protection and Participation in Emergencies* (Sweden: Save the Children).

Trimble, J. E. (1977), 'The Sojourner in the American Indian Community: Methodological Issues and Concerns', *Journal of Social Issues*, 33: 159–74.

Turton, D. (2003), *Conceptualising Forced Migration*, RSC Working Paper no. 12 (Refugee Studies Centre, University of Oxford). www.rsc.ox.ac.uk/PDFs/workingpaper12.pdf

United Nations High Commission for Refugees (1994), *Refugee Children: Guidelines for Protection and Care* (Geneva: UNHCR).

United Nations High Commission for Refugees (1997), *State of the World's Refugees: A Humanitarian Agenda* (Oxford: Oxford University Press).

United Nations High Commission for Refugees (2000), *Trends in Unaccompanied and Separated Children Seeking Asylum in Europe, 2000* (Geneva: UNHCR). www.unhcr.org/statistics

United Nations High Commission for Refugees (2001), *New Directions for Resettlement Policy and Practice*, EC/51/SC/INF.2, 14 June 2001 (Geneva: UNHCR).

United Nations High Commission for Refugees (2002), *Refugees, Asylum-Seekers and Other Persons of Concern – Trends in Displacement,*

Protection and Solutions: Statistical Yearbook 2001 (Geneva: UNHCR).

United Nations High Commission for Refugees (2004), *Trends in Unaccompanied and Separated Children Seeking Asylum in Industrialised Countries, 2001–2003* (Geneva: UNHCR). www.unhcr.org/statistics

Utting, W. (1997), *People Like Us: The Report of the Review of the Safeguards for Children Living Away from Home* (London: The Stationery Office).

Utting, W. (2003), 'The Role of the Child's Social Worker', in K. Bilton, *Be My Social Worker: The Role of the Child's Social Worker* (Birmingham: British Association of Social Workers/Venture Press).

Valois, N. (2001), 'Does the Community Care?' *Community Care*, 25–31 January 2001.

Valtonen, K. (1994), 'The Adaptation of Vietnamese Refugees in Finland', *Journal of Refugee Studies*, 7 (1): 63–78.

Weisner, T. (1987), 'Socialization for Parenthood in Sibling Caretaking Societies', in J. Lancaster, J. Altmann, A. S. Rossi and L. R. Sherrod (eds), *Parenting Across the Lifespan: Biosocial Dimensions* (New York: Aldine).

White, M. (1995), *Re-Authoring Lives: Interviews and Essays* (Adelaide: Dulwich Centre Publications).

White, M. (1997), *Narratives of Therapists' Lives* (Adelaide: Dulwich Centre Publications).

White, M. and Epston, D. (1990), *Narrative Means to Therapeutic Ends* (New York: Norton).

Williamson, L. (1995), 'A Safe Haven? The Development of British Policy Concerning Unaccompanied Refugee Children, 1933–93', *Immigrants and Minorities*, 14 (1): 47–66.

Williamson, L. (1998), 'Unaccompanied – but Not Unsupported', in J. Rutter and C. Jones (eds), *Refugee Education: Mapping the Field* (Stoke-on-Trent: Trentham Books).

Williamson, L. (1999), 'Unaccompanied Refugee Children: Legal Framework and Local Applications in Britain', in A. Bloch and C. Levy (eds), *Refugees, Citizenship and Social Policy* (Basingstoke: Macmillan).

Yule, W. (1992), 'Resilience and Vulnerability in Child Survivors of Disasters', in B. Tizard and V. Varma (eds), *Vulnerability and Resilience* (London: Jessica Kingsley).

Yule, W. and Gold, A. (1993), *Wise Before the Event: Coping with Crises in Schools* (London: Calouste Gulbenkian Foundation).

Zetter, R., Griffiths, D., Ferretti, S. and Pearl, M. (2003), *An Assessment of the Impact of Asylum Policies in Europe, 1990–2000*, Home Office Research Study 259 (London: Home Office RDS Directorate).

Zivic, I. (1993) 'Emotional Reactions of Children to War Stress in Croatia', *Journal of the American Academy of Child and Adolescent Psychiatry*, 32 (4): 709–13.

Zulfacar, D. (1987), 'Alternative Forms of Care for Unaccompanied Refugee Minors: a Comparison of US and Australian Experience', *International Social Work*, 30: 61–75.

Index